WHITE LIES
ABOUT THE
THE INUIT

White Lies about the Inuit

John L. Steckley

University of Toronto Press

Previously published by Broadview Press in 2008 © John L. Steckley

LIBRARY AND ARCHIVES CANADA CATALOGUING IN PUBLICATION

Steckley, John, 1949–
White lies about the Inuit / John L. Steckley.
Includes bibliographical references and index.

ISBN 978-1-55111-875-8

1. Inuit—Canada—History—Errors, inventions, etc. 2. Common fallacies.
I. Title.
E99.E7E797 2007   971.004'9712   C2007-906149-4

We welcome comments and suggestions regarding any aspect of our publications—please feel free to contact us at news@utphighereducation.com or visit our Internet site at www.utphighereducation.com.

North America
5201 Dufferin Street
North York, Ontario, Canada, M3H 5T8

UK, Ireland, and continental Europe
NBN International
Estover Road, Plymouth, PL6 7PY, UK
TEL: 44 (0) 1752 202301

2250 Military Road
Tonawanda, New York, USA, 14150

FAX ORDER LINE: 44 (0) 1752 202333
enquiries@nbninternational.com

ORDERS PHONE: 1-800-565-9523
ORDERS FAX: 1-800-221-9985
ORDERS E-MAIL: utpbooks@utpress.utoronto.ca

The University of Toronto Press acknowledges the financial support for its publishing activities of the Government of Canada through the Book Publishing Industry Development Program (BPIDP).

Cover design and interior by Em Dash Design
Copy-edited by Catherine Dorton

Printed in Canada

Contents

CHAPTER ONE

Imagining the Inuit

LEARNING OBJECTIVES

After reading this chapter, you will be able to

» describe the ways in which the Inuit have been treated as collectors' items or showpieces.
» outline the history of the portrayal of Inuit in the movies.
» critically discuss the four stereotypes of the Inuit described in this chapter.
» critically evaluate interpretations of the meaning of the word *Eskimo*.
» connect the story of John Rae and his findings about the fate of the Franklin expedition to the notion that the Inuit were cannibals.

> I dreamed I was an eskimo in my Maidenform bra. Guess whose figure is going around in Arctic circles? It's mine and it's marvelous—so sleek and smooth, so fabulously curved. Here on top of the world we know what makes the world go round ... it's Maidenform.
> —1954 Maidenform Bra ad (quoted in D'Souza 2004)

THIS BOOK HAS BEEN a personal journey for me. It has not been easy to knock the heroes of my youth and early academic career from their pedestals. But it needed to be done. In my early teens, Farley Mowat inspired me to become an author myself, and yet here I am writing a book that takes shots at him. In the academic sphere, anthropologist Franz Boas was one of my first heroes. In my later career, I have been forced to undertake a long hard reappraisal of his material.

Until recently, I would not have called myself an Inuit specialist. Yet when I look at it, my life and academic career have often taken me back to the people. My first anthropological paper as an undergraduate reviewed Farley Mowat's *People of the Deer*. It was filled with praise for my then hero. I still highly respect the fact that he brought the world's attention, however briefly, to the Caribou Inuit, the people who traditionally hunted caribou west of Hudson Bay. An examination question in an introductory class on Aboriginal people intrigued me at the time, as it does now: "Why is it that the Inuit are conceived of in ways different from those of Indians?" How many exam questions do you think you will remember 30 years from now? At Memorial University of Newfoundland, I worked as a research assistant for Jean Briggs from 1974–75, coding the field notes from her psychological and linguistic studies of a small Inuit population. She had then only recently published *Never in Anger: Portrait of an Eskimo Family*, an excellent ethnography based on her time among the Uktu on a remote Arctic shore—a brilliant exception to the "White lies" rule discussed here. In it, she examined how the people she studied virtually never expressed anger. At the anthropology department at Memorial, the joke was that her sequel would be called *Sometimes in Anger*.

In 1980, I volunteered in St. John's, Newfoundland, to act as a guide for school tours in the Inuit section of the city's museum. I still remember the challenging questions the students asked and how I scrambled in ignorance for answers. In 1985, I published a piece on the early eighteenth-century Labrador Inuit girl Acoutsina for *Them Days*, the often quirky but always interesting Labrador publication. Shortly afterwards, the Labrador school board asked to use my piece in their curriculum. At the time, I found this ironic. I had written frequently about the Huron—I was a Huron specialist after all—and no such request had ever come concerning those articles. This is still true.

Inuit stories have been a feature of my anthropology classes at Humber College in Toronto over the last 20 years. So it is hard to admit that for years, I taught lies—White lies. I should have known better. I should have checked the facts. However, my stories came from textbooks and other so-called reliable sources, and the lies were so useful in teaching about a culture different from my own.

Generally, though, my discussions of the Inuit have come to be useful in my teaching. Through the Inuit, I have learned well to beware what I read in textbooks, a lesson I pass on to my students. Such information concerning the Inuit provides a good cautionary tale for my students, teaching them how important it is to be critical of what they read.

Arctic Urban Legends

Truth is not a popularity contest. Repetition, like imitation, might flatter an earlier author, but it doesn't necessarily lead to truth. Just because there is a huge literature about a subject, does not mean that many truths are told. Often what you get are the same falsehoods repeated over and over again. Over the last three centuries, White explorers and adventurers, police officers, missionaries, traders, and especially anthropologists, sociologists, and other scholars have spun many a twisted story about the Inuit. Some have become Arctic urban legends without a city. White-created myths about the

Inuit abound like five-year-olds' theories about where babies come from. Ignorance abhors a vacuum.

In her discussion of one of these myths—Inuktitut terms for snow—Laura Martin put forward the following ideas:

> Arctic peoples, among the most easily recognized ethnographic populations, remain a poorly understood group about whom other easy generalizations are routine: they eat only raw meat, they give their wives as gifts to strangers, they rub noses instead of kissing, they send their elderly out on ice floes to die. We are prepared to believe almost anything about such an unfamiliar and peculiar group. (Martin 1986: 420)

The problem of distorted perceptions about the Inuit has long been recognized and written about. Unfortunately, the impact of these writings is rather like that of the corrections to front-page news stories that are buried somewhere in the back pages. To my knowledge, an 1887 issue of *The American Naturalist* contained the first published piece attempting to correct such errors. The author was naturalist John Murdoch, a member of the Point Barrow, Alaska, research expedition of 1881–83, headed by Captain Patrick Henry Ray. Murdoch's scientifically trained mind could not abide the myths he was hearing. In concluding his insightful article, he wrote, not without a little humour:

> I trust that I have presented sufficient evidence to show that the popular picture of the dwarfish Eskimo, dozing in an underground den, keeping up his internal heat by enormous meals of raw blubber washed down with draughts of lamp oil [made from boiled blubber], is based on exaggeration, to say the least, rather than on actual facts. (Murdoch 1887: 16)

The notions that Inuit are dwarf-sized and dig underground homes have thankfully disappeared. However, the idea that they only eat their meat and fish, not to mention blubber, raw persists. This has been encouraged, of course, by the outsider-imposed term *Eskimo*, which means "eaters of raw flesh."

When most of us hear an Inuit story, we lack any critical framework with which to judge it, much like with urban legends. I know I digested, as a southern Ontario child and young adult, pretty much every Arctic story I was fed, no matter what the narrative ingredients. The vast majority of North Americans have never been to the Arctic or even the Subarctic of the Inuit and have never even met an Inuk (singular of *Inuit*). They meet paper Inuit only, in elementary school two-dimensional picture-book images of igloos, parkas, dogsleds, and kayaks. How could they know better than they do?

Tear down the igloo, strip off the parka, take away the harpoon, and Whites would not recognize an Inuk. In an anthropology class at Humber College in the late 1980s, I had an Inuk student. She was born in Pelly Bay (officially known since 2000 as Kugaaruk, a traditional place name referring to a nearby river) in the extreme North and had been adopted when she was still a baby. Culturally, she was raised as a Toronto suburbanite. Throughout the four months of the course, no one in the class ever guessed that she was an Inuk. She wanted it kept a secret, so I never told. She was full of enthusiasm for everything Inuit taught in the course, and when she did well on an exercise in Inuktitut, she referred to it as "my language" several times. Still, despite these hints, she remained invisible as an Inuk. She was presumed to be White.

As we will see from our discussion of the Inuit in movies, southerners readily perceive non-Inuit actors as Inuit. Canadian football fans are familiar with the Edmonton Eskimos. Their history goes back to a rugby team formed in 1892, which acquired the name "Esquimaux." The name was changed to reflect the conventional spelling in 1910. Normie Kwong was a star player with the Eskimos for three Grey Cups during the 1950s. He was born in 1929 to Chinese immigrants and was named Lieutenant Governor of Alberta in January 2005. When a television reporter asked him for funny stories concerning his career, he recalled a child pointing to him in his uniform and saying, "See, some of them really are Eskimos."

Learning about the Eskimo

It is not hard to determine why distorted images of the Inuit have spread. The reasons grow quickly, as do the number of Inuktitut terms for snow reported in the popular literature, which stretches from 20 to more than 500. Part of this mythologizing process comes from the romanticism of the North itself. Canada has long looked to the "Great White North" for its images. I grew up with the romance of Robert Service's poetry—I have a copy of his works in my library still. I vividly remember having "The Cremation of Sam McGee" read to my class in grade five. My early reading included the northern adventure books of Jack London (especially *White Fang* and *The Call of the Wild*), Farley Mowat, and Pierre Berton. From 1955 to 1958, I watched "Sergeant Preston of the Yukon," an adventure series that featured an officer of the Royal Canadian Mounted Police and his dog, Yukon King. I dreamed of having my own dogsled team. Now I can only fantasize as I walk my border collie, my border collie cross, and my Jack Russell cross over newly fallen snow in southern Ontario.

Europeans early on made the Inuit exotic. Russians once believed they had tails. They may have seen just their coats and parkas, not much more, but from there used their imagination. The earliest published portrayal of an Inuk was in Swedish archbishop Olaus Magnus's 1539 *Carta Marina*. It was indicative of the distorting writings to come. According to Danish anthropologist Kaj Birket-Smith, it depicts "a bearded Greenland 'pygmy' [so that's where the idea started!] wearing a broad-brimmed hat and engaged in a spear fight with a good-sized European" (Birket-Smith 1959).

The centuries-long European practice of treating the Inuit themselves as collectors' items or showpieces contributed to the exoticizing process. They were "exotic talking booty," to use American archaeologist J.M. Adovasio's apt terminology for all Natives brought to Europe in such a way (Adovasio and Page 2003). After his voyage to Baffin Island in 1577, Martin Frobisher gave Queen Elizabeth of England several exotic presents: a six-foot-long narwhal tusk and an Inuit man, woman, and child, all of whom died shortly afterwards. At various times during the nineteenth century and early twentieth century, Inuit were shown off as living museum exhibits.

In 1824, American whaleboat captain Samuel Hadlock brought two Inuit from Baffin Island, a man and a woman, with appropriate artifacts, to display on show first in England, then on the European continent. When the woman died, he replaced her with a series of women that to his mind (and the minds of his audience) "looked Eskimo." When the Inuk man died, Hadlock closed the show and returned to the United States.

In 1847, British captain John Parker brought another Baffin Island couple, Memiadluk and Ucklaluk, reported to be 17 and 15 respectively, to put on show in England. Flyers reported in large letters that visitors to the show could see "The Two Esquimaux or Yacks, Male and Female, brought here by Captain Parker of the Ship *Truelore* of Hull.... They Will Appear in Their Native Costume." Ucklaluk died of measles, and Memiadluk was returned home with a large supply of gifts.

Tookoolito (1838–76) from Cumberland Sound, Baffin Island, travelled with the ill-fated Arctic explorer Charles Francis Hall, who was killed by arsenic poisoning in 1871. Partially as a fundraiser for Hall's exploits, Tookoolito (generally referred to as "Hannah") and her family were presented at P.T. Barnum's ("Never give a sucker an even break") American Museum in New York for two weeks. The following is the text from a ticket. It was accompanied by a sketch of Tookoolito, her husband, Ebierbing (known as "Joe" or "Eskimo Joe"), and the baby girl they adopted.

Amusements
Barnum's American Museum
Thursday, November 20, 1862
ONLY THREE DAYS MORE
ONLY THREE DAYS MORE
OF THOSE WONDERFUL
ESQUIMAUX INDIANS
ESQUIMAUX INDIANS
ESQUIMAUX INDIANS
which have just arrived in this country
FROM THE ARCTIC REGIONS
Where they were brought by

> C.F. Hall, Esc., ARCTIC EXPLORER
> being the first and only
> INHABITANTS OF THE FROZEN REGIONS
> Ever brought to this country, they are objects
> of universal interest; but they can remain
> only this week
> SEE THEM NOW, OR YOU'RE TOO LATE
> They are on exhibition from 10 a.m. till
> 12 p.m. from 2 till 4 and from 7 to 10 p.m.

Joining them on display were "Commodore Nutt" (a man who stood 29 inches tall, whom P.T. Barnum had acquired for $30,000 earlier that year) a Madagascar albino family, wax figures of famous people, "monster snakes," and tropical fish.

In 1880, eight Labrador Inuit men, women, and children were hired for exhibit in European zoos. They all died of smallpox within five months of their arrival in Europe. Another woman was able to make a living by combining the fact-free fantasies of North Americans about the Inuit with their love for them as circus freaks. Her name was Ólöf Krarer. A white woman born in 1858 in Iceland, Ólöf was about 40 inches tall and weighed about 120 pounds. Her family travelled to North America in 1876, and the parents of Vilhjalmur Stefansson, a major figure in this book, were fellow passengers on the ship.

She made her money first by joining the circus charging 10 cents a look. Pictures of her in books, postcards, and "cabinet cards" (photographic prints stuck onto cardboard) show her either in a white parka or in the formal clothes of the time. She had graduated from circus to lecture circuit by the end of 1884, when she appeared before 300 people in a town in Indiana. She later came to work for the Slayton Lyceum Bureau, which arranged for lecturers, including well-known scholars, to present in small towns and big cities. In her stories about her supposed Inuit culture, she mixed fairly common Icelandic knowledge about the North with her own inventions: bones heated up to burn children as punishment and bags into which people put a single bone each time they saw the first sun after the six months of Arctic darkness (so they would know how old they were). These bones were supposed to be collected in bundles of 10 since she claimed her people could not count above that number. She claimed that her family and her people in Greenland were short like her and were getting shorter due to malnutrition (Murdoch was probably responding to this aspect of her presentation in his comment on "dwarfish" Inuit). These stories became influential not just among the tens of thousands of people who heard her. They were also incorporated into American textbooks for elementary school children of her time (the late nineteenth century and first third of the twentieth century).

In 1893, at the World's Columbian Exposition in Chicago, 59 of the ever-popular Labrador Inuit and 35 of their dogs formed an exhibit:

For fifty cents the public could enter the midway, and for an additional quarter they could see fur-clad Eskimos posing by papier-mâché igloos. The exhibit subsequently incorporated three children born following the group's arrival, and the remains of the Eskimos who died during their tenure in Chicago were preserved in museum collections established in the exhibition's wake. (Fienup-Riordan 1995: 39)

Franz Boas, who will be discussed in detail later, was the chief assistant in anthropology at this show. Eleven years afterwards, Inuit were featured in the St. Louis Exposition in an "Eskimo village" of 9 Inuit families, 26 dogs, and "Mac, the Wise Bear." To get some idea of the exposure this gave to stereotypes about the Inuit, consider the following statistics. Some 200,000 people attended the exposition on the opening day. Average daily attendance was 85,197. Over the seven-month period of the St. Louis Exposition, nearly 20 million people passed through the turnstiles. Ice cream cones and air conditioning made their public debut as well. In 1909 at the Alaska-Yukon-Pacific Exposition in Seattle, the "Eskimo Village" featuring Inuit from Labrador, Siberia, and Alaska was one of the most popular attractions.

See You in the Movies

Then came the movies. If you went to the 1901 Pan-American Exposition in Buffalo, you could view film footage of an "Eskimo Village," a dogsled, and Inuit playing leapfrog and generally acting like fun-loving children. The American inventor Thomas Edison shot the pictures. Between 1909 and 1911, the Carnegie Museum Expedition in Alaska and Siberia, led by Captain Frank Kleinschmidt, shot some 10,000 feet of Inuit film. The film series, entitled "Tip Top of the World," included shots from 1912–19, and was used by teacher and missionary William Van Valin to good financial effect on his travel lecture circuit.

Robert Flaherty's *Nanook of the North* (1922) was a highly successful documentary, grossing $251,000 worldwide. Nanook, an Inuk hunter whose name means "polar bear," became a short-lived star, literally. But the educational value of this documentary was limited. The scenes were highly staged, primarily following Flaherty's images of what the culture should look like.

The movie also helped to sell another commodity: the Eskimo Pie, the original snack food with chocolate-covered ice cream invented in 1921 by a Danish-born American named Christian Kent Nelson. (The Inuit have a hard time escaping the Danes—see Chapter Four: The Myth of the Blond Eskimo.) By the spring of 1922, 1 million Eskimo Pies were being sold each day in the United States. Nelson even patented the name *Eskimo Pie*.

The combined appeal of the movie and the ice cream is well described by Judy Jones and William Wilson in *An Incomplete Education*. In their words, *Nanook of the North* was

[u]npredictably, a big commercial, as well as critical, hit. Of course, it helped that the picture opened in New York in the middle of one of the hottest Junes on record; but beyond that, viewers couldn't get over the way they were invited not only to travel to a distant clime, but to look into somebody else's mind and heart....Within a matter of months, Eskimo pies were being sold on both sides of the Atlantic, and words like "igloo," "kayak," and "anorak," formerly known only to anthropologists, were popping up in grade-school civics tests and sporting-goods store windows. Too bad Nanook couldn't have basked in his new fame: He died of starvation, out there on the ice, shortly after the film was released. (Jones and Wilson 1987: 135)

A spate of Inuit-themed, stereotype-reproducing films would follow throughout the 1920s and 1930s, including *Kivalina of the Ice Lands* (1925), *Justice of the Far North* (1926), *Frozen Justice* (1929), and *Igloo* (1932). The advertising for *Igloo* gave a good indication of what you would have seen in the theatre.

Away, Far Away, ADVENTURE CALLS. To the top of the World for the Screen's Mightiest Thrills. The Strangest Adventure Ever Filmed. A Love Story of a Forgotten Land. The Romance of Chee-ak, the Great Hunter, and Kyatuk, his Eskimo Beauty. See: The raging, roaring, freezing Arctic Blizzards. A fight for life so thrilling you will gasp and wonder at its drama. See: The hunger-maddened Eskimos' walrus hunt. See: The old sealed in tombs of ice and left to die. Primitive Passions. Stark Drama. Mighty thrills. (Fienup-Riordan 1995: 67)

"In This Movie, You Will Be an Eskimo"

In movies, Inuit have been played by Greeks, Mexicans, Japanese, Chinese—anyone who is not blond haired and blue eyed (although as we will see in a later chapter, even that test failed for a while). A great variety of actors have enhanced their resumés pretending to be Inuit. A classic example of this was a joint production between France and Canada in 1992. *Shadow of the Wolf* is based on Yves Thériault's prizewinning novel *Agaguk*, published in 1958. Lou Diamond Phillips, the Philippine-born actor who claims Hawaiian, Filipino, Cherokee, and Scots-Irish descent, played the lead role of Agaguk. Japanese actor Toshirô Mifune, who is dressed like an aging ninja in the movie, plays Kroomak, his dangerous shaman father. Their common love interest is Igiyook, played by Jennifer Tilly. You could hardly find someone who looks less like an Inuk. With a shaman among the characters, the bizarre mysticism of the movie is predictable. Shamans (based on the Siberian Tungus term meaning "one who knows") traditionally combine traits of doctors, psychiatrists, magicians, musicians, and outright entertainers. They have been popular figures among non-Aboriginal people since anthropology student Carlos Castaneda took drugs with a Yaqui shaman (a First Nation in Mexico and the American southwest) and described his trips in his best-selling books of the early 1970s. Now the term *shaman* is even associated with the popular Japanese manga (that's an expensive Japanese comic book to anyone older than their early 20s) and animé; for example, the video game figure Shaman King is a 13-year-old Japanese figure who can channel spirits to fight the forces of evil.

My favourite absurd Inuit impersonator is Anthony Quinn. Born in Mexico, with an Irish-Mexican name, he played Zorba the Greek, Attila the Hun, "Indian" and Hawaiian chiefs, a Chinese guerrilla, and an Arab sheik. In 1959, he played an Inuk in *The Savage Innocents*.

White Lies Not Included

The White lies that I will debunk in this section (and in this book) do not form an exhaustive list of White stereotypes about the Inuit. What follows here is only intended as a short series of cautionary tales. The longer stories in chapters three, four, and five are lies that I have been lucky enough to discover in my research. Two of them (the number of Inuit words for snow and elder abandonment and suicide) have a special significance to me, as I once not only believed them but also taught them. I hate to think how many other such fables and half-truths exist that I still might believe in.

FEMALE INFANTICIDE

The myth of Inuit elder abandonment, which we will discuss later, is often paired with the myth of female infanticide. Knud Rasmussen, an early anthropologist of mixed Danish-Inuit heritage, presented the classic explanation for this practice. Like the myth of Inuit elder abandonment, it is set in the Darwinian construct of the struggle for existence so often manufactured by White writers when describing Inuit life. In an Arctic environment that has proven such an obstacle to non-Aboriginal people, how else could life be? Both the Inuit people and environment are portrayed in the harshest light possible. This representation helps the reputation of White adventurers when they master both, however briefly:

> The most glaring consequence of the struggle for existence is manifested in the way in which [the Netsilik] try to breed the greatest possible number of boys and the fewest possible girls. For it is solely economy that lies behind the custom that girls are killed at birth ... The reasoning that lies behind infanticide is as follows: A female infant is only a trouble and an expense to the household as long as she cannot make herself useful. But the moment she is able to help she is married and leaves her family; for it is the rule that the woman goes with the family into which she has married. For this reason they try to regulate births in

order to get as many boys as possible. (Rasmussen 1931, in Smith and Smith 1994: 595)

Female infanticide was especially featured in *The Incredible Eskimo*, by Father Raymond de Coccola and Paul King (1986: 8–18).

The subject of Inuit female infanticide became the focus of the dramatic conclusion of Yves Thériault's *Agaguk*, the most popular post-World War II novel in Quebec. Not only was the novel made into the movie *Shadow of the Wolf*, it was also the subject of a book that presented a highly esoteric social-semiotic analysis: *Towards a Semiotics of the Modern Quebec Novel: "Agaguk," by Yves Thériault* (Perron 1996) looked at it as a metaphor for Quebec society. When I write about you, it's all about me.

Undoubtedly, female infanticide did take place in some circumstances. However, we must question how extensive it was and the reasons behind it, and seek out possible links between its practice and European intrusion into Inuit land. In Eric A. Smith and S. Abigail Smith's 1994 publication of "Inuit Sex Ratio Variation: Population Control, Ethnographic Error, or Parental Manipulation?" they noted a fairly significant variation in both female infanticide and the sex ratio from place to place. They also challenged some of the explanations that had been put forward. Unfortunately, they did not come up with a clear hypothesis of their own. Their census data came from 1880–1930, which would not have enabled them to look directly at the differences between practices before and after European and North American non-Aboriginal whaling and other intrusions into Inuit lands and waters. As good as the article is, it was not able to address whether this practice was adopted only after the impact of White intrusion. To explore that question, we would need physical anthropologists and archaeologists to investigate sex ratios and infant burials, and such might not even be possible.

WIFE SHARING

Another myth is wife sharing, which from another gender perspective might of course be considered husband sharing, or in a more neutral way, spouse swapping. The at least occasionally active role of the woman is suggested in the following quotation from Asen Balikci: "In case two wives wanted to exchange husbands, no direct proposition was made, but the possibility was gently suggested with the hope that the husbands would agree, while thinking themselves masters of the situation" (Balikci 1970: 141). Again, something was definitely happening, but what it actually was and what it meant to the people deserves more serious analysis. The notion has entered North American culture in some bad places. It entered the plot line of an episode of *Love, American Style* entitled "Love and the Eskimo's Wife" that aired on December 3, 1971. Do an Internet search under "Eskimo wife sharing," and you will get that reference, plus a lot of sites advertising swinging couples and other sexual adventures. Apparently, Eskimo wife-sharing stories are a staple of these sites. Of course, Inuit women are not the only non-White females who are so treated. The highly sexualized non-White female "other" is a stock (perhaps that should be "stocking") figure in North American media.

RUBBING NOSES

Q: What do Eskimos get from rubbing noses?
A: Snif-fles (rhymes with syphilis).

Another of the stock features of the Inuit stereotype is nose rubbing. This practice was not unique to the Inuit; some of the South Pacific peoples did it as well. Nor was it a feature of all Inuit cultures, but it did become identified with the Inuit. In 2005, two award-nominated television ads featured Inuit actors rubbing noses. A Scope mouthwash commercial showed several couples rubbing noses as they began their day. One couple started to make out with heavy passion, the woman climbing on top of the man. The idea was that the fresh breath provided by Scope was a turn-on.

On December 6 of the same year, a Chap Stick television commercial was featured in the *Globe and Mail*'s "Hard Sell," a feature that discusses and rates television advertisements. It was entitled "Inuit Kiss." The following is part of the *Globe*'s presentation. Little commentary is necessary. The stereotyping speaks for itself:

THE BRIEF: Create a television commercial to remind Canadians that we have tough winters, so they shouldn't forget their Chap Stick.

THE KUNIK: "Once we knew we were honing in on Canadian winters, that made us wonder why Inuit do this kind of nose kissing, called the kunik," said Jane Pritchard, the art director who worked on the spot ... "We said: Wouldn't that be a funny advertising idea if we implied that maybe Inuit kunik because they didn't have Chap Stick?"

THE AUTHENTICITY: The agency consulted with Inuit in the Yukon to make sure the kunik in the ad was authentic.

PIBLOKTUQ

Not to be forgotten is the subject of the so-called "Eskimo psyche." It was discussed in the 1892 journal of Josephine, the wife of Arctic explorer Robert Peary. Historical rumours claim that she went with him because she had heard stories—true—of his Eskimo wife: a little White husband sharing. Josephine was the first to describe the "crazy" acts of Inuit women who would suddenly scream, tear their clothes off, imitate the sound of a bird or animal, and go running around until they dropped. The name *pibloktuq* (and linguistically-challenged variations thereof) emerged, an Inuktitut word distorted by White visitors who then began to record this phenomenon.

The name first entered the historical record, then the psychiatric medical record, as a form of "Arctic hysteria" (Brill 1913). It still exists as a psychological disorder legitimated by a medical name and "authenticated" by case studies. It also became enshrined in anthropology, from Seymour Parker's explanation of the phenomenon in an article in the prestigious *American Anthropologist* (1962) to ethnographies such as Jean Malaurie's *The Last Kings of Thule* (1982), in which he wrote the term as *Perlerorneq*, and textbooks (e.g., Barnouw 1987: 207; Harris 1987: 328–29; and Holmes 1965: 315). As such, it is one of a number of culturally specific syndromes or psychoses, like the Malay *amok*, which became used in the English phrase "running amok."

In a 1995 article in *Arctic Anthropology* entitled "'Pibloktuq' (Arctic Hysteria): A Construction of European-Inuit Relations?" historian Lyle Dick challenged whether the phenomenon existed as a part of traditional Inuit culture. He suspects (and I concur) that it is more likely the creature of the White-Inuit power imbalance embodied in specific contexts, such as when the obsessively driven Robert Peary forced the Inuit to participate in risky exploration that they would not normally have done and when White men sexually abused Inuit women.

It is significant for me to mention this alleged disorder. I used to teach it. I was recently looking through my computer files for material to teach a class on medical anthropology. I spotted a lecture from 2001 that discussed possible physical explanations for *pibloktuq* such as calcium deficiency and hypervitaminosis A resulting from ingesting the livers of hunted animals. Maybe I should have trusted that the people could see medical cause and effect over thousands of years. In my defence, I had set up the colonial situation as a potential explanation, but I see from my notes that I did not explore that possibility.

THE IGLOO

The igloo stands (at least in the winter) as a good illustration for southerner lack of knowledge about the Inuit. I am not going to say that White men invented the igloo, although they did invent Styrofoam ones for early expositions and movies. Despite what we learned in elementary school, the igloo was not the only traditional Inuit home. The earliest Arctic dwellings appear to have been single-family tents, something that archaeologists can see by the circle of stones that were used instead of wooden pegs (hard to drive in through the permafrost and difficult to acquire north of the tree line). When whaling flourished for the Inuit and their antecessors, semi-subterranean houses with whalebone A-frames and sod in the construction commonly appeared. This was before the Little Ice Age, roughly from 1400 to the early

1800s. White intrusion also forced many Inuit to abandon or to diminish whaling as a way of life.

The image of the igloo is often reproduced in the public domain. In the summer of 2006, billboards in Ontario showed a picture of an igloo surrounded by middle-class suburban homes. The message was that you should save energy by not keeping your air conditioning on all the time. More subtly, it reinforces the message taught in school that Eskimos live in igloos.

The Word *Eskimo* and Its Meanings

Even the meaning of the word *Eskimo* has been open to question recently. This does not mean, however, that the new meanings are "new and improved." The word *Eskimo* was first recorded by the sixteenth-century English explorer Richard Hakluyt in 1584 as "Esquimawes." About a century later, Pierre Radisson, a French fur trader who later worked for the English through the Hudson's Bay Company, wrote the name as "Esquimos" and "Esquimaux." The spelling "Eskimo" is of more recent vintage.

Two types of proof are useful in developing a good etymology (historical development of meaning) of a word:

1. Credibility in terms of the mechanical processes of linguistic reconstruction (this is what linguists are best at).
2. Credibility in terms of the cultural logic of the people (this is what cultural anthropologists are best at).

Linguists who are not N/native speakers do a great job of the former, but often fall down in terms of the latter. The first is best demonstrated through strict adherence to linguistic rules, although as prominent linguist Edward Sapir once said famously, "all grammars leak." (Don't you wish you could have quoted that to your high school English teacher?) The second kind of proof requires closer attendance to how the people and their traditional neighbours thought.

There is a long written tradition of interpretation of the word *Eskimo* that is supported by Aboriginal oral tradition. It thus has credibility following both rules given above. Following the first form of proof, the word is based on a root in Algonquian languages that means "raw." The form that this root takes in the hypothesized ancestor language Proto-Algonquian, from which all Algonquian languages are said to have developed, is -*ašk*-. This root is also found in the -sq- of the borrowed-from-Algonquian-then-mangled-into-English word *squash* (the Aboriginal domesticated plant not the action). Most commentators or writers combine -*ašk*- with the hypothesized verb root meaning "to eat," which takes the form *-IMO- in Proto-Algonquian. The asterisk before the root means that it is a linguist's hypothetical construction. It has not been attested, meaning that it has not been heard by a native speaker or seen written in a text. The Montagnais (and their fellow Innu, the Naskapi) are an Algonquian people who speak a language closely related to Cree and were historically in contact with the Inuit. The North Shore Montagnais (along the Gulf of St. Lawrence) have been recorded as using the forms *kachikushu* or *kachekweshu*, which have been interpreted by speakers of the language as meaning "eater of raw meat" (Goddard 1984).

This Montagnais tradition is supported by the term for Inuit that comes from the Huron people, historic allies and trading partners of the Montagnais. It is a loan translation of the Inuit term, meaning the Huron (an Iroquoian-speaking people) translated the term used by the Montagnais into their own language. The Huron often loan translated names.[1] There are several forms of the Huron term for Inuit, depending on the dialect. The Huron of Lorette, now located at the outskirts of Quebec City, used *ok8ch iechronnon*, while the Wyandot of the Detroit/Windsor area used *ok8chtronnon*. Both expressions use the Huron verb *-ok8ch-* meaning "to be raw" (Potier 1920: 408) and the populative suffix *-ronnon-* "people," giving the literal meaning of the Wyandot word "people of the raw." The Lorette term adds the verb form *iech* that means "one, they eat it," giving the longer term the meaning "people who eat something raw."

Interestingly, the verb *-ok8ch-* is not used by any other Iroquoian language (e.g., Mohawk, Oneida, Onondaga, Cayuga, or Seneca), since the five (which later became six) nations of the Confederacy did not have a close, positive relationship with the Montagnais. The Huron along with the Algonquin were the Montagnais's allies in their seventeenth-century struggles with the Iroquois Confederacy of the Five Nations of the Mohawk, Oneida, Onondaga, Cayuga, and Seneca. The Iroquois had no such close relationship to an Algonquian-speaking people.

It is not unusual for Aboriginal groups to refer to their neighbours in terms of what they eat. The Mi'kmaq of the Atlantic provinces and Quebec called their Maliseet neighbours "porcupine people," and the Maliseet, who live in New Brunswick, reciprocated by calling the Mi'kmaq "muskrat people," based on their slightly different preferences in meat. The Mohawk called their Algonquian neighbours "Adirondack" ("they eat trees"), supposedly because those peoples boiled the inside bark of evergreens for the vitamin C in winter. In return, their Algonquian neighbours referred to the Mohawk as something more sinister: *Mohawk* derived from a word meaning "eaters of living things," implying that they were cannibals. Of course, it is not just Aboriginal peoples that use such names, as the English term *frogs* for the French, *sausage-eaters* for the Germans, and the Italian-Canadian term *mange cake* ("cake eaters") for English Canadians will attest. The list goes on.

The standard interpretation of the word *Eskimo* has changed since two linguistic heavyweights have entered the field. The first and foremost is Ives Goddard, the much-respected long-time curator of the department of anthropology at the Smithsonian Institution in Washington. He came up with a new idea, published prominently in 1984, that puts emphasis on the Montagnais word *ayassimew*, used with reference to their Mi'kmaq neighbours. In Goddard's brook-no-contradiction words:

> In spite of the tenacity of the belief, both among Algonquian speakers and in the anthropological and general literature ... that Eskimo means "raw-meat eaters," this explanation fits only the cited Ojibwa forms (containing Proto-Algonquian *ashk-* "raw" and *po-* "eat") and cannot be correct for the presumed Montagnais source of the word Eskimo itself.... The Montagnais word *ayassimew* [signifying the Mi'kmaq] (of which *ay-* is a reduplication) and its unreduplicated Attikamek cognate exactly match Montagnais *assimew*, Ojibwa *ashkime* "she nets a snowshoe," and an origin from a form meaning "snowshoe-netter" could be considered if the original Montagnais application (presumably before Montagnais contact with Eskimos) were to Algonquians. (Goddard 1984: 5–7)

His sole evidence is an intellectually tidy match between words and linguistic reconstruction. He is talented in forming those matches, and is usually right. However, such etymologies can be historically dodgy when they are not supported, as this is not, by the people's own interpretation. No historical source cites any Native group giving this meaning to the word *Eskimo*. That doesn't make Goddard's interpretation automatically wrong, but it does weaken the case for his hypothesis. He does not even mention that his hypothesis has no support in oral tradition. This expert assumption that "I know more than you do about your own traditions" is one that anthropologists of all types, including linguistic anthropologists, have to be careful before making.

The second linguist to challenge the interpretation of the word *Eskimo* was Jose Mailhot, a skilled linguist with an impressive knowledge of Cree. Her proposed etymology was similarly well crafted, following proof type one, but weak in terms of the cultural logic of the people. Referring to the East Cree word for Inuit, *ischiimeu...iischiimaau* (Cree School Board 1987: 23), Mailhot constructed another interpretation for *Eskimo*. She utilized the Proto-Algonquian forms *aya(ch)-* "other," *axkyi* "land" + *me* "by mouth" + animate suffix *-w* to come up with the suggested meaning "other-land speaker." Again we have a credible construction with this form, but this interpretation too suffers from not coming from Native speakers. It is just a linguist's logical construction. It is built on highly competent linguistic techniques. Sometimes, however, such constructions have to take a back seat to how the people interpret their own words. This is one of those times.

Taking this all into consideration, I still support the traditional interpretation. The burden of proof is on the shoulders of the linguists. The fat lady has yet to appear on the stage. And as far as I am concerned, when she appears, she will be singing the traditional verses.

Does Eating Raw Mean Eating *People* Raw?

One persistent story about the Inuit is that they practise cannibalism. This notion was featured in two Canadian classics: Farley Mowat's *Snow Walker* and Yves Thériault's *Agaguk*. Inuit cannibalism was popularized in Britain, in large measure to shift blame from English gentlemen. Ken McGoogan's excellent *Fatal Passage: The Untold Story of John Rae, the Arctic Adventurer Who Discovered the Fate of Franklin* (2001) tells the story of John Rae, one of many British explorers who ventured to find survivors and discover the fate of Sir John Franklin's well-financed but ill-starred attempt to sail across the Arctic in 1845. Rae was shamed for even suggesting English gentlemen would practise such a thing as cannibalism. When he talked and actually listened to the Inuit (a rare occurrence among writers of early literature), he heard them mention cannibalism among the last survivors of the Franklin expedition. As he heard it from a number of different Inuit sources, he was prepared to accept it. When he returned to Britain in 1854, he reported his findings to the British public. His upper class readers were not amused. It was simply not on for English gentlemen to behave in such a manner. But "savages," well that was something different. Even Charles Dickens, much to his discredit, held this belief. Dickens was a friend to the White downtrodden, but not to colonized peoples. In his popular magazine *Household Words*, he attacked Rae's assertion several times. The following shows Dickens's clear racism:

> [Nobody can rationally affirm] that this sad remnant of Franklin's gallant band were not set upon and slain by the Esquimaux themselves. It is impossible to form an estimate of the character of any race of savages, from their deferential behaviour to the white man while he is strong....We believe every savage to be in his heart covetous, treacherous, and cruel; and we have yet to learn what knowledge the white man—lost, houseless, shipless; apparently forgotten by his race; plainly famine-stricken, weak, frozen, helpless and dying—has of the gentleness of the Esquimaux nature. (as quoted in McGoogan 2001: 227)

Rae's reports were ripped apart by other writers. It didn't help his cause that he was working class. Neither did the fact that he wasn't English. (His family came from the Orkney Islands.) Recently, however, archaeologists Keenleyside, Bertulli, and Frike have vindicated the Scottish working class upstart. In the conclusion to their article on the subject, they wrote: "To date, the skeletal remains of less than two-thirds of the 105 crewmen who abandoned ship in the spring of 1848 have been located.... The presence of cut marks on approximately one-quarter of the remains support nineteenth-century Inuit accounts of cannibalism on the expedition" (Keenleyside et al. 1997).

Who Are You Calling Inuit, White Man?

Another question regarding the term *Eskimo* is why we changed the name we'd been calling the people. There are several reasons to support the change. The basic one, of course, is that *Eskimo* is not a term in the people's own language. It was never their choice. Imagine if your name came from what your unfriendly neighbours called you? There is an implied insult in the origin of the name. Further, some White people in the North historically used another derived version of the Algonquian word, *husky* (as in the dog's name), as an insulting term of reference and address for the Inuit.

While we are talking about names for the people, we should take a look at the word *Inuit*, which means "people" in Inuktitut. It is important to recognize that *Inuit* is a plural form of *Inuk*. Writers of sociology textbooks (e.g., Spencer 1981: 294 and 1996: 378) and students who use *Inuits* should be cautioned that the term is as incorrect as *phenomenas*, *datas*, or *childrens*. There is also a dual form of the word *Inuit*. Inuktitut (like other Aboriginal languages, such as Huron and Mohawk) distinguishes among three numbers: singular, dual, and plural.

While many of you may be nodding your heads in agreement, do you also know that not all the people that used to be called Eskimos should be called Inuit? Fundamentally, *Inuit* is only really appropriate for those people who live in Canada, and not all of those, either. In the Mackenzie Delta, the plural for the people should be *Inuvialuit*, meaning "real, genuine people." The singular is *Inuvialuk*. Note the parallel -uk (Inuk and Inuvialuk) and -uit (Inuit and Inuvialuit). In Alaska, two terms tend to be used: *Inupiaq* (singular for "real, genuine person") and *Inupiat* (plural) in the north, and *Yup'ik* in the southwest (singular and plural). In Greenland, you can use *Katladlit* and *Kalaallisut*. In the far west, Siberia and St. Lawrence Island, try using *Yuk* (meaning "person"; not pronounced as *yuck*, but more like the beginning of the word *euchre*) and *Yuit* ("people"). Confused? Here is a chart.

AREA	SINGULAR	PLURAL
Most of the Canadian Arctic	Inuk	Inuit
Mackenzie Delta	Inuvialuk	Inuvialuit
North Alaska	Inupiaq	Inupiat
South Alaska	Yup'ik	Yup'ik
Siberia and St. Lawrence Island	Yuk	Yuit

To keep things in perspective, here is a European parallel. People who speak German and live in Germany are called Germans. People who speak German in the Netherlands are called Dutch, and in Belgium they are called Flemish. In Austria, they are called Austrians; in Switzerland they are called Swiss Germans. It is just as confusing to outsiders as the different names for the *Inuit* are.

Part of a Larger Picture

The White lies about the Inuit do not stand as isolated phenomena. They came about as a result of Canadian ignorance of Aboriginal people, the conservative and additive nature of introductory textbooks, and colonialism.

CANADIAN IGNORANCE OF ABORIGINAL PEOPLE

I have several times heard Aboriginal speakers say that Canadian knowledge about Aboriginal people is like the soil of the Prairies: It's very broad, in that everybody knows something, but regrettably very shallow, in that few people know more than a little. To further the analogy, the winds of opinion also blow the soil from place to place periodically. Very little is taught in the Canadian school system, from elementary school, to secondary school, to colleges and universities. Those who become teachers in Canadian schools are typically products of the system, so they are not likely to know much and have little to pass on to the next generation of learners. Ignorance is as communicable as knowledge.

Here is an example to illustrate. After I tried for years to get my article on the Iroquois Great Law of Peace included in the textbook used for a course that is a kind of compulsory elective for students in my college, it was finally accepted. The article was placed in the politics unit, along with the usual suspects: Hobbes, Locke, Mills, and Marx. When I was part of a group teaching the course, I made sure my article was taught (by me). Other groups rarely used it, as it was beyond the knowledge and comfort of my colleagues. It was eventually dropped from the textbook. Our students will pass through the course with the same ignorance of Aboriginal people that they brought to it.

The Canadian educational system is one good reason why we don't have a critical (in both senses) mass of people who can judge good from bad information about Aboriginal people. Most people will believe almost anything about Aboriginal people.

THE CONSERVATIVE, ADDITIVE NATURE OF INTRODUCTORY TEXTBOOKS

"None of us will ever accomplish anything excellent or commanding except when he listens to this whisper which is heard by him alone." Textbook writers would do well to listen to these words of Thomas Carlyle. Introductory textbooks in social sciences such as anthropology and sociology have strong conservative tendencies. Rethinking is rare. Dorothy Smith's important and useful critique of sociology in *The Conceptual Practices of Power: A Feminist Sociology of Knowledge* (1990) is applicable to the construction of both sociological and anthropological textbooks. She asserts that newly and differently developed knowledge is primarily inserted as an addendum rather than presented as a cause to rethink what is already there: "It is not enough to supplement an established sociology by addressing ourselves to what has been left out or overlooked, or by making women's issues into sociological issues. That does not change the standpoint built into existing sociological procedures, but merely makes the sociology of women an addendum to the body of knowledge" (Smith 1990: 12–14).

This addendum principle has been applied directly to the study of textbooks in Michael Apple and Linda Christian-Smith's *The Politics of the Textbook* (1991). They refer to the addendum process as "mentioning":

> As disenfranchised groups have fought to have their knowledge take center stage in the debates over cultural legitimacy, one trend has dominated in text production. In essence, very little tends to be dropped from textbooks. Major ideological frameworks do not get markedly changed. Textbook publishers are under considerable and constant pressure to include *more* in their books. Progressive *items* are perhaps mentioned, then, but not developed in depth. Dominance is partly maintained here through compromise and the process of "mentioning." (Apple and Christian-Smith 1991: 10)

What Smith and Apple and Christian-Smith are saying is that textbooks are additive. More is added than taken away. Old paradigms tend to be repeated. The only way in which textbooks can be made smaller is to have brief introduction books, some of which are over 300 pages long. These don't usually introduce radically new thought. I have a measure of recent expertise here as I have co-written a couple of textbooks: one in Native studies and one in sociology. The past weighs heavily on a newly written textbook. Like new parents who repeat in small ways how they were parented, teachers repeat to a significant extent how they were taught. For a textbook writer, teachers are your first market because they are the ones who choose what to buy; the students merely comply. Also, the dynamics of contemporary post-secondary education create conservative tendencies. Many introductory courses are now taught by young teachers under single-term contracts. They don't tend to make waves when choosing a textbook. They want to be hired full time. Textbook editors tend to solicit older teachers to read and judge proposals for new textbooks and to suggest what should be left out or added. Editors can use these opinions to strongly influence the content of a book by claiming to reflect the market. Older teachers tend to structure their courses as they have taught them in the past. I know that *I* do. It is easy to link such a practice with textbook structure. Judging from their reactions when I break the "rules," students generally expect courses and textbooks to proceed together in order. This adds to the conservative drag on textbook innovation.

Frequently taught courses have more conservative drag on the textbooks than ones that are offered less often. In writing the Native studies textbook, I was fairly free from the weight of the past. However, I felt the pull when I recently (2005–06) began revising the work for its second edition: Teacher-reviewers suggested adding things that they typically taught. But this was lightweight resistance. Editors of Native studies textbooks have to trust the writer as the "expert" because they probably have never taken a Native studies course and their background knowledge is slight. They can't comment because they don't know much about what you are writing. There is no set pattern. I felt tremendous freedom in what I wrote.

In writing the introductory sociology textbook, I found much more resistance from editors and teacher-reviewers, but fortunately not much from colleagues at my college. I tried to follow the method of economist and mathematician John Nash, the Nobel Prize-winning subject of the book *A Beautiful Mind*. Nash would find out what the significant problems were and attempt to solve them while deliberately not looking at how others had tried. He produced first the weird and then the wonderful. I gave that something of a try. I composed chapters without looking at what other people had written. Introductory textbook writers generally aren't permitted that kind of intellectual freedom. My biggest innovation, a chapter devoted to Canadian sociology, was the first victim of the forces of conservatism. (I try not to think of them as the forces of evil.) Nobody taught that subject, so nobody wanted it included in the book. The whole got sacrificed for parts to go in different chapters, like an old car going to the wrecker.

REPETITIONS AND THE HYPERREAL

Repetition gives credibility to a story. If you hear the phrase "weapons of mass destruction" often enough, you may think they exist. When such myths are perceived as more real than concrete evidence-based constructions of reality in a culture, they are called *hyperreal*, a term coined by sociologist Pierre Baudrillard. The White lie about the cultural custom of the Inuit to abandon their elders to die when the going got tough is one example of the hyperreal. The often-repeated textbook tales of Inuit elder abandonment magnified the presence of the practice. They made it appear more frequent, "more real" to students than it actually was.

Teacher lecture notes can follow the same path. If teachers do not question what they have taught before, they will repeat the errors of the past, in the discipline and in the standard textbooks. As an anthropology teacher for more than 25 years, I have had to seriously check up on what I have traditionally taught. Some of our most important figures have been taken to task, but news of these challenges to traditional thinking spreads slowly into introductory classrooms and textbooks, and even more slowly into public knowledge through media such as the Internet. The Internet is often a place where old, discredited ideas go not to die, but to live on in a home for the intellectually aged.

Three important figures in American cultural anthropology have had their works seriously questioned. Franz Boas, one of the main White players that I will be examining in this book, has been challenged for his recording of Tsimshian myths. In 2000, Simon Fraser University English professor

Ralph Maud published *Transmission Difficulties: Franz Boas and Tsimshian Mythology*, which presented severe and valid criticism of one of Boas's most substantial works, *Tsimshian Mythology*—an examination of the BC-based First Nation published in 1916. First, one of the "transmission difficulties" was that Henry Tate, Boas's informant for these texts, wrote the myths first in English and then translated them, although not completely, into Tsimshian. However, Boas claimed in his Introduction that the text was recorded in Tsimshian and that he translated it. Second, Boas (and Tate, with Boas's subtle prompting) greatly toned down the sexuality of the stories. Boas sometimes recorded the "dirty words" in Tsimshian, sometimes in Latin.[2] Third, Boas removed the Christian sensibility and biblical phrasing of Tate's English, making the myths look less influenced by European contact than they were. Fourth, Tate copied (we would say plagiarized today) some myths and parts of others from Boas's earlier work with a Tsimshian informant from another community (Nass River to Tate's Port Simpson) and from another language group, Kwakiutl. Boas noted that there might be outside influences, but did not say that some of them came from material that he sent to Tate. The list goes on.

In her dissertation and later her book, Boas's prize student Margaret Mead challenged the notion of adolescence as a universally stormy time by comparing the North American experience with the Samoan. First published in 1928, *Coming of Age in Samoa* portrays Samoan teenage females as sexually active and free living. This idea has itself been seriously and convincingly questioned by Derek Freeman in *The Fateful Hoaxing of Margaret Mead: A Historical Analysis of Her Samoan Research* (1999). It seems to me fairly clear that the value of Mead's classic book is severely compromised in a few key ways. First, Freeman ably demonstrates that she had preconceived notions of Polynesian promiscuity (I love the alliteration of that phrase), and, if he is to be believed, she was hoaxed by the sexual joking of her main informant. Second, she ascribed to an overwhelmingly strong cultural determinist ideology (see discussion of Boas in chapter two for what this entails). Third, her research interests were conflicted; unknown to Boas, her thesis supervisor, she had signed a contract with a museum to research and write a Samoan ethnography.

From the time of its first publication in 1968 until 1983, Napoleon Chagnon's *Yanomamo: The Fierce People* sold four million copies (Tierney 2000: 7). In addition, many collections of readings include a selection from that work. According to Patrick Tierney's carefully constructed *Darkness in El Dorado: How Scientists and Journalists Devastated the Amazon* (2000) Chagnon's book involved "both a riveting account of warfare among Stone Age people and a sobering assessment of what life may have been like for much of prehistory. *The Fierce People* made the Yanomami the most famous tribe in the world—a model of primitive man and a synonym for aggression. It made Napoleon Chagnon the best-known American anthropologist since Margaret Mead" (Tierney 2000: 7–8).

Tierney asserts that Chagnon's construction of the fierce Yanomamo image was, among other violations of anthropological ethics, stage-managed by his masterly hand. Yet Chagnon's educational construct still lives on unfettered. Just do an Internet search on the Yanomamo and see how often the construct is offered up with no challenge in sight. Word and picture images of this construct are being reproduced over and over in websites (some of them for anthropology courses), blogs, educational videos, textbooks, and lesson plans. These images are educational commodities being sold in the market-place. It is safe to say that the force of their hyperreality is stronger than any intellectual challenge that has been made on their original creator.

COLONIALISM

A key concept for understanding the manufacture and long-term distribu-tion of White lies about the Inuit is colonialism. Colonialism refers not just to societies reaching out to grab and control the lands and bodies of peoples from other societies. It also refers to grabbing and controlling the story of these lands and peoples. This has happened all over the world: the Americas, Africa, Siberia (see Reid 2003 and Slezkine 1994), South Asia, and what is increasingly being called (for tourism and intellectual purposes) the "Wild West" of China in Tibet and in Xinjiang (see Tyler 2004) are primary exam-ples. As a result, scholarly and non-scholarly information that can distort the people's history and contemporary culture in a number of ways is being produced and distributed. One kind of colonial distortion shows people as victims or inferior beings needing our help. The false story of the Inuit aban-doning their elders fits comfortably into this conceptualization. Secondly, there is the exoticization of the colonized people, making them look strange and different. This type of distortion includes stories of Inuit elder abandon-ment and the multitude of snow terms. Third, although it seems to contradict exoticization, there is the sense that "we came here long before, and aspects of the colonized culture (typically the best bits) are really ours." That this notion fits well with the idea of conquering land and people should not pass unnoticed. In South Africa and Zimbabwe, the idea that "they are really part of us" was called forth to "explain" the massive stone structure of the Great Zimbabwe. This archaeological marvel was hypothesized to be an ancient (at least 3,000 years) White-made structure possibly constructed by the Phoeni-cians, rather than the more accurate 800- to 600-year-old construction of the local Shona people (Beach 1994). When late eighteenth-century linguist Wil-liam Jones established that Sanskrit, the sacred language of Hinduism, was related to Classical Greek and Latin as well as most contemporary European languages, and that modern South Asian languages such as Hindi, Urdu, Punjabi, and Bengali also shared that linguistic family relationship, the Aryan race of "superior" Europeans, later made famous by Hitler, claimed to have invaded India and brought high culture to it. (This claim has now been fairly successfully challenged since it has been proven that "civilization" was there before the Aryans arrived.) This made for a good justification for Britain's colonial control of India. More recently, China has claimed inaccurately that the significantly different Tibetans and the Muslim Turkic peoples of Xinjiang have been part of China for at least the last two millennia. The example of the Blond Eskimo (chapter four), while perhaps not actively used for colonial justification, fits into the "really part of us" storyline.

Notes

1   They did this sometimes with personal names of the French. Guillaume Couture was called *ihandich* "he sews" as a loan translation of his last name. Father Pierre Chastelain had his first name translated by a Huron name meaning "rock."

2   This was not unique to Boas. Jesuit missionary linguists translated "dirty" Huron body part names into Latin in the seventeenth and eighteenth centuries. Pioneering Canadian anthropologist Thomas McIllwraith engaged in extensive fieldwork with the Bella Coola (now called Nuxalt) in 1922 and 1924. When he attempted to have it published through the National Museum, he followed the advice of Edward Sapir and Diamond Jenness (who well knew the minds of government officials) and translated from Nuxalt into Latin the more explicit descriptions of sexual practices. The supervisor of government publications wouldn't even allow that. It wasn't until 1948 that McIllwraith's classic work *The Bella Coola Indians* was published by the University of Toronto Press.

CONTENT QUESTIONS

1. How were Inuit put on display during the nineteenth and early twentieth centuries?
2. Outline the history of the portrayal of the Inuit in the movies.
3. What "White lies" are discussed in this chapter?
4. What does the word *Eskimo* mean, and what other interpretations have been given?
5. What names are given to the Inuit in different areas?
6. What form of research is necessary before the female infanticide stereotype can be meaningfully discussed?
7. What two forms of evidence are necessary to "prove" the etymology or original meaning of a name in an Aboriginal language?
8. Why do White lies about the Inuit exist and persist?

DISCUSSION QUESTIONS

1. What kind of research should the ad agency have done to discover the authenticity of the practice of rubbing noses as a general Inuit practice?
2. Why is it easier to develop theories of culturally specific psychoses than to seek historically or individually specific explanations for so-called strange behaviour?

3. Why do you think that Boas exhibited what we would think of today as a harsh or callous attitude towards the suffering of the Inuit he encountered, both in the Arctic and as museum exhibits?
4. Why might discussions of the Inuit be more susceptible to stereotyping than discussions of more southerly Aboriginal people?
5. Why might the demands of good storytelling and good anthropology sometimes clash?

KEY TERMS

Algonquian languages	Caribou Inuit	colonialism
cultural logic	exotic/exoticize/exoticization	
etymology	female infanticide	fieldwork
hyperreal	Iroquoian languages	loan translation
nose rubbing	*pibloktuq*	wife sharing

CHAPTER TWO

Four Major White Figures

LEARNING OBJECTIVES

After reading this chapter, you will be able to
» present and critique the anthropological ideas and work of Franz Boas.
» critique the idea of the ethnographic present.
» distinguish between biological and cultural determinism.
» compare and contrast the occupations of the explorer and the anthropologist during the late nineteenth and early twentieth centuries.
» outline Diamond Jenness's contribution to our knowledge of the Inuit.
» outline the weaknesses and strengths of Farley Mowat's subjective non-fiction.

> No sooner does a great man depart, and leave his character as public property, than a crowd of little men rushes towards it. There they are gathered together, blinking up to it with such vision as they have, scanning it from afar, hovering round it this way and that, each cunningly endeavoring, by all arts, to catch some reflex of it in the little mirror of himself.
>
> —Thomas Carlyle

FOUR WHITE FIGURES WILL appear regularly in the chapters that follow: Franz Boas, Diamond Jenness, Vilhjalmur Stefansson and Farley Mowat. All four had strong ties to Canada: Mowat and Stefansson were born here; Jenness spent most of his life here; and Boas did the majority of his research here. What follows is a brief introduction to the men and their contributions to our understanding of the Inuit. All four are implicated in the production and reproduction of White lies, some more than others. My assessments of these men will have their biases. While all four men have accomplished things that are to be admired, my feelings about them are varied and conflicted, and intersect with my sense of what is right and wrong and what is good and bad scholarship. And these feelings are interwoven into my sense of right and wrong, good scholar and bad scholar.

However, despite the prevalence of White lies in so much of the scholarship about the Inuit, some non-Inuit anthropologists and other scholars have produced excellent, relatively bias-free works. A short list would include Brody (1975), Dahl (2000), Dorais (1997), Minor (1992), Rasing (1994), and Tester and Kulchyski (1994). The Inuit themselves are developing a growing literature, including Freeman (1978), Okpik (1964), and prolific Inuk journalist Rachel Qitsualik, whose articles have appeared in magazines such as *Indian Country Today*, and *Nunatsiaq News*.

Franz Boas: A Paternalistic Father of Anthropology

Franz Boas (1858–1942), who lived on Baffin Island in 1883 and 1884, was the first scholar to engage in prolonged fieldwork with the Inuit. Born in what is now Germany, Boas earned a doctorate in physics before he began studying geography and decided to go to the Arctic. At the time, mapping "unknown lands" (that is, those not familiar to Europeans) was a rite of passage for German geographers aspiring to academic success. His stay on Baffin Island was his only ethnographic research among the Inuit, but it profoundly influenced how the Inuit were perceived and studied, particularly in the discipline of anthropology. It also affected how anthropology itself was practised, particularly in the United States. His field notes map out the development of the concept of cultural relativism, which would play such a large part in his thinking. For example:

> *October 3, 1883*: I can tell you that the Eskimos are far from being uncivilized people.

> *December 23, 1883*: I believe that if this trip has a significant impact on me as a thinking person, then it is the strengthening of my notion of the relativity of all education. (Müller-White 1998: 110, 159)

After staying on Baffin Island, Boas wrote his classic *The Central Eskimo* (1888), the first detailed anthropological account of an Inuit group. Beginning in 1896 and while at Columbia University in New York, he did much to shape North American anthropology. Boas and his many American followers (e.g., Margaret Mead, Ruth Benedict, Alfred Kroeber, Ralph Linton, and Robert Lowie) engaged in a school of thought sometimes referred to as *historical particularism*. As with all schools of thought, it made use of ideas that enabled its followers to see some things more clearly (even if the seeing was hallucinating) and to be blind to others. Boas's historical particularism had several elements. One, it stood in opposition to cultural evolution: a then-popular notion that cultures, like biological entities, evolve from simple forms to the more complex, advancing in stages like those of biological evolution. In its early and most insulting form, the stages were called savagery, barbarism, and civilization. Establishing the stage of a particular culture involved engaging in a far-reaching comparative study of different cultures.

Boas opposed this often crudely speculative practice, as the title of his 1896 book *The Limitations of the Comparative Method of Anthropology* suggests. He and his followers believed in intensely focusing on one specific culture, or most broadly, one culture area (a group of peoples having similar cultures).[1] This is the "particularism" part of the school of thought. The "historical" part involved reconstructing the history of the people to form a hypothesized "ethnographic present." (i.e., the present of the culture at the time it was studied).[2] This kind of study often involved two flawed assumptions. First, the culture was described as if the people were not and had never been in contact with the broader world, typically Western society. Second, it was portrayed as if the society had been static prior to contact. The anthropologists had a salvage mentality, wanting to quickly record the pristine, untouched culture before it disappeared completely under Western influence.

Modern criticism of Boas and his contemporaries on this score is well articulated in the introductory chapter to Conrad Phillip Kottak's *Mirror for Humanity: A Concise Introduction to Cultural Anthropology* (1999):

> Recent ethnographic writers have ... attempted to correct the deficiency of *romanticized timelessness*, which is obvious in the classics. Linked to salvage ethnography was the idea of the *ethnographic present*—the present before Westernization, when the "true" native culture flourished. This notion gives classic ethnographies an eternal, timeless quality. The cultures they describe seem frozen in the ethnographic present. Providing the only jarring note in this idealized picture are occasional comments by the author about traders or missionaries, suggesting that in actuality the natives were already part of the world system.
>
> Anthropologists now recognize that the ethnographic present is a rather unrealistic and romantic construct. Cultures have been in contact—and have been changing—throughout history. Most native cultures had at least one major foreign encounter before any anthropologist ever came their way. Most of them had already been incorporated in some fashion into nation-states or colonial systems. (Kottak 1999: 21)

This criticism aptly applies to Boas's work with the Inuit. The Baffin Island Inuit that Boas encountered had experienced a significant amount of contact by that time, with whalers and explorers of the German Polar Commission that had arrived the year prior to his fieldwork. Boas made virtually no reference to the presence of whalers in his ethnography *The Central Eskimo*. They were almost anthropologically invisible. But Boas alludes to the influence of their presence in journal entries, which refer to sudden illnesses and deaths, particularly among children. The harsh hand of White disease was having a profound effect on the people. Yet Boas took no significant anthropological notice.

In his work in physical anthropology, Boas was an avid skull collector and measurer. To be fair, this was common practice at the time, and he used his findings to oppose the scientific racism of his day. He resisted racist theories that equated intelligence with skull configuration by using his research on immigrants to New York to show how the skulls of subsequent generations changed: race was not a fixed or permanent construct.

In the summer of 1888, Boas worked for the Canadian government with the Kwakiutl of the Northwest Coast, and his writings about these people were voluminous. Few other Canadian Aboriginal groups would be so "anthropologized." But he didn't just study the Kwakiutl—he was a kind of "headhunter." According to David Hurst Thomas:

> Discouraged at his inability to become associated with any of the established natural history museums, Boas also used the trip to build up a personal Northwest Coast Indian skull collection as a speculative business venture. He described himself as "just like a merchant," who was hoping that a carefully documented collection, at the going rate of $5 for a skull and $20 for a complete skeleton, might return "a tidy profit"—as well as finally open the door to a permanent curatorship.

> While digging a burial ground near Victoria, British Columbia, Boas used a photographer to distract the Indians while he was doing his grave robbing. On June 6, 1888, he wrote in frustration that "someone had stolen all the skulls, but we found a complete skeleton without head. I hope to get another one either today or tomorrow.... It is most unpleasant work to steal bones from a grave, but what is the use, someone has to do it." (Rohner 1966: 188)

Some of the skulls collected would join the Labrador Inuit on exhibit at the 1893 World's Columbian Exposition in Chicago.

By 1896, Franz Boas had been appointed assistant curator of the prestigious American Museum of Natural History in New York as well as professor at Columbia University. Boas sent a request to intrepid Arctic explorer Robert Peary to bring back a living middle-aged Inuk from northwestern Greenland so that he and other anthropologists could study this person in the museum. Peary brought back six.

The six were Nuktaq, his wife Atangana, and their twelve-year-old adopted daughter, Aviaq; Qisuk and his five-year-old son Minik; and Uisaakassak. The six were initially housed in the cold and damp basement of the museum, and people gathered to gawk at them through the grating of the window. They had arrived on September 30, 1897, but by the beginning of November, all six were in Bellevue Hospital, with various degrees of pneumonia. When they returned to the museum, they were moved up to an apartment on the sixth floor, a place usually reserved for the caretaker.

Their deaths were not long in coming. Qisuk was first, dying on February 17, 1898. Atangana was next, on March 16. Two others would follow shortly. Only Uisaakassak, who later returned to Greenland, and Minik were able to survive. As living exhibits, their grief was not to be private. In 1901, soon-to-be-prominent physical anthropologist Ales Hrdlicka published an article entitled "An Eskimo Brain" in the *American Anthropologist*. The brain was identified as belonging to Qisuk. It did not remain anonymous, as was the usual practice. Alfred Kroeber, then 21 years old and also destined to become a prominent anthropologist, published a detailed account of the mourning behaviour of the Inuit in 1899. He would later stage a famous living exhibit of his own on the other side of the United States: Ishi, "the last wild Indian." Ishi's brain was preserved upon death and kept it at the Smithsonian. It has only recently been buried.

Perhaps the grimmest tragedy to the Inuit from Greenland was revealed in the New York press in 1907. On January 6, the headline of *New York World* (the paper after which the World Series is named) read "Give Me My Father's Body." In 1986, Kenn Harper would use this headline as the title for his best-selling book that revealed Qisuk's fate. After Qisuk died, the museum people, including Boas, staged a fake burial for Minik's benefit, using a covered log so he would think his father was respectfully buried. Qisuk was actually being kept in the museum. Following a dispute over the body, the museum and Bellevue Hospital reached a compromise to allow medical students to dissect the body, while the skeleton would be preserved and mounted in the museum.

What was Boas's attitude to the deception? As reported by Harper, it was as follows:

> The purpose of the burial, Boas claimed, was "to appease the boy, and keep him from discovering that his father's body had been chopped up and the bones placed in the collection of the institution." Not only did Boas confirm the story of the fake burial, though, he defended it. He said that he saw "nothing particularly deserving severe criticism" in the act. "The other Eskimos who were still alive were not very well, and then there was Minik, and of course it was only reasonable to spare them any shock or uneasiness. The burial accomplished that purpose I suppose."
>
> The reporter questioned the right of the museum to claim the body of a man whose relatives were still alive, but Boas responded, "Oh, that was perfectly legitimate. There was no one to bury the body, and the museum had as good a right to it as any other institution authorised to claim bodies." But, protested the reporter, did not that body belong rightfully to Minik, the son of the deceased? "Well," was Boas's reply, "Minik was just a little boy, and he did not ask for the body. If he had, he might have got it." (Harper 1986: 93–94)

Qisuk's bones, along with those of the other three who died, would not be returned to their Greenland home until 1993. Minik died in 1917. He, too, was buried in the south.

Boas and his students infused their anthropological work with a strong sense of the power of culture (see Freeman 1999: 17–27). Race in the name of biology was the alternative, and they fought hard against the "scientific racism" of their time by using cultural determinism to combat biological determinism. But in so doing, they overstated their case, arguing too strongly for the power and the uniformity of culture, particularly in societies they deemed "primitive." In her notes from her first anthropology class, taught by Boas, Margaret Mead wrote "in primitive society the ideal is conformity, and any attempt to deviate is not tolerated" (Freeman 1999: 34). Boas and his high profile students committed the fallacy we now refer to as "culturist": making culture an anonymous deterministic force that denies members the opportunity to choose or contest. This will be discussed further in looking at the three main issues of this work: the exaggerated number of Inuit snow terms, the myth of the Blond Eskimo, and the myth of Inuit elder abandonment.

Stefansson and Jenness: Two Polar Opposites

Vilhjalmur Stefansson and Diamond Jenness are two physically small but figuratively big characters in the study of the Arctic. I would label the former as small part anthropologist and large part explorer, self-promoter, and media darling. The latter was a quietly competent government anthropologist. In their own ways, the men epitomized the stereotypical differences between the two countries in which they spent most of their lives: Stefansson in the United States and Jenness in Canada.

VILHJALMUR STEFANSSON: THE ICEMAN

Vilhjalmur Stefansson (1879–1962) began life in Manitoba, the son of two Icelandic immigrants. When Stefansson was a small child, his family moved to an Icelandic farming community in North Dakota. He began his university studies at the State University of North Dakota in Grand Forks, but later dropped out. He then enrolled at the University of Iowa in 1901 and graduated from the faculty of theology in 1903. That year, he shifted to anthropology and received a scholarship to study at Harvard. He initially intended to research Africa, but changed to Arctic studies by 1905. He conducted his first archaeological fieldwork in Iceland that summer and stirred up local controversy by taking 88 skulls and some other bones from old, abandoned Icelandic cemeteries. In 1906, he became engaged to drama student Orpha Cecil Smith from Toronto (one of two lives he would ruin for people from my home town—the second was a man from Toronto who was recruited to Wrangel Island). Shortly afterwards, he was hired as anthropologist for his first expedition, directed by Einar Mikkelsen from Denmark and American Ernest de Koven Leffingwell. Stefansson stayed in the North for 16 months, the shortest expedition he participated in. In 1908, not long after his return, he was off on the Stefansson-Anderson expedition, this time for four years.

Dr. Rudolph Anderson, the second-named figure, was an American zoologist and a former classmate of Stefansson's, and a man who would later become one of his leading critics. Stefansson hired Fanny Pannigabluk as a seamstress, and she soon became his lover. In 1909, Miss Smith broke off the engagement by letter. In 1910, Pannigabluk gave birth to a son, Alex. Purportedly on the advice of his lawyers, Stefansson did not officially acknowledge his son, until the magazine *North* published a piece in 1961 written by one of his young grandchildren: "My Grandfather, Dr. Vilhjalmur Stefansson" (Pálsson 2005: 272).

After struggling to secure adequate funding from American sources for a third expedition, Stefansson struck it rich by convincing the Canadian government to support his next project, which was called the Canadian Arctic Expedition, although Stefansson sometimes named it the Stefansson Expedition after himself.

When pleading for funding for his research, Stefansson didn't hesitate to play upon Canadian fears that American money might lead to American control of the Arctic. Throughout the twentieth century, the idea that Americans (or Russians or Danes) would control "their" Arctic consistently motivated lethargic Canadian governments into action. It forced them into assuming the court-ordered responsibility for the Inuit that they naturally provided for other Canadians. Their fear sometimes led to foolish decisions, such as moving whole Inuit communities farther north into dangerously different environments to make the claim that "Canadians are here." But on one occasion, they were not so moved when Stefansson played that card—and four young men would die on that expedition, three of them never to be found. More of that sad story later.

Polar expeditions, to the Arctic or Antarctic, were highly romanticized adventures at the turn of the twentieth century. They were the near equivalents to rocket trips to Mars, or the Survivor series today. Heroes abounded in the frozen extremities of the planet 100 years ago. There was American naval officer Admiral Robert Peary (1856–1920), generally recognized for being the first person to reach the North Pole, in 1909. Significantly less recognition went to his "assistant," African-American Matthew Henson (1866–1955), who published *A Negro Explorer at the North Pole* in 1912, or to the four, usually nameless, Inuit—Egingwah, Ooqueah, Ootah, and Seeglo—who travelled all the way with Peary and enabled him to stake his claim to lasting fame. Norwegian explorer Roald Amundsen was the first to cross the Arctic by boat, sailing the fabled Northwest Passage from 1903 to 1905, across the Arctic waters that had charmed centuries of earlier explorers to their deaths. Not finished with exploration, Amundsen was the first to reach the South Pole, in late 1911.

DIAMOND JENNESS: A NORTHERN GEM

Among the eager young men hired to accompany Stefansson on the Canadian Arctic Expedition was New Zealand-born anthropologist Diamond Jenness (1886–1969). Like his sister Pearl, he was named to honour his father's trade as a jeweller and watchmaker. Jenness was trained in classical studies at the newly founded university in his native town of Wellington. Like a number of classical scholars of his time, he converted to anthropology when a student at Oxford. Like other famous Wellington-born anthropologists—Reo Fortune (Margaret Mead's second husband) and Derek Freeman (Mead's biggest critic)—Jenness conducted his first fieldwork in the Pacific Islands. With the help of his missionary brother-in-law, he studied the people he referred to as the Northern D'Entrecasteaux of Papua New Guinea (the big island just north of Australia). Afterwards, he went back to New Zealand to recoup from malarial fever. While convalescing, he looked for work. Fortunately, he had a Canadian connection: his fellow Oxonian Marius Barbeau. Quebec-born Barbeau would eventually become one of the most prolific anthropologists in Canada. Through Barbeau, Jenness began work in a climate that was the exact opposite of what he had endured in Papua New Guinea. Out of the frying pan and into the freezer.

Jenness signed on to Stefansson's Canadian Arctic Expedition, which lasted from 1913 to 1916. He produced a good number of reports from his work with the Copper Inuit, as well as *People of the Twilight* (1928), a highly readable work that has long been considered a classic. In 1932, he wrote *Indians of Canada*, the canonical work in Native studies during the twentieth century. During the 1960s, he published another monumental work, the five-part *Eskimo Administration* (1962, 1964, 1965, 1967, and 1968), which included discussions on the Inuit in the USSR, Alaska, Canada, and Greenland.

Diamond Jenness was a true anthropological Renaissance man. In North American anthropology, we generally say that there are four sub-disciplines of the field: archaeology (cast adrift in Europe or linked with Classics), socio-cultural anthropology, linguistic anthropology (which has the fewest students and is the least taught in introductory classes), and physical or biological anthropology (currently very popular because of the forensic aspect—CSI: An Introduction). Jenness made significant achievements in all four sub-disciplines in his research on the Inuit. No one else can claim that, not even Boas.

Jenness and Stefansson can be called the founding figures of Arctic archaeology, although Canadians tend to support the former (see Morrison 1991: Preface) and Americans the latter (see Collins 1962). I have read the field notes of both, and I find Jenness to be the most systematic, more like a modern archaeologist. But then, I am Canadian, and I greatly prefer the quiet professional Jenness to the bombastic Stefansson who was careless with other people's lives. Jenness's main lasting contributions to the field are twofold. In

the Preface to Jenness's field notes (edited by his son, Stuart Jenness), archaeologist William Taylor of the Canadian Museum of Civilization talked about
these contributions in the context of Jenness's modesty: "Although he always
denied being an archaeologist, Jenness first identified two very important
prehistoric Eskimo cultures, the Dorset in Canada and Old Bering Sea culture
in Alaska" (Jenness 1991: xvi).

Jenness's work on the Cape Dorset culture was his best-known contribution to archaeology. In 1924, he was sent a collection of artifacts discovered
by Inuit at Cape Dorset in the area of the community of Kingait (which
means "mountains") on the southwest corner of Baffin Island. He noticed
that although some of the artifacts fit into the newly named Thule culture,
which began about 1,000 years ago, some were distinctly different and from
an earlier time. He named this earlier tradition "Dorset," and in 1925, published his groundbreaking (always something archaeologists want to do!) "A
New Eskimo Culture in Hudson Bay" in the *Geographical Review*—his first
archaeological publication. His findings were contested for about 10 years,
but are accepted today. By comparison, Stefansson's archaeological contributions are forgettable.

One of Jenness's main interests was the Inuit's use of string figures, also
known as cat's cradles, and how these figures were used to tell stories and
sing songs. Jenness appears to have been gifted in learning the figures quickly.
His field notes are filled with references to them and the times when it was
deemed culturally appropriate to make them; that is, in the dark days of
winter and not when the sun is over the horizon (1924: 503 and 540–41).
"A Woman Pulling Another by the Hair" (1928: 51), which appeared in his
book *People of the Twilight*, shows how string figures can be used as part
of a show. First, you create a figure that looks like two women pulling each
other's hair. Then, you move your hands to make them pull farther apart or
come closer together. While doing this, you chant:

Hair pulling
Hair pulling
The other wife's hair she pulled it
Because she would not bring water,
Because she would not bring wood,
She pulled her hair. (Jenness 1928: 51)

According to his son Stuart, Jenness developed his interest in string figures
while doing his first fieldwork in Papua New Guinea. "Papuan Cat's Cradles," his first publication about the people of Papua New Guinea, appeared
in the prestigious *Journal of the Royal Anthropological Institute of Great
Britain and Ireland*. Interest in string figures wasn't peculiar to him; it was
an anthropological fad at the time. Studies of the subject spanned the world
in the first half of the twentieth century and looked at the Aboriginal people
of the Americas, Africa, Australia, India, Japan, Scotland, Malaysia, Papua

New Guinea, and of course, the Maori of Jenness's native New Zealand, among others. Anthropological students included E. Evans-Pritchard (most famous for his work with the Nuer of the Sudan), Raymond Firth (author of *We, the Tikopia*), W.H. Rivers (instrumental in setting up Oxford's impressive collection of cultural artifacts), and Louis and Mary Leakey (famous for their early prehuman finds in Olduvai Gorge in Kenya). In 1920, British mathematician W.W. Rouse Ball wrote that a piece of string was an anthropological tool "without which to-day no self-respecting anthropologist ought to travel" (quoted in Ratajczak 1998). Jenness published an article on Inuit string figures in 1923; a book called *Eskimo Folklore* (with a major section on string figures) followed the next year. It is a much-respected work among people who study the subject now (such as the International String Figures Association).

Jenness entered the Arctic with a solid background in languages, if not in linguistics per se. He had studied French in high school, as well as Latin and Greek as a Classics scholar at the University of Wellington in New Zealand. After studying the Bwaidogan language of the Northern D'Entrecasteaux with his brother-in-law, he published an article on its grammar in 1926. In 1928, 13 years after the death of his brother-in-law, whom he cites as his co-author, he published a 270-page study called "Language, Mythology, and Songs of Bwaidoga, Goodenough Island, S.E. Papua" (Jenness and Ballantyne 1928).

He published several times on Inuktitut over a span of more than a quarter century. His work appeared twice in the prestigious *International Journal of American Linguistics*. He published two reports on the Canadian Arctic Expedition: a 134-page study on comparative vocabulary of dialects (1928) and a shorter work, 34 pages, on grammar (1944). Both stand as state-of-the-art Inuktitut linguistics for the time. The former is a good source of ethnographic data as well, since many entries are not just simple one-word translations, but descriptions that include context (e.g., distinguishing between usual names and song names for animals).

The impact of Jenness's work in archaeology, socio-cultural anthropology, and physical anthropology transcended that of his contemporary Stefansson. But few references to Jenness's work appear in contemporary anthropological literature, partly because he was employed by the government rather than a university. So it's more difficult to find criticism of Jenness. In her recent master's thesis, Aluki Rojas, an Inuit woman, examined Jenness's interpretation of gender roles and questioned whether he was too rigid, possibly downplaying the respect owed to Inuit women's work:

Jenness comments on the tasks of the genders when he described how when "Icehouse wanted to cook, Ikpuck, forgetting the pride of a hunter, would fill her bag with dryads and bring her water from the lake. No eye but mine saw his undignified conduct, and I was one of the family" (1928: 142). Ikpuck having "forgotten the pride of a hunter" according to Jenness was able to accomplish "undignified" tasks. Jenness has subtly judged Ikpuck for doing tasks Jenness believes to be strictly tasks for women—tasks that should be accomplished by Icehouse. (Rojas 2001: 44–45)

The strongest critique of Jenness's work comes from Peter Kulchyski, who accuses him of being an anthropologist "in the service of the state" (Kulchyski 1993). Kulchyski analyses a partial selection of Jenness's work, focusing on four pieces: his 1947 presentation to the Special Joint Committee of the Senate and House of Commons set up to examine the Indian Act and recommend revisions (which were enacted in part in 1951), his canonical *Indians of Canada* (1932), his *Eskimo Administration* series (1962, 1964, 1965, 1967, and 1968), and his field notes edited by his son, Stuart Jenness (1991). As we will see later, Kulchyski biased the discussion to favour his own hypothesis by examining only the above works and especially by excluding Jenness's ethnographies.

He does, however, make some valid criticisms. Jenness's 1947 presentation shows a strong tendency to support assimilation, which was in line with what the federal government would also be advocating, and particularly foreshadowed the infamous "White Paper" of 1969, proposed by Jean Chrétien, who was then minister of Indian affairs. Jenness stated that the reserves should be "liquidated" (an unfortunate word so soon after World War II) and that the government should "abolish the separate political social status of the Indians (and) Eskimos" (Kulchyski 1993). Kulchyski's assessment of *Indians of Canada* also brings to light some real flaws. Jenness tends to use the voice of the "outsider expert" to the exclusion of the voices of his Aboriginal subjects. He speaks of Aboriginal cultures in terms of their absences—the lack of agricultural tools and crops,[3] central governing authority, organized priesthood, "true"[4] creation stories[5] with a single creator, and musical instruments. (It is a European bias to downplay drums in this way.)

However, because *Indians of Canada* was an "encyclopedia" or textbook about Aboriginal people in Canada, built in pressures or restrictions made it different from the more personal and inclusive anthropological approach that Jenness employed in his ethnographies. His audience for *Indians of Canada* would have been less academic than that of his ethnographies, and their ignorance of Aboriginal people and lack of background knowledge would have restricted his options and made the work more distant and scientific sounding than it otherwise might have been. As a teacher, I know that I have more flexibility with a class that has background knowledge than I do with a class without that knowledge. I know that when I taught Native studies courses to an Aboriginal audience, I was able to include more Aboriginal voices than I could when teaching similar courses to non-Aboriginal students.

To do justice to any anthropologist, you need to compare him or her with peers of the time. To do otherwise would be to commit the mistake of presentism, a method of historical or literary analysis in which present-day ideas, issues, or perspectives are projected back into the past. For example, Kulchynski claims that Jenness felt a "general disdain towards Native women," (1993: 12) when in fact his writing reflected the male gender preoccupations of anthropologists of his time. Kulchyski's interpretation of Jenness is typical of his own time in that he was embedded in the obscuring sediment of the postmodernism of the early 1990s. Unclear definitions coming from continental European authors (e.g., French Marxist Louis Pierre Althusser and his definition of ideology) and the use of *sic* when a phrase is politically rather than grammatically incorrect were common diagnostic traits at the time. More recent scholarship has identified this as a problem that was prevalent in previous analyses of early anthropology and anthropologists (see Barnhart 2005).

If you perceive Jenness in the context of his time, the picture changes. Yes, he seemed to be subscribing to the early anthropological view of the "vanishing Indian" by believing that Native empowerment could only come from assimilation, rather than by maintaining a distinct culture. However, his ethnographies (1923, 1928, 1935, 1937, 1938, 1943, and 1955) show him to be ahead of his time regarding inclusiveness of voice. He acknowledged the contributions of his individual informants to such an extent that his ethnographies are useful tools for developing biographies of those informants. (See Steckley and Cummins 2005 for a biography of Ojibwa war hero Pegahmagabow, developed from one of Jenness's ethnographies.)

Kulchyski makes a postmodern meal of Jenness's response to Inuit partner swapping. Jenness reacted with embarrassment when invited to participate and pleaded "anthropological inadequacy" because his emotions would get in the way of what would have then been called "scientific detachment." Kulchyski felt that Jenness's feelings exposed his "weakness in this respect as an ethnologist," and claimed that the situation "destablized" Jenness's "patriarchal," "imperial" narrative and upset his "imperial desires for mastery." I feel that Kulchyski exaggerates, and it would be more accurate to say that Jenness responded true to his culture as a Victorian gentleman raised in a middle class home. Contrast his response to sexual overtures to that of Stefansson, who fathered children but did not admit to it, not even in his field notes. Jenness did not want to exploit Inuit women for sex without responsibility, as he doubtless saw others, including Stefansson, do. In fact, his stance can be considered less patriarchal for his time than that of his peers.

STEFANSSON AS DEADLY EXPEDITION LEADER

Stefansson and Jenness could hardly have been more different. Risking a bad pun, you could say that the two men were polar opposites. Jenness was a shy man of great modesty, not given to blowing his own horn. Stefansson was an extroverted self-promoter, at times shamelessly so. In his writing and speaking, quality of information often took a back seat to quantity of self-aggrandizement. His best-selling *The Friendly Arctic* (1921), for example, contained little if any anthropological significance. The author filled most of the pages with tales of his brave exploits and tried to justify his often-untenable opinions. He is perhaps most clearly portrayed in his own words, taken from an article appearing in *Harper's Monthly Magazine* in January 1936. He was describing someone else—the early twentieth-century Antarctic explorer Ernest Henry Shackleton (1874–1922)—but the picture fits. (However, unlike Stefansson, Shackleton managed to bring his co-adventurers back alive in his furthest trip south in 1909):

> He was a Hawkins or a Drake, a buccaneer in spirit and method. He talked louder and more than is good form in modern England. He approached near to brag and swagger. He caused frictions, aroused and fanned jealousies, and won the breathless admiration of youngsters who would have followed Dampier and Frobisher with equal enthusiasm in their piracies and in their explorations. (Stefansson 1936)

Some of the differences between Stefansson and Jenness led to ill feelings, even conflict. Jenness was a meticulous, methodical man, very well organized and careful. Perhaps because he was one of the youngest of a large group of brothers and sisters, he was sensitive to the feelings and concerns of those around him. Stefansson likened his role of expedition leader to that of "lead Arctic adventurer," instead of putting his best efforts into planning and attending to the safety needs of those he led. Stefansson exhibited a cavalier attitude toward the dangers of the Arctic, which Jenness did not share. This came in part from Stefansson's sense of adventure and in part from the notion of "the friendly Arctic," after which he named his popular book.

Stefansson did not believe that the Arctic was the barren, dangerous, and bitterly cold wilderness that people in the south thought it was. For him, it was not only rich in minerals and animals, it was also a place where adventurous young men of stout heart and good sense could live off of the land like an Eskimo. Extensive practical experience and careful thought as to supplies were relatively unimportant in his opinion.

Although his attitude exposed those who believed his stories to incredible risks, Stefansson himself did not suffer personally. He seemed to have led a charmed existence as an Arctic traveller. No matter how ultimately foolish his choices were, he always survived, with stories to tell that would help him earn a living. Some who responded to his call were not so fortunate. They died. Even then, Stefansson felt it important to constantly convey the idea that it was their own decisions, not the friendly Arctic, that caused their demise.

Stefansson's somewhat carefree disregard for the lives of those under his charge stemmed from his belief that the glory of the goal comes first for an explorer, before life itself. He was not unlike his contemporary at the other end of the globe, the British explorer Robert Falcon Scott (1868–1912) who died along with his men in 1912 on his second voyage to reach the Antarctic. Stefansson expressed this "glory before life" attitude in the following fatally predictive statement, quoted in a book written by one of those who survived Stefansson's leadership:

> [T]he attainment of the purposes of this expedition is more important than the bringing-back safe of the ship in which it sails. This means that while every reasonable precaution will be taken to safeguard the lives of the party, it is realised both by the backers of the expedition and the members of it, that even the lives of the party are secondary to the accomplishment of the work! (Stefansson as quoted in McKinlay 1999: 6)

I'm sure both the backers and the members of the expedition *would* have been surprised to learn that such was their attitude. Stefansson wouldn't have stated directly that lives were secondary—that aspect was kept secret.

Stefansson divided the expedition into a northern and southern party. Jenness would be part of the latter, and live a long life. Such could not be said for 11 members of the northern party. The *Karluk*, the 20-year-old whaling ship hastily chosen by Stefansson, was trapped and crushed in the ice the year after the *Titanic* had its own "ice issues." The 11 died on or near Wrangel Island—later to be an island of death for others heeding Stefansson's call.

While Stefansson was not too keen on the details of running the expedition, he did want absolute control over the diaries of the participants (i.e., complete publication and censorship rights). He earned his bread and butter giving talks and writing articles and books, and he needed material. After the expedition, he earned $1,000 a week as the headline performer and lecturer in the American travelling entertainment and education shows known as Chautauqua. Jenness, who was not receiving any money for the enterprise, took exception to Stefansson's policy of control. As an anthropologist who wanted to write up his observations, he resented having someone else try to take own work from him. Stefansson also did not want anyone to question his authority or his actions. Although he was not normally critical of others, Jenness wrote the following to his friend and colleague Marius Barbeau on July 11, 1913:

> Between ourselves I have no confidence whatever in Stefannsen [sic] as leader.... I believe that we in the southern party will do good work & get along very satisfactorily unless Stefannson [sic] returns from the North & wishes to take over the charge of the southern party. I think the Geological Survey will treat us fairly, although the terms of the contract were most unusually severe considering that our services are to all intents & purposes unpaid. We shall be 4 years older when we return & financially in no better position than now—worse in fact in my case at least for I practically gave up a post to which a salary of $550 a year was attached in order to go on this expedition. Of course one expects contracts to appear harsher on paper than they are in practice interpreted. But at Victoria Stefannson seemed to interpret mine harsher than the words implied.

The two men would disagree in print over a number of intellectual issues. None was so prominent or so vehement as their conflict over the notion of the Blond Eskimo (see chapter four).

Despite the deaths during his previous endeavour in the North, Stefansson still believed in the friendly Arctic. He organized another tragic expedition in 1921, to the same place as the first: Wrangel Island. The island is off the northeast coast of Siberia, and, since 1976, a Russian wildlife preserve. Spinning tales of the romance of northern adventure, he persuaded three young American men to make the journey. Stefansson would stay in the south to obtain more funding, which he hoped to accomplish by forcing the Canadian or British government to claim the island and assume responsibility for the expedition.

He needed a Canadian or a Briton to at least nominally lead the expedition, so he wrote a letter on March 13, 1921 to Sir Robert Falconer, the president of the University of Toronto. He wanted a young man fresh out of college for the role. Stefansson's cavalier attitude toward possible dangers of the expedition is reflected in this statement of the main qualification he was looking for in his leader: "The chief qualification is temperamental. There should be no tendency to imagine that you are a hero or that it constitutes remarkable hardships to be away from movies and operas for a year or two" (Niven 2003: 29). The young man who responded was Allan Rudyard Crawford, the 20-year-old son of a University of Toronto mathematics professor.

Having been told they should have at least one Eskimo to assist them, Crawford and his crew obtained the services of Ada Blackjack, a city-raised 23-year-old Inuk woman from Nome, Alaska, who also worked for them as a seamstress. She too was poorly prepared for the adventure, with only a little experience in the wild. The crew took with them a mere six months' worth of supplies because they believed Stefansson's sales job that they could survive on their own. When the anxious parents of these young men expressed concern about what was happening to their sons, Stefansson reiterated his dogma of the friendly Arctic. Crawford's father wrote to Stefansson, and he replied by writing:

> There is ... no more need to worry about them than if they were in some European city or an ordinary place and were merely not in the habit of communicating with you. In other words, the only worries you need have for Allan are the same which he may reasonably have about you, and his chance of being safe and well next fall is the same as your own. (Niven 2003: 120)

All four men died. Three tried a desperate push to Siberia. They were never found, despite persistent rumours that they were sighted. The fourth died of scurvy. Ada Blackjack survived, but her story of hardship was dismissed after Stefansson wrote *The Adventure of Wrangel Island*, in which he denied culpability and placed the blame on the young adventurers and their Inuk companion.

The human tragedies did not end there. But those that followed cannot be blamed on Stefansson, at least not directly. In 1926, the Russians took a few dozen Inuit with them on an expedition as personal markers to claim the island. Whether Stefansson inspired this move, it is hard to tell. In 1936, two White men in charge of the station at Wrangel Island, Semenchuk and Startsev, were put on trial for murder. In the words of Russian anthropologist Yuri Slezkine:

> [T]he court proceedings revealed that Semenchuk and Startsev ... had been robbing and exploiting the "natives" just like the old traders, trappers, and colonists. Semenchuk had allegedly forced them to work for the station at the expense of hunting, refused them credit, refused them medical help, and eventually starved twelve people to death. Both men were executed. (Slezkine 1994: 288)

With his Wrangel Island expeditions and other dodgy endeavours in the North—such as a failed attempt to raise reindeer on Baffin Island—Stefansson eventually became persona non grata with the Canadian government. But in other ways, he flourished. Through all his misadventures and the misfortunes of those who followed him, Stefansson landed on his feet. He managed to maintain his reputation in the United States as an Arctic explorer, adventurer, and anthropologist. From 1929 onward, he was associated with Dartmouth College in Boston and eventually became director of polar studies. He sold to that prestigious institution his 25,000-volume library. Most websites bearing his name are quick to praise him, and ready to omit his death-dealing failures. The Centre for Canadian Studies hosts a site on which he is listed as one of the "Great Canadian Explorers."

However, a number of recent books take a more critical stance toward Stefansson. Most damning is William Laird McKinlay's *The Last Voyage of the Karluk*, first published in 1976 but reissued in 2001. He was a survivor of the last voyage of the *Karluk* and lays all the blame on Stefansson for the tragedy. Jennifer Niven has recently written two books, one about the *Karluk* (2000) and one about Ada Blackjack (2003), the sole survivor of the second Wrangel Island expedition. Both are quite critical of the entrepreneurial explorer.

Rising to his defence is Icelandic anthropologist Gísli Pálsson, who has written two books about him. The first one, *Written on Ice: The Ethnographic Notebooks of Vilhjalmur Stefansson*, was based on Stefansson's field notes and published in 2003, not surprisingly by Dartmouth College. The second book, seductively named *Travelling Passions: The Hidden Life of Vilhjalmur Stefansson*, adds to the discussion a collection of letters, many of which were written by his Toronto fiancée, Miss Smith. It was published in 2005 by the University of Manitoba Press. McKinlay's work is not included in either of his bibliographies.

While both books are relatively thorough, Pálsson takes a kinder reading of the damning events than most scholars would, missing significant opportunities to probe deeper. Ultimately, when it comes to the deaths associated with the two Stefansson expeditions to Wrangel Island, Pálsson is little more than an apologist. Take the following paragraph, for example, when he first takes the uncritical "some people say *this*, while others say *that*" approach characteristic of unenlightened journalism on controversial subjects, such as the shroud of Turin. He also indirectly attempts to blame the victims:

> Jennifer Niven suggests in a recent book about Blackjack's endurance that the responsibility for the tragedy lies with Stefansson. As in the case of the *Karluk* disaster, human mistakes had fatal consequences and it is difficult to decide who was ultimately responsible for them. It has also been suggested that the Wrangel Island expedition would have succeeded if the expedition team had followed Stefansson's plan to buy Inuit boats, *umiaks*, before leaving Nome, which they failed to do. (Pálsson 2005: 183–84)

I don't think that it is at all difficult to assign blame, and the academically anonymous suggestion (Pálsson's perhaps?) that the expedition team is at fault is without serious merit. Inuit boats would not have been useful in the iced-over sea surrounding the island, and the crew had little say in what they could and could not bring. Apologist not accepted.

Farley Mowat: Subjective Non-fiction, Essential Truths, or Fxxx the Facts?[6]

Farley Mowat (b. 1921) is a big admirer of Stefansson. Mowat heard Stefansson speak in 1938, and after hearing his bombastic style and mandatory flaunting of conventional wisdom, he must have felt a kinship that led to an unrequited intellectual love affair (as far as I know, Stefansson never wrote to or about Mowat). Mowat dedicated his book *Farfarers* (1998) to his hero.

While I cannot be counted among those enchanted by Stefansson, I *am* a fan of Farley Mowat. Like many Canadians over the last half-century, I was raised with Farley Mowat's exciting stories of the North. I wondered whether I could eat mice, as he allegedly did to follow wolf dietary practices in *Never Cry Wolf* (1963). I was horrified by the callous shooting and slow killing of the whale in *A Whale for the Killing* (1972). I was outraged when Mowat was banned from the United States because he supposedly shot a bullet at an American bomber flying over his head in Newfoundland (see *My Discovery of America*, 1985). When I wrote my book review of *People of the Deer* (1952) for my first anthropology class, I had nothing but good things to say about him. He was one of my first writing role models. I still think of him as an excellent storyteller. From 1951 to 2004, he published 39 books. By 2001, there were 460 translations of his books into 24 languages.

Farley Mowat and I share a great deal. When he wrote his first books, he lived on Highway 50 in Palgrave, Ontario, just down the road from where

I wrote my first books in Bolton. We both have lived in Newfoundland and share a great respect for its heritage and people. We are both bearded radicals who have trouble with authority figures, especially those running big corporations and governments. Strongly opposing American governments and their policies comes easily to the two of us. As children, we both brought home a menagerie of animals. Each of us has been paid to do a biologist's work, without extensive training or degrees in biology. My wife, Angie, knew his first wife, Fran.

However, students should exercise caution when citing Farley Mowat in a course on the Arctic or in anthropology. (My first anthropology professor, John Price, was more forgiving than I might be!) Why? There is the matter of his truth. I tell my students that truth is a destination you cannot reach. You can get closer to it or further away, and you can see the destination from different perspectives or angles. But Mowat's truths are what his very sympathetic biographer James King (2002) several times refers to as essential truths: basic truths that are broader and more important than mere isolated facts. For example, wolves are misunderstood to be predators, and are made to pay for that misunderstanding. The Ihalmiut (or people of the little hills, the Caribou Inuit group that Mowat visited but never really lived with as a good anthropologist would) experienced extreme hardship brought on by government neglect and White visitors, whose foolish, destructive practices compromised the caribou herds, among other things. These are essential truths. They are not wrong. However, in trying to tell the story of these essential truths, Farley Mowat uses what he calls subjective non-fiction (1974 in King 2002: 361). This technique involves trying to make you feel what he feels, making his subjectivity your subjectivity. He uses rhetorical tools to tell a good story and the creative imagination of fiction to communicate the essential truths he wants people to know. Events that are told of do not happen. Exaggerations and other distortions make the plain look more interesting (like makeup). Mowat's field notes and his stories do not tell the same tale. John Goddard wrote a critical article in *Saturday Night* (1996) that emphasized this point. Mowat's books about the Caribou Inuit—*People of the Deer* (1952), *The Desperate People* (1959), *The Snow Walker* (1975), *Walking the Land* (2000), and *No Man's River* (2004)—are not scientific ethnographies based on extensive participant observation. They are works that give a sense of a particular time, place, and situation: a tragic but very particular time in which the extreme measures of murder and abandonment were practised in response to severe deprivation and starvation, uncharacteristic of pre-contact Inuit history. It exemplifies the destructiveness of colonialism upon an indigenous Canadian people. Note to students: Read him, but don't quote him, unless it is in a critical manner.

Conclusion

To a greater or lesser extent, each of these four people—Boas, Stefansson, Jenness, and Mowat—served the cause of colonialism. However, to varying degrees, they also served the needs of the people they studied. They taught lessons about the Inuit that filled a void. They aimed squarely at the huge mainstream ignorance about the Inuit and hit the target at least a few times (some more often than others, of course). They all established close, genuine human relations with Inuit and could at least be called good friends. The Inuit people sincerely mourned the deaths of Boas, Stefansson, and Jenness, much as they mourned deaths of those close to them.

By its very nature, colonialism exploits the colonized, and it is difficult for a member of the colonizing group to side with or assist in empowering the colonized group (Memmi 1991). However, the word *exploitation* needs to be problematized in any discussion of anthropology and colonialism. The more-blatant colonial exploitation practised by missionaries, traders, and government officials was opposed by all four of the major players criticized in this chapter. Although they themselves "exploited" the Inuit to gain knowledge, stories, and reputation, two things should be considered. Knowledge, stories, and reputation were exchanged by both sides. The Inuit who were involved with these four White men were not all merely victims: They were able to broker these three commodities from the storytellers who talked about them. The balance sheet was uneven, perhaps in favour of the White men, but debits and credits appeared on each side. This should not be lost in any discussion of colonialism. Anthropologists of today must aim to make sure that the sheet is more even in their time.

Notes

1 For example, anthropologists developed a seven-culture area study of Aboriginal Canada, including Arctic, Eastern Subarctic, Eastern Woodland, Plains, Western Subarctic, Plateau, and Northwest Coast. Boas's specialty was the Northwest Coast, with long works written about the Tsimshian and the Kwakiutl.

2 The term *ethnographic present* is also used to refer to the time when data was collected.

3 This is ironic considering all the contributions to world agriculture from crops that the Aboriginal peoples of the Americas domesticated. These include potatoes, tomatoes, corn, beans, squash, peppers (hot and sweet), chocolate, sunflowers, and vanilla.

4 Using the word *true* to refer to a practice can readily be a form of ethnocentrism, in which one culture's ways are considered the standard for all.

5 We use the more neutral and culturally inclusive term *origin stories* today.

6 According to Mowat biographer James King, "When the writer and broadcaster Peter Gzowski interviewed him at the Harbourfront International Festival of Authors in 1999 and debated with him about the number of facts a non-fiction writer owed his readers, Farley bellowed, 'Fuck the facts!'" (King 2002: xv).

CONTENT QUESTIONS

1. Identify the four major White players in this book.
2. What school of thought is linked to Franz Boas?
3. What idea did this school of thought oppose?
4. What is the "ethnographic present"?
5. Why can Diamond Jenness be called a true anthropological Renaissance man?
6. What is "presentism"?
7. What does it mean to be an apologist for someone from an earlier time?
8. What is subjective non-fiction?

DISCUSSION QUESTIONS

1. Critique the notion of the "ethnographic present" as it applied to Boas's work.
2. Would you say that Boas's work benefited the Inuit?
3. Compare and contrast the occupations of the explorer and the anthropologist during the late nineteenth and early twentieth centuries.
4. To what extent can individual anthropologists of an earlier time be criticized today, given the changes in the intellectual climate over the years? Keep in mind the concepts of "presentism" and the idea of being someone's apologist.
5. Outline the weaknesses and strengths of Farley Mowat's subjective non-fiction.

KEY TERMS

apologist	archaeology
cultural determinism	cultural evolution
essential truths	ethnographic present
historical particularism	linguistic anthropology
physical/biological anthropology	presentism
socio-cultural anthropology	subjective non-fiction

CHAPTER THREE

Fifty-two Words for Snow

LEARNING OBJECTIVES

After reading this chapter, you will be able to
» distinguish between linguistic determinism and linguistic relativity.
» outline the development of the idea that there are 20 Inuit terms for snow.
» contrast the word and sentence structure of English and Inuktitut.
» identify the seven primary Inuktitut terms for snow.

> The Eskimo has 52 names for snow because it is important to them; there ought to be as many for love.
>
> —Margaret Atwood

ONE OF THE MOST POPULAR so-called facts about the Inuit is that they have an extraordinarily large number of terms for snow. People from all walks of life, including academics, spout this myth. The above quote from Atwood is a classic Canadian example.

Atwood, Inuit, and snow—you could scarcely get more Canadian than this. But the belief is not limited to Canadians. In the strange, innovative 1999 movie *Being John Malkovich*, one of the actors asks another, "Do you know that Eskimos have not 1 but 49 words for snow?" Don't be surprised that the numbers clash. Various numbers are quoted, and they often include a two. Twenty is a particular favourite, as we will see. Forty-nine is less popular, coming from the dictionary *West Greenlandic* (a dialect of Inuktitut, the language of the Inuit), written by Michael Fortescue in 1984. That number includes terms for both snow and ice, so it is a bit of a cheat.

Where did this idea come from? Why do the numbers vary? Is Inuktitut structurally better equipped than English to name and describe snow? Does this belief reflect misunderstanding about the language of the Inuit?

The idea that the Inuit have many snow terms is a White tradition that goes back nearly 100 years, illustrating the basic premise of this book: people are quite prepared to believe almost anything about the Inuit. It also carries with it an element of negative judgment about the Inuit language, even though it is usually meant as something of a compliment or statement of respect.

A Source of Humour: Jokes about Inuit Snow Terms

As part of popular culture, comments about Inuit snow terms are often used in humorous ways (not that there is anything wrong with that). Two kinds of jokes can be found in Inuit snow term humour. One type begins by telling how many Inuit terms there are for snow, and then follows with a parallel commentary on another group of people, who are ultimately the butt of the joke. Following the general practice with these jokes (it is good to be anthropologically precise), I will use the word *Eskimo* rather than the more respectful *Inuit* in the following examples. These jokes will cross Canada, west to east. It is a snow term road trip.

» There are 52 Eskimo terms for snow, which is about as many terms as British Columbians have for marijuana (or Vancouverites for rain).
» There are 52 Eskimo terms for snow, and 104 insulting terms that Albertans have for federal Liberals.
» There are 52 Eskimo terms for snow, but twice as many ways of saying *flat* in Saskatchewan.
» There are 52 Eskimo terms for snow, and 104 adjectives that can be used before cold to describe January at Portage and Main in Winnipeg.
» There are 52 Eskimo terms for snow, which roughly equals the number of excuses Toronto fans have for why the Leafs haven't won the Stanley Cup in a long time.
» There are 52 Eskimo terms for snow, about the average attendance for the last year of the Montreal Expos.
» There are 52 Eskimo terms for snow, but only one word for potato in New Brunswick: McCain's.
» There are 52 Eskimo terms for snow, about the same number of bed and breakfast places in PEI that claim that Lucy Maud Montgomery slept there.
» There are 52 Eskimo terms for snow, about the same as the number of terms for *bleak* in Sydney, Nova Scotia.
» There are 52 Eskimo terms for snow, half the number of terms for *mainlanders* in Newfoundland or for *fog* in St. John's.

The other kind of Inuit snow term joke is a little more complicated and clever. To understand it (and the more serious issues that follow) requires a short linguistics lesson on morphemes. When you see "morph" as part of an English word, it means *structure*. The morphology of something is its structure. The *Mighty Morphin Power Rangers* changed their structure. Morphemes are the building blocks of words, contributing either meaning or grammatical function to the words they form part (or all) of. For example, in the word *snowing* (to keep on topic), there are two morphemes: -snow-, the verb root (for white stuff to come tumbling out of the sky) and -ing-, which refers to a continuous action (sometimes an all too continuous one!).

The second type of snow term humour involves inventing a morpheme for snow and adding funny English prefixes or suffixes to it. For example, musician and entertainer Phil James composed the following, which is found on many Internet sites (see for example <http://www.firstpeople.us/glossary/ Fake-Eskimo-Snow-Words.html>). The morphing morpheme is -tla- (warning: this is not a real Inuktitut morpheme).

tla	ordinary snow
gristla	deep-fried snow
Mactla	snow burgers
Hahatla	small packages of snow given as gag gifts
mextla	snow used to make an Eskimo Margarita
briktla	good building snow
maxtla	snow that hides the whole village
tidtla	snow used for cleaning

To which I would add:

hooptla	outdoor basketball court in Nunavut
pooptla	dog walkers hiding dog turds under snow rather than picking them up
scooptla	what the dog walkers should do with the mixture of dog turds and snow
stooptla	describes jokes about Inuit terms for snow

It All Began with Boas

How did this story begin? Linguist Laura Martin was the first to identify the essential weakness of this White lie about Inuit snow terms in her 1986 *American Anthropologist* article "'Eskimo Words for Snow': A Case Study in the Genesis and Decay of an Anthropological Example." For her, it all began with Franz Boas, as do a number of similar clichés, as well as the questionable practices we saw in previous chapters. Before he travelled to Baffin Island in 1883, Boas studied Inuktitut. He corresponded with Heinrich J. Rink, a Danish explorer and "Eskimo expert," and read all he could about Greenland dialects of Inuktitut. He was somewhat cocky about his learning early on, claiming in 1882 that he had "already made relatively good progress" in the language. Later, the harsh reality of the field set in. In his journal entry on December 2, 1883, he admitted, "The language is very difficult to learn," and later that month he said, "Their language is horribly difficult."

But he steadily progressed. By May 1884, Inuktitut words were becoming regular entries in his journal. Still, he was linguistically humbled by the experience. After his fieldwork, he conceded that he felt he never mastered Inuktitut adequately. His sense of his own limitations prevented him from writing on Inuktitut grammar in his masterful compilation *Handbook of American Indian Languages* (1911). Instead, he asked the Danish linguist William Thalbitzer to write it (Stocking 1974: 178–79). As we shall see, Thalbitzer himself played a role in spreading untruths about the Inuktitut language. Interestingly, when Boas wrote to Thalbitzer asking him to write about peculiar characteristics of Inuktitut vocabulary for the piece, he suggested looking at the fact that there were "a great number of special stems expressing different kinds of motion" (Stocking 1974: 179). That was in 1905. No reference was made to the number of snow terms.

That changed in 1911 when the *Handbook of American Indian Languages* was published. In his Introduction, Boas identified four distinct words for snow in Inuktitut. He did so after elaborating on terms for water in English (including rain, dew, mist, lake, brook, river, foam, wave, and liquid). He was discussing linguistic relativity, the idea that languages differ not because of a general superiority or inferiority, but because they are constructed to meet the challenges faced by the speakers: "Another example of the same kind, the words for SNOW in Eskimo, may be given. Here we find one word, *aput*, expressing SNOW ON THE GROUND; another one, *qana*, FALLING SNOW; a third one, *piqsirpoq*, DRIFTING SNOW; and a fourth one, *qimuqsuq*, A SNOWDRIFT" (Boas 1911: 21–22).

He then entered into a similar discussion about Inuit terms for *seal*. In his book *The Mind of Primitive Man*, based on lectures he gave from 1910 to 1911, he repeated these examples, without using the actual Inuktitut words (Boas 1916: 145–46). The first two terms he presented in the quotes above (*aput* and *qana*) are nouns that turn up in most discussions of Inuit snow terms. They are written in their most basic form. *Piqsirpoq*, the third term, is a verb that should probably be translated as "it (snow or rain) is drifting, moving." The last term, *qimuqsuq*, does not seem to appear in the Inuktitut dictionaries that I consulted. Curiously, he did not mention the noun *mauja*, which refers to deep, soft, hard-to-walk-in snow. This word appears twice in the midst of German words in his journal:

May 24, 1884: It is still abominably cold, unfriendly weather ... and abominable mauja.

June 21, 1884: We travelled between Atteraelling and Alikdjua ... but could scarcely see Alikdjua and Manitung from here. Maujadlu [deep, soft snow]. (Müller-White 1998: 223, 232–33)

Clearly, he was no fan of *mauja*.

Enter Diamond Jenness

Although Laura Martin failed to identify him as such, the second important scholar to make special mention of the Inuit terms for snow was Diamond Jenness. In the 1920s, he spent quite some time with several groups of Inuit. His *People of the Twilight* (1928), a highly readable account of his stay with the Copper Inuit, has long been considered a classic. In 1928, he also published what appears to have been the second major Inuktitut-English dictionary, entitled *Comparative Vocabulary of the Western Eskimo Dialects* (Jenness 1928). The first such dictionary was penned by a Danish Lutheran minister born in Greenland, C.W. Schultz-Lorentzen, and was published in English in 1927 as the *Dictionary of the West Greenland Eskimo Language* (preceding Jenness's dictionary by just a year). Schultz-Lorentzen was in communication with Jenness about his work and acknowledged his help.

In 1932, Jenness published the most influential work ever written about Canadian Aboriginal people: *Indians of Canada*. Copies of this masterwork continued to be printed as late as 1989. It is still very influential, as it is often found in university and public libraries and has influenced the current generation of scholars. In this book, he expressed his belief in linguistic relativity, which he shared with Boas:

> It has often been thought that because an Indian distinguishes perhaps only three or four colours, and possesses few abstract nouns, his vocabulary is very limited. Nothing could be farther from the truth. If he distinguishes few colours it is because fine discrimination in colour has no value in his life. He will differentiate, in matters that are important to him, where Europeans may make no distinction. Thus Eskimo has one term for falling snow, another for granular snow, a third for a snow-drift, and several others; whereas English possesses but the one word "snow," and must employ descriptive phrases to separate its varieties or manifestations. (Jenness 1932: 24–25)

In his dictionary, Jenness listed five nouns and one verb for snow. In common with Boas, he included a noun for falling snow, *qänik* (Jenness 1928: 61), and another for snow lying on the ground, *apun* (22). Jenness added the nouns *pukAq* for granular snow (98), *äniu* for snow used in the house (e.g., for water) (18), and *mauyaq* for soft snow, Boas's favourite (76). As with Boas, he listed a verb for drifting snow, *mingulik* (78). Two of Jenness's terms (*apun* and *qänik*) roughly match those of Boas (*aput* and *qana*).

Benjamin Whorf

When Benjamin Whorf entered the picture, the number of terms grew. Whorf, an important twentieth-century linguist, is most famous for the Sapir-Whorf hypothesis, which he developed with his teacher and mentor Edward Sapir (also a mentor to Jenness and a student of Boas). In a 1929 paper, Sapir wrote that "our language affects how we perceive things: Even comparatively simple acts of perception are very much more at the mercy of the social patterns called words than we might suppose.... We see and hear and otherwise experience very largely as we do because the language habits of our community predispose certain choices of interpretation" (Sapir 1929: 210).

There are about as many definitions, more properly termed *interpretations*, for the Sapir-Whorf hypothesis as there are Inuit terms for snow (see how easy it is to use this cliché!). The wording of the interpretations often reflects the biases of the writer. The hypothesis involved two elements: linguistic relativism and linguistic determinism. The latter element is the most controversial. It suggests that by limiting or stressing particular elements, language determines what the speakers can see or perceive. Interpretations differ on the degree of linguistic determinism in languages. The way I see it—and I believe in the linguistic relativism of the Sapir-Whorf hypothesis—the relationship between culture and language can be likened to a dialogue. Sometimes culture speaks and language listens. Sometimes it is the other way around. There is no one-way determinism.

In his article "Science and Linguistics," which first appeared in 1940 in the prestigious Massachusetts Institute of Technology's *Technology Review*, Whorf began with a discussion of his favourite exemplary language, Hopi (spoken by an Aboriginal people of the American Southwest), and moved on to Inuktitut:

> We have the same word for falling snow, snow on the ground, snow packed hard like ice, slushy snow, wind-driven flying snow—whatever the situation may be. To an Eskimo, this all-inclusive word would be almost unthinkable; he would say falling snow, slushy snow, and so on, are sensuously and operationally different, different things to contend with; he uses different words for them and for other kinds of snow. The Aztecs go even farther than we in the opposite direction, with "cold," "ice," and "snow" all represented by the same basic word with different terminations; "ice" is the noun form; "cold," the adjectival form; and for "snow," "ice mist." (Whorf 1956: 216)

He did not cite his source for Inuit terms, so we do not know where he got them. Interestingly, the first two translations he provides match those found in Boas and Jenness.

Downplaying the Number of Inuit Snow Terms: An Ignored Source

In many anthropology and sociology textbooks, the Sapir-Whorf hypothesis is set up as a clay target bird to be cast skyward and shot down with ease by the author. One simple way to do this is to aim at examples such as Eskimo snow terms. Linguist Roger Brown did this in his book *Words and Things*

(1958), shortly after the publication of a well-circulated 1956 collection of Whorf's major works. While Brown stated that there were three terms for snow in Inuktitut, he only bothered to identify two roots:

> There seems no reason to posit more than two distinct *roots* that can be properly said to refer to snow itself (and not, for example, to drifts, ice, storms or moisture) in any Eskimo language. In West Greenlandic, these roots are *qanik* "snow in the air, snowflake" and *aput* "snow (on the ground)" (Schultz-Lorentzen 1927; c.f., Boas's data). Other varieties have cognate [i.e., related] forms. Thus Eskimo has about as much differentiation as English does for "snow" at the monolexemic level: snow and flake. (Brown 1958: 422 fn2; emphasis mine)

Brown made the point that the distinct grammars of English and Inuktitut are rather like the proverbial apples and oranges, and showed how making an apple-to-apple comparison concerning snow terms is difficult. I will make essentially the same point shortly, adding how an apple-to-apple comparison can and should be made. However, Brown's good work seems to have been ignored by most writers on the subject. The literature is just as silent about his too-harsh trimming of the roots of Inuit snow terms tree. I believe that he cut too much. It should be noted the two roots that he mentioned are those shared by all the previous sources.

The Birth of 20 Snow Terms: A Sociological Tradition Since 1968

Many classroom teachers find it too imprecise to tell students that there are many snow terms and merely allude to what that number might be. Teachers like concrete numbers with which to illustrate the point of linguistic relativism. Numbers are good for multiple-choice questions on tests. As far as I can figure, this numerical "precision" was first provided by Peter Farb in his extravagantly titled 1968 book *Man's Rise to Civilization: As Shown by the Indians of North America from Primeval Times to the Coming of the Industrial State*. Referring only to Boas and Whorf, he made the following claim without sourcing where he got his high number: "The Eskimo can draw upon an inventory of about twenty very precise words for the subtle differences in a snowfall. The best a speaker of English can manage are distinctions between sticky snow, sleet, hail, and ice" (Farb 1968: 237).

After this, many introductory sociology textbooks made reference to the same number, although sometimes adding qualifiers. In their 1977 textbook, Smith and Preston simply quote Farb (1977: 21). Six years later, Federico and Schwartz pushed the figure a bit higher in their text called *Sociology*, but still kept 20 as the base figure. Like many textbook writers, they also highlighted the fact that there is no general term for snow, as if that were somehow a strange thing. I believe this to be an artifact of the old idea that since they have no general category or abstract term, something must be deficient with them.

One of Sapir and Whorf's most striking examples involves the word "snow." Those who speak English have only one word for it. Although active skiers refer to "powder," "base" and maybe "slush," most people in our culture, most of the time, say "snow." Eskimos, on the other hand, have no general word for snow. Instead, they know *between twenty and thirty* different kinds of snow, each expressed by a different word. Since snow is such an important element in their lives, they are forced to make distinctions that are meaningless to us. (Federico and Schwartz 1983: 56; emphasis mine)

In their *Sociology: An Introduction*, published two years later, Eshleman and Cashion are less adventurous: "The Eskimos ... have no general word for snow, but they have *more than twenty* words for different kinds of snow, depending on whether it is falling, drifting, fresh, crumbling, and so on" (1985: 85; emphasis mine).

In his 1989 publication *Society: A Brief Introduction*, Ian Robertson not only reproduced this number, but also made the same exotic contrast with the Aztec that Whorf did. Note the linguistic determinism in his writing, as well as the reference to Boas's favourite Inuktitut snow terms:

The Aztecs, for example, used a single word for snow, frost, ice, and cold, and only one word for snow; the Eskimo have no general word for snow at all, but have *over twenty words* for different kinds of snow—snow on ground, snow falling, snow drifting, and so on. Their language forces them to perceive these distinctions, while our language predisposes us to ignore them. (Robertson 1989: 45; emphasis mine)

The creators of modern websites seem to really like the figure 20. Whether they are selling religion, Hawaiian holidays, or all-you-need-is-baby-boomer love, the one number fits all:

Just as the Eskimos of North America have more than 20 words for "snow," the Hebrew in the Old Testament had many words to describe the act of worshiping god. (McEachern Memorial <http://www.mceachernumc.org/praise/>)

While some say Eskimos have over 20 words for snow, Hawaiians should have over a hundred words for romance considering the islands' idyllic surroundings, luxurious hotels, celebrated restaurants and relaxing spas. (Travel Sense <http://www.travelsense.org/destinations/hawaii.asp>)

(To be completely parallel, the travel sense quote should include "romance on the ground," "falling or flaky romance," "soft, deep romance," "dry romance," "mushy romance," and "drifting romance"!)

The Eskimos have more than 20 words for snow. Surely, we need at least 20 words for love, to cover all the aspects and variations and nuances of

the emotion. (*Boomer Times & Senior Life* <http://www.babyboomeresand
seniors.com/feb02/love.html>)

According to linguist Laura Martin, 20 wasn't high enough for Cleveland weather forecasters during the hard winter of 1984. When predicting snowstorms, they claimed that there were "two hundred words" for snow in Inuktitut (Martin 1986: 420).

Numbers Ending with Two: 52, 42, 32, 22

The number 20 is not the only one that is commonly found. So are numbers that end with two. The number 52 is frequently found on the Internet, as in the Margaret Atwood quotation that opens the chapter. Fifty-two also appears in the following quotation found on the Internet: If Eskimos have 52 words for snow, how many words might the Warriors have for losing night after night? (*San Francisco Chronicle* <http://www.csli.stanford.edu/~nunberg/snow.html>).

Those more comfortable with lower numbers ending in two may choose from the following, among others:

Like the Eskimo who has 42 words for snow, the glider pilot needs a dozen different names to describe convergences in mountain regions. (British Gliding Association <http://www.gliding.co.uk/sailplaneandgliding/articles/febmar02exploitingopposingairmasses.pdf>)

Like the Eskimos who have 22 words for snow, astrologers have 12 basic energy patterns and many variations and colorations beyond that. (Astrology Software Shop <http://www.astrologysoftwareshop.com>)

Notice how the authors of these quotations prefer the older term *Eskimo* rather than the more respectful *Inuit*. Disrespect needs company.

Farley Mowat Takes the Number to an Artistic High: 100

It should not be surprising that the author who quotes the highest number of snow terms is Farley Mowat. This is consistent with his bombastic style and with his performance in the other White lies about the Inuit. In his introductory piece in *Snow Walker* (1975), simply called "Snow," he wrote the following. As usual, he makes his claim in opposition to orthodox scientists, favourite targets of his diatribes:

With vast expenditures of time and money, the scientists have begun to separate the innumerable varieties of snow and to give them names. They could have saved themselves the trouble. Eskimos have more than a hundred compound words to express different varieties and conditions of snow. The Lapps [Saami] have almost as many. (Mowat 1975: 17)

This number seems to have influenced the arts community to new creative heights. In the late 1990s, Québécois dance diva Dominique Dumais choreographed *One Hundred Words for Snow* for the National Ballet of Canada, set to music by the highly regarded Canadian composer Alexine Louie. A recent CD released by Irish musician Adrian Crowley, entitled *A Northern Country*, has "One Hundred Words for Snow" as its first piece.

How Do Inuktitut and English Differ in Terms for Snow?

A distinct problem with contrasting Inuktitut and English lies in how the two languages differ structurally. Inuktitut is an agglutinative or polysynthetic (isn't that some kind of fat?) language. That means its words are constructed using a relatively high number of morphemes. Words can often be quite long and sentences typically have few words. English is not such a language. My word processing software will tell me how many words are in each sentence I write and how many letters are in each word. It seems always to say that my words are averaging five letters. Although I know I am not one to use a lot of big words, I suspect that such a figure is fairly typical for writers of English. The number of words in my sentences varies, from about 15 (when I am trying to write for a general audience) to more than 20 (when I am writing more academically). In Inuktitut, those numbers would probably be reversed, with more letters (and ultimately sounds) per word and fewer numbers of words in a sentence.

Kublu and Mallon (1999) present a good analogy for this distinction between English (and related European languages) and Inuktitut:

In English, and in most other European languages, a sentence is a string of beads. Each bead is a tiny little word, and the beads are strung together to make meaning.
I am happy to be here.
Je suis content d'être ici.
Yo estoy contento de estar aquí.

But in Inuktitut the words are like Lego™ blocks, intricate pieces locked together to produce a nugget of meaning.
quviasuktunga tamaaniinnama
(happy + I here + in + be + because I)

Calling a language agglutinative means that most words are constructed from an often relatively large number of meaningful parts or morphemes.

Morphemes can be prefixes, suffixes, infixes (appearing within a root or stem), or roots. Here is an English example:

Uncooperative
- un-   prefix that negates the meaning of the word
- -co-   prefix meaning "together"
- -operat-   verb root meaning "to do"
- -ive   suffix that changes a verb into an adjective

Learning Inuktitut involves looking at the morphology or composition of verbs and nouns. The syntax or word order within sentences requires less study. There are fewer words in a sentence. Again, it is the opposite of English. Inuktitut is a suffixing language. This means that parts are added after the verb or noun base, not before it. For example, the personal pronouns come after the base. Many common Inuktitut words appear to end with a -k- in their borrowed English form. Technically, these endings are not really like the English -k-, as they are pronounced farther back in the mouth, by the uvula (the fleshy lobe that is found in the back of your mouth). So they would be more accurate written as a -q-.

kayak	single person skin boat
mukluk	warm footwear (from an Inuktitut word for bearded seal and for sealskin boots)
anorak	waterproof, originally sealskin jacket
nanook	polar bear
inuksuk	human image made of piled stones

The -k- in English represents an Inuktitut suffix that marks the third person singular: she/he/it. For example, the word *Inuk* is the singular for the plural *Inuit*. Like almost every Aboriginal language in Canada, Inuktitut does not use gender specific pronouns like *he* and *she*.

Canada's newest territory, Nunavut, has the noun root or base *-nuna-* meaning "land" followed by *-vut-* meaning "our." As we will see later, a lot can be made of the root *nuna*. It all depends on what comes after it. The following is a relatively short list of suffixes added to the noun root for caribou, *tu'tu* (or *tuktu* in some dialects of Inuktitut), presented in Jenness's dictionary of western Inuktitut dialects:

Tu'tuayaq	caribou fawn	with *-ayaq*	young, little, small (of animals)
tu'tuleqiroq	he goes after caribou	with *-leqiroq*	goes after, pursues
tu'tuvak	a moose	with *-vak*	big, large

tu'tuqaqtoq	there are caribou	with -*qaqtoq*	has, contains
tu'turaruit	many caribou	with -*raruit*	many
tu'tusioqtoq	he is hunting caribou	with -*sioqtoq*	goes after, searches or hunts for
tu'tusuatciamik	a piece of caribou meat	with a morpheme that is represented in Jenness as -*suatciaq* piece or portion of	
tu'turoq	caribou are abundant	with a morpheme that is represented in Jenness as -*turoq* has much, many, abundant	
tu'tutoq	[s]/he has killed a caribou	with a morpheme that is represented in Jenness as -*tuq* [s]/he obtained, killed	

(Jenness 1928: 20, 22, 24, 25, 26, 27)

Inuktitut words can be quite long compared to the undemanding word lengths in the English language. The following is an often-repeated example of a long Inuktitut word, which comes from Louis-Jacques Dorais's excellent 1988 study of Inuktitut grammar, *Tukilik: An Inuktitut Grammar for All*:

illujuaraalummuulaursimaanginamalittauq

I would like to point out that English speakers bring a visual bias to their understanding of Inuktitut words. Keep in mind that English speakers don't usually pause between words (unless they are speaking slowly when asking for directions in Quebec). So when I speak the English translation of this word, it could be written as:

butalsobecauseIneverwenttothereallybighouse

The English sentence is slightly longer than the Inuktitut word it represents (42 letters as opposed to 39). However, the number of letters or symbols used in writing does not make for a truly accurate comparison of languages. This is particularly true for English, as the number of letters does not efficiently reflect the number of sounds they represent. For example, the words *straight* and *strait* have the same number of sounds but differ by two letters in their representation. Phonemes—the meaningful sound units used to distinguish between words—would provide a better comparison. (For example, the separate phonemes -d- and -t- differentiate *bit* from *bid*.) A phoneme count of a sentence in English and Inuktitut would yield pretty much the same number.

The second thing to consider when viewing the "lengthy" word above is that Inuktitut was purely oral until not much more than 100 years ago, and primarily oral until much more recently. There would be no problem with lengthy words because they were heard and not seen. This visual bias of the written word affects how English speakers (including Aboriginal people) perceive Aboriginal languages such as Inuktitut. They look more complicated than they sound. For comparison, think of some activity that you do every day; say, boil water. Imagine how much more complicated the process would appear if you had to write out precise instructions. No wonder you have difficulty with your DVD player.

Now for the full translation of the long Inuktitut word. First, we will do it morpheme by morpheme; then full flowing:

illu-	"house" (n.b. this word is cognate with *igloo*)
-juar-	big
-alum-	emphatic
-mu-	allative case (expressing motion towards the noun's referent) singular "go"
-laur-	past
-sima-	perfect
-ngi-	negative
-nama-	causative first person singular (i.e., I)
-li-	"but"
-ttauq	"also"

The flowing, sentence-long English translation: "But also, because I never went to the [really] big house."

The essential point is that it is unreasonable to compare words or terms for things in English and Inuktitut. To abuse an old expression a bit to fit the story, it would be like comparing apples (English words or terms) to watermelons (Inuktitut words). The better comparison would be English nouns to Inuktitut noun roots or bases. They are both about the same length and can be modified to further describe the noun or root/base. In English, this is done primarily by verbs and adjectives—separate words in their own right. In Inuktitut, it is done primarily by suffixes following the noun root.

English Is Good in the Snow, Too[1]

As some commentators on the subject are apt to point out, English does pretty well with snow terms. James Myers, an old farmer from the Cornwall area of eastern Ontario, once taught me a particularly vivid expression he had learned for describing very fluffy snow that falls in large flakes: "The old woman plucking the goose." (Of course, he also used to say that smokers with cigarettes hanging from their mouths looked a lot like pigs with straw hanging out of their back ends!) In Newfoundland English, the dreaded freezing rain may be called "silver thaw" or "glitter."

English has a long list of words built from the morpheme -snow- plus a qualifier. Here are 18 examples that my spell check would accept: snowball, snowbank, snowbird (a drug addict in old slang, or an older Canadian who migrates to Florida for the cold months, or the subject of an Anne Murray song), snowblind, snowboard (how Canadians feel in May!), snowbound (Canadian bondage), snow-bunting (a bird, not a way to get on base in Yukon baseball), snowdrift, snowdrop (a white spring flower that never became popular in Canada because it looks like snow), snowfall, snowfield, snow-flake, snowman, snowmobile (what you are when you can still move in a cold, snowy day), snowplow (a device for making hills in front of driveways), snowshoe, snowstorm, and snowsuit. All but two (snowbound and snow-bunting) are composed of two nouns forming a single compound noun.

In English, whether or not two nouns act as morphemes to form one word or remain as two separate nouns is sometimes rather arbitrary. There is no hard and fast rule about when you can combine two nouns to form one noun. Therefore, any list that reflects the productivity of the English noun *snow* should include the following: snow angel, snow belt (a drink taken before going out to shovel the snow), snow blower, snow bunny, snow cone, snow crystal, snow day (a schoolchild's favourite), snow fence, snow flurries, snow fort, snow goggles, snow goose, snow job, and snow shovel. I have seen most of these terms written as one word at one time or another.

None of these compounds really tells us anything about the snow. They only use *snow* as a modifier, telling us, for example, what kind of ball, bird, or shoe is being referred to. This is different from Inuktitut: If a snow morpheme comes first, snow is what is being modified. To describe snow in English, we put the word *snow* second; for example: corn snow, granular snow, packing snow, powder snow, and slush snow (or just slush).

So How Many "Words" Are There for Snow?

I am sure by now you've realized that the answer to the question "How many 'words' are there for snow?" is a difficult one. The fact that Inuktitut is not just one uniform language is not the least of the problems. This problem varies, in some ways significantly, among the dialects of Inuktitut, which is spoken all the way from Siberia to Alaska, and from the Canadian Arctic to Greenland. To even give a ballpark figure to the question, it is useful to examine one more term from linguistics, a discipline that has more esoteric terms than the Inuit have words for ... (I fell into the trap again!). The term is *lexeme*, which differs from both the previously used terms *word* and *morpheme* in subtle but important ways. In an article entitled "Counting Eskimo Words for Snow: A Citizen's Guide: Lexemes Referring to Snow and Snow-related Notions in Steven A. Jacobson's (1984) Yup'ik Eskimo Dictionary,"

Anthony C. Woodbury of the University of Texas at Austin discusses how this term can be used in looking at Inuktitut words for snow:

> Roughly, a lexeme can be thought of as an independent vocabulary item or dictionary entry. It's different from a word since a lexeme can give rise to more than one distinctly inflected word. Thus English has a single lexeme -speak- which gives rise to inflected forms like -speaks-, -spoke-, and -spoken-. It's especially important to count lexemes rather than words when talking about Eskimo languages. That's because they are inflectionally so complicated that each single noun lexeme may have about 280 distinct inflected forms, while each verb lexeme may have over 1000! Obviously, that would put the number of snow words through the roof very quickly. (Woodbury 1994)

A lexeme differs from a morpheme in that a morpheme can indicate a grammatical function that is not a "meaning" per se (e.g., such as the -s- for noun plurals in English), and a lexeme does not.

To give you a very basic sense of how much the lexeme of the Inuktitut noun root can be inflected, look at the following list from Jenness, using *nuna* or "land" (Jenness 1928: 7–9):

nuna	land
nunat	lands
nunami	on the land
nunatni	on the lands
nunamin	from the land
nunannin	from the lands
nunakun	through the land
nunatigun	through the lands
nunamun	to the land
nunannun	to the lands
nunamik	with the land
nunannik	with the lands
nunatun	like a land
nunattun	like the lands
nunaga	my land
nunakka	my two lands
nunatka	my lands
nunan	your (sing.) land
nunakin	your (sing.) two lands
nunatin	your (sing.) lands
nunanga	his/her land
nunak	his/her two lands
nungangi	his/her lands

nunakpuk	our (two of us) land
nunavuk	our (two of us) two or more lands
nunaktik	your (two) land
nunatik	your (two) two or more lands
nunangak	their (two) land
nunangik	their (two) two lands
nunangit	their (two) lands
nunaktik	their (two) own land or two lands
nunatik	their (two) own lands
nunakput	our (plural) land
nunavut	our (plural) lands
nunaksi	your (plural) land or two lands
nunasi	your (plural) lands
nunangat	their (plural) land
nunangit	their (plural) lands
nunating	their (plural) own land(s)
nunatik	their (plural) own two lands

(when the noun is the subject of a verb that takes an object)

nunama	my land(s)
nunangma	my two lands
nunavit	your (sing.) land(s)
nunakpit	your (sing.) two lands
nunangat(a)	his/her land
nunakita	his/her two lands
nunangita	his/her lands
nunami	his/her own land
nunakmi	his/her own two lands
nunami	his/her own lands
nunapta	our land or lands
nunapsi	your land or lands
nunangata	their land
nunagikta	their two lands
nunagita	their lands
nunaming	their own land or lands

For those of you who are counting, this incomplete list of inflections adds up to 56. Of course, this is a list of inflections only, with no other morphemes added. It does not include more complicated word constructions such as the following, which can also differ depending upon inflection:

nunaqtivut   our fellow countrymen (with the morpheme generally represented by Jenness as -*qat* "partner, companion")

nunasuatciaq   a piece of earth (with -*suatciaq* "piece or portion of")

(Jenness 1928: 25, 26)

Seven Primary Terms for Snow

Below is my list of seven primary Inuktitut snow terms. Please do not regard it as definitive. I have put together a list of nouns concerning snow that you could expect to find in a dialect of Inuktitut. The list also can function, as we will see shortly, as a tool for cutting down the number of terms that other writers list. To make my list, a term had to appear frequently in the Inuktitut sources I consulted, in dialects across the Arctic. There are, of course, others that crop up ("drift across" might be a better analogy in the Arctic context), but in many cases they do not seem to refer to snow exclusively or primarily. While I consider mine to be a conservative estimate, I do not believe it is too far off of the mark.

1. *aput* or *apun*   snow lying on the ground
2. *qaniq*   snowflake, falling snow
3. *aniu*   (packed) snow (on the ground) used for something, especially for making water, but also for building
4. *mauya*   soft, deep, (newly fallen) snow that is difficult to walk in
5. *pukaq*   dry, granular, sandy, sugar or salt snow; snow crystals
6. *massak* or *mahak*   mushy, wet, saturated snow
7. *minguliq*   powdery snow that drifts or is drifting

Each of these terms can be used in a good number of different constructions. You can fairly readily see how terms based on these nouns find their way onto lists of Inuit snow terms. For example, *Images of Society: Introduction to Anthropology, Psychology, and Sociology* (Hawkes et al. 2001: 86) presents a list of 17 Inuktitut "words" (but without references—not an unusual trick for textbook writers talking about Aboriginal materials). In what follows, I show how some of them can be grouped, easily cutting four terms from the list, leaving the first two from my list remaining:

aput   snow (on ground)

aput masannartuq   slush (on ground) [note that this also includes a derivative of the sixth term, *massak*]

aputitaq   snow patch (on mountain, etc.)

qaniit   snow in air/falling

qanipalaat   feather clumps of falling snow

qannirsuq   snowy weather

"Eskimo Snow: From Aput to Aputaitok," a list of 30 snow terms found on The Inquiry Net, includes the following that are all derived from *aput*, the first term on my list:

aput	the general term for a spread of snow
aputainnarowok	much snow on clothes
aputierpok	cleaned off snow
aputaitok	no snow

(<http://www.inquiry.net/outdoor/winter/snow/eskimo_snow.htm>)

For the second term on my list, *qaniit*, we have the following words from Lowe's 1984 Siglit dictionary:

qaniaraq	light falling snow
qaniaraqtuq	light snow is falling
qanikłuktuq	wet snow is falling

For my third term, most lists include an additional: *aniuvak*, which is translated in different dialects as "snow lying on the slopes of hills" (Spalding 1998: 10) and "snowbank" (Lowe 1984: 48). For the fourth, there can be *mauvarpoq*, which means "is soft, loose to tread on" (Schultz-Lorentzen 1967: 137), with the *-rpoq* suffix making the noun into a verb. Add just *-poq* to my fifth term, which was recorded by Schultz-Lorentzen as meaning "snow crust," and you get *pukagpoq*, meaning "has formed a snow crust" (1967: 198). In Lowe's Siglit dictionary, the verb form *masaguqtuaq*, derived from my sixth term *masak*, means "snow is turning into *masak*" (1984: 49).

In Schneider's dictionary (1985: 171), he demonstrates how that last noun, *minguliq*, can be used in a number of constructions in the Inuktitut spoken in Northern Quebec:

mingulirikkut	balaclava ... (... [which is sometimes used] to prevent fine snow from being deposited)
mingulirpaa	(the weather) covers the ground with a fine coat of powdery snow
mingulirtaq	object covered with a light coat of powdery snow
mingulirtuq	(the weather, the wind) makes a fine coat of powdery snow fall and cover the ground
minguliuvuq	it is covered with a fine coat of powdered snow

Negative Implications of the Inuit Snow Term Cliché

Why do I view the "Eskimo" snow term cliché negatively? Why is it not merely inaccurate, a "mistake"? My reason is simple. The cliché too readily connects linguistic difference with intellectual deficiency. The larger myth that language difference is akin to intellectual deficiency is evident in another feature mistakenly attributed to Inuktitut over the years.

BY NOUNS ALONE SHALL YOU KNOW THEM

University of Chicago linguist Jerrold M. Sadock identified the birth and spread of the false notion that, unlike all other known languages, Inuktitut does not distinguish between nouns and verbs, having only nouns. According to Sadock, Danish Inuit specialist William Thalbitzer (1873–1958) initiated this story. In his contribution to Boas's influential *Handbook of American Indian Languages* (1911), Thalbitzer made the following spurious claim about Inuktitut and the minds of its speakers:

> In the Eskimo mind the line of demarcation between the noun and the verb seems to be extremely vague, as appears from the whole structure of the language, and from the fact that the inflectional endings [e.g., suffixes] are, partially at any rate, the same for both nouns and verbs. (Thalbitzer 1911: 1057)

This argument, as well as the dubious connection to the so-called Eskimo mind, was unfortunately taken up by C.W. Schultz-Lorentzen, who was the first to write a comprehensive Inuktitut-English dictionary, as we have seen. In his short grammar of Inuktitut, he penned the following misleading and inaccurate description:

> In our discussion here of stems and stem words we have not drawn any distinction between word classes as in other languages, not even between nouns and verbs. It is true that there occur noun-like and verb-like forms among constructed stem words.... But the difference between the forms is quite small, and the words are formed with the same endings. This would seem to show clearly that the Greenlandic mind draws no decisive distinction between the two word classes, but expresses itself by means of a single class, corresponding approximately to what we call nouns. (Schultz-Lorentzen 1967: 15–16)

Generally speaking, if it smells like a verb (i.e., is verb-like), it is a verb. Verbs and nouns take a different set of endings.

It is ironic that some White linguists should identify nouns as the only form in an Aboriginal language and that they should suggest that this indicates some kind of cognitive deficiency. Generally speaking, Aboriginal languages have far more verb roots and inflections than noun roots and inflections. For example, in a 53-page text written in Huron called "De Religione" (see Steckley 2004), I identified the presence of 445 different verb roots, but only 136 noun roots, plus 15 noun stems formed from verb roots. European languages, in fact, have far more nouns than verbs and use them more often in sentences. The preceding sentence had four nouns (plus a pronoun), and two verbs.

By my rough calculation, Inuktitut has a roughly equal number of nouns and verbs, but still has fully functioning structural distinctions between the two different kinds of words.

INUKTITUT METAPHORS FOR SNOW

While the perceived number of Inuktitut snow terms may be used as a metaphor by English speakers, speakers of Inuktitut use a number of different metaphors for describing snow. Why isn't this generally known? It may be because people generally associate written languages with literature and metaphors, but they not do not make such an association for oral languages. There is also the problem of labels. Say that a couple has a child, Angelika (I promised my wife that she would be in this book), and she gets labelled as "the family musician" because she plays the piano well. Say also that she has other talents that are at least equal to her musical gifts: dancing, drawing, acting, writing, and cooking. These are ignored because she has been labelled as being good at one thing—music—and not others. I think this happens with Inuktitut. With so much written about the high number of snow terms, other capacities of the language and its speakers get ignored. I think the Inuit aptitude for metaphor, especially metaphor concerning snow, is overlooked in such a way.

The following examples are meant to illustrate how metaphor is used to describe snow. The various Inuktitut dialects have a number of terms for snowdrifts. These developed, at least in part, from the metaphors used to describe them. My favourite is the Yup'ik word *iqalluguaq*. Used to describe a "snowdrift in the lee of an object," it literally means "imitation dog salmon," so called from its shape (Jacobson 1984: 173). The word for a dog or chum salmon is *iqallak* (Jacobson 1984: 173). It is not unusual for speakers of Inuktitut to use fish metaphors. In Lucien Schneider's dictionary of the Inuktitut of Northern Quebec, Labrador and the Eastern Arctic, he gave the following:

> *katakartanaq*   Snow rendered rough by rain and freezing (which has many little scales) (Schneider 1985: 125)

A spookier metaphor is found in Spalding and Kusugaz's dictionary of Aivilik (the Inuktitut dialect of Repulse Bay). The term *ijaruvak*, which refers to eyeballs, is used to describe "melting snow which has formed ice crystals in the spring" (Spalding and Kusugaz 1998: 19). That leaves an image in the back of my mind that will return to haunt me some March (or May, given our strange climate).

Of course, the metaphors can also work the other way: Snow terms can be used to denote things that are similar. Edmund Peck noted that the term for wet snow, which he recorded as *machak*, also referred to "loam, clay ... porcelain, china, earthenware" (Peck 1925: 124).

I DON'T KNOW MUCH ABOUT ABSTRACT QUALITIES, BUT I KNOW WHAT I LIKE

When people talk about Inuktitut snow terms, they often open with the comment, "They don't have one general term for snow." (Only once have I encountered a suggestion that there is such a term, and he was misreading the meaning of *aput* [Gagne 1968: 32]). I believe that this idea is related to the general trend among early European commentators, such as missionaries, explorers, fur traders, governors, and soldiers, of describing Aboriginal languages largely in terms of what they do not express. The same was true of how they described Inuit material culture. Imagine being described as a potential date for someone in terms of what you are not: "Well, he isn't tall; he isn't rich; and he doesn't own a fancy car; but he knows a lot of terms for snow." These early commentators would say, for example, that the languages and their speakers lacked common European sounds or grammatical features. Significantly, the languages were frequently said to be deficient in so-called abstract terms, typically in reference to European abstract terms for European cultural items, physical and metaphysical.

The following quotation, from the Jesuit Father Jean de Brébeuf's often-cited statement about the Huron language, is illustrative:

> They are not acquainted with B. F. L. M. P. X. Z; and I. E. V are never consonants to them [e.g., "i" as representing "j"]. The greater part of their words are composed of vowels. They lack the labial letters [i.e., those such as b, f, m, and v that are made with the lips]. This is probably the reason why they all open their lips so awkwardly, and why we can scarcely understand them when they whistle or when they speak low. As they have hardly any virtue or Religion, or any learning or government, they have consequently no simple words suitable to express what is connected with these. (Thwaites 1959: 117)

To be fair to Brébeuf and his fellow missionaries, they would eventually write comprehensive grammars and dictionaries of the Huron language that were far superior to anything that existed for the English language until well into the eighteenth century. Unfortunately, these works, unlike the quotation above, were not published. Later writers would uncritically copy these first impressions. In his 1956 biography of Brébeuf, *Saint Among the Hurons*, Father Francis X. Talbot wrote that the seventeenth-century Jesuit missionary was "puzzled as to how he could express abstract and spiritual concepts. Their vocabulary was limited to specialized, concrete, material things that they knew through their senses" (Talbot 1956: 78). Talbot never read the unpublished works that would have readily contradicted such a statement.

It seems to me that the essential message of these types of early statements and their imitators is fairly clear, whether conscious or not: Aboriginal languages are deficient in abstract or generalizing terms because the thinking of the people is primitive. They are like animals, capable of sensory perceptions only, not the abstract philosophical, political, religious, and scientific discourse of Europeans.

Mario Pei's influential work *The Story of Language* (1965) provides a good example of this bias. He lumped the Inuit's development and use of snow terms with other examples of so-called "primitive" languages when he referred "those very numerous cases where a less developed language makes fine distinctions essential to its speakers and their activities but not to us" (Pei 1965: 119). He clearly attributes the diversity of Inuit snow terms to Inuit intellectual inferiority.

There is no such thing as a "less-developed language" in terms of structure. All "natural" languages (i.e., languages that are someone's first language, not a pidgin or trade language) are roughly equal in complexity, albeit each has unique and intricate twists and turns that make it tricky for the second-language learner. Based on my undistinguished high school career as a French student, I would say that the use of gender in Romance languages is one of those complex twists and turns. I also know that when I taught English as a second language, explaining to students when to use *the* and why they could not use it before *these* or *those* made for an interesting challenge. "You just don't" was my initial response.

Aboriginal languages *do* have general categories. They just differ from those found in English and French. The Huron noun root *-rh-* means *forest*, but often only referred to deciduous trees—maple, ash, and beech in particular. Different terms applied to collectivities of evergreens. Of course, the outsider commentator is also likely to say that the Huron fail to make distinctions where such distinctions exist for the presumably more intelligent English speaker. The commentator has it both ways.

In an indirect way, the notion of innumerable Inuit terms for snow but no general one helps to support, if not to reproduce, a prejudicial discourse against Inuktitut and its speakers. We hear that the Inuit are so in tune with their environment that all their words are about that environment. While on one hand that is something of a compliment, it is also comparable to the notion that "the Eskimo are good with their hands" ("but not with their minds")—frequently implied by early writers. The people's capacity to develop more abstract concepts through their language, such as the idea of *ihuma* so well discussed by anthropologist Jean Briggs in *Never in Anger* (1970), is downplayed or ignored by such a discourse. We, the non-Inuit readers, are cut off from such a world of the Inuit mind. Here we will take two short visits to that world—visits that will give us hints about what we might be missing with our ignorance of Aboriginal languages.

IHUMA/ISUMA

First there is *ihuma* (*isuma* in some dialects), as interpreted by Briggs, who specialized in psychological and linguistic anthropology. She conducted her research over a 17-month period, between June 1963 and March 1965, with a small community of 20 to 35 Inuit who lived northwest of Hudson Bay.

The nearest neighbours lived about 150 miles away. According to Briggs, the people's concept of *ihuma* was used in a number of ways:

1. *ihuma*
This term applies to

> a person who has (or uses) *ihuma* is cheerful but not giddy. He is patient in the face of difficulties and accepts unpleasant but uncontrollable events with calmness.... A person who lacks *ihuma*, on the other hand ... will be immoderately happy ... and playful and will laugh too easily. He will be easily upset ... and frightened ... unable to distinguish between real physical danger and imaginary danger; and he will be easily angered or annoyed. He will cry, scold, and hit on slight provocation.... His perception of his environment and his judgments concerning the future will be confused and unrealistic.... If a person grossly misjudges the length of a familiar trip, repeatedly sees imaginary caribou in the distance or hears non-existent airplanes ... such errors are attributed to lack of *ihuma*. (Briggs 1970: 360)

2. *ihumaqaruiqtuq*: "complete disappearance of *ihuma*"
This term applies to "sick people who are unconscious or delirious, unaware of their surroundings, and insane people during psychotic episodes. Such loss of consciousness is thought to be caused by the intervention or intrusion of evil spirits and is, naturally, feared" (Briggs 1970: 362).

3. *ihumaquqtuuq*: "too much *ihuma*"
This term applies to people who are considered to be focusing too much on one idea (e.g., anthropologists such as Briggs, asking questions of Inuit) and in a mild form are merely thought to be "inconsiderate." It is dangerous in particular when such a person becomes angry:

> When a person who has "too much *ihuma*" gets angry ... he gets very angry, and he stays angry. He does not recover easily ... he broods, and the angry thoughts can make the person who is brooded about fall ill or die. For this reason, people say they are careful not to arouse resentment in a person who has "too much *ihuma*." Old people, in particular, are thought to be *ihumaquqtuuq*, so when an old person is ill or housebound, people will take care to visit him and be kind to him, so that he will not begin to "think (*ihumagi-*)." (Briggs 1970: 363)

SILA/HILA

The idea of *Sila* (*hila* in the western dialects) is an apt example because it is the term for weather. It is the noun root in both *siläluk*, which means "rain," and *silalutoq*, which means "it rains" when referring to snow's warmer cousin (Jenness 1928: 108). It is a concept that combines the concrete and the abstract, a concept that has many complexities to it. It can be simply translated as weather, but there is much more to it than that. It also relates to knowledge and the spirit world. A whole chapter could be dedicated to this word.

In an op-ed piece in *Nunatsiaq News* entitled "Word and Will—Part Two: Words and the Substance of Life," Inuk writer Rachel Qitsualik wrote about the meanings of *sila*. She interwove the meanings with logical connections, much like a modern Western philosopher would do with the works of Plato or Aristotle. She writes as an heir to an intellectual tradition, picking up threads of links through generations of interpretation. It is not exactly what the ancestors would have said, but that doesn't make it wrong. They didn't face the same challenges of presenting their ideas to English-speaking readers, both Inuit and non-Inuit. It is tradition informed, and doesn't need to be anthropology-approved as authentic. She writes as follows, first commenting on and then lamenting the weakness of translation and its effects on her people:

> Although translated as "air" or "weather" or even "outside," the modern translations of *sila* only convey to us non-Inuit ideas associated with English words. When I speak of "air" to a southerner, what immediately comes to his or her mind is the idea of invisible, breathable gas: the nitrogen, oxygen, and other gases that make up Earth's atmosphere. Today the vast majority of Inuit will think of the same thing, as well as wind and weather.

She then picks up strings of meaning and constructs figures, rather like the string figures of her culture's tradition that take shape and move to illustrate story and song. *Sila* is breath, and life itself:

> Eventually, *sila* became associated with incorporeal power, quite understandable, since not only does *sila*—through breath—convey the energy that drives life, but *sila* also manifests itself as tangible weather phenomena, such as the slightest touch of breeze, or as the flesh-stripping power of a storm. *Sila*, for Inuit, became a raw life force that lay over the entire land; that could be felt as air, seen as sky, and lived as breath.

From there, through the visions and intuitions of the *angakuit*, which she insists were "wrongly termed 'shamans,'" but for which no other English word exists, she comes to talk about *sila* and the intelligence *angakuit* and other wise Inuit gather through observing it. They also learn from the powerful weather spirit called *Sila*, to whom respect and taboos were directed, and to whom the *angakuit* directed their familiar spirits for insights.

Through this broad interpretation of *Sila*, with its tangible and intangible elements of wind, breath, life, spirit, intelligence, and meteorological phenomena, we can see how reductionist the missionary priest Raymond de Coccola's interpretation was: He translated Hilla as "Weather Spirit," "the Spirit of Earth and Air," more provincially "The Evil Spirit of great snowstorms and winds," or simply "the malevolent spirit" (de Coccola and King 1986: 28, 45, 298, and 303). Even the anthropologist Edmund Carpenter, in his *Eskimo Realities*, diminishes *sila* through specific strict translations of the terms he gathered that employed the noun root:

> Perhaps the most ambiguous Eskimo concept, to Western minds, is expressed in the term *sila*, which means both thought and outside. In one sense, it refers to the world outside man, especially weather, elements, the natural order. *Silakrertok* means fair weather; *silalutok*, bad weather; *silami*, outdoors; *silata*, outside; *silapak*, outer garment; *silalereit*, neighbors; *silalleq*, the one farther out; *silaller-paaq*, the outermost one. But *sila* also refers to the state of the inner mind: *sila-tunerk*, has intelligence, shrewdness; *silaitok*, has not intelligence; *silatusurpok*, prudent, thinks ahead. (Carpenter 1973: 44)

Perhaps we should change the popular notion that "Eskimo" have many terms for snow to the reality that the Inuit have many ways of modifying the root *sila*.

Summary

First, it bears repeating that because Inuktitut has a highly developed capacity to build words—a capacity that English generally lacks—it is impossible to accurately determine the number of words for snow. Although vocabulary is developed where need is felt, such a vocabulary does not require stand-alone nouns, as often occur in English and other European, noun-dominated languages. The term *word* here is imprecise and has a European grammatical bias built into it. This bias comes from the fact that comparatively speaking (and certainly when compared with Inuktitut), English is an underachiever in word-building but an overachiever in vocabulary, particularly nouns (many of them borrowed from other languages such as Inuktitut: *igloo, anorak, kayak, mukluk, muktuk,* and *parka* come quickly to mind). Second, we are not saying that the Inuit did not and do not have a capacity to distinguish between types of snow in ways that southern Canadians might find amazing. We *are* saying that the language is not constructed in such a way that enables them to better make those distinctions. Structurally and lexically, Inuktitut is no better equipped than English to describe snow. Third, we are trying to establish that the language and the people are not programmed to make only, or even primarily, specific concrete distinctions rather than abstract, generalizing ones. Their metaphors, generalizations, and abstractions have been generated as time and need has required them. They are not constrained by their minds, their language, or their differences in culture. The Arctic sky is the limit.

Note

1 English is also good with ice. Just using the same basic formula of "word + ice," we have specialist terms such as fast ice, frazil ice, glacier ice, grease ice, new ice, old ice, pack ice, pancake ice, sea ice, and young ice (see <http://www.worldwidelearn.com/northpole/thepole/glossary.htm>).

CONTENT QUESTIONS

1. Distinguish between linguistic determinism and linguistic relativity.
2. How did the idea that there are 20 Inuit terms for snow develop?
3. How did the number expand to 100 terms?
4. Contrast word and sentence structure in English and Inuktitut.
5. What is the visual bias concerning Inuktitut and other agglutinative languages?
6. What were the seven primary Inuktitut terms for snow and what do they refer to?
7. What deficiency did early European observers think that Aboriginal languages had? Why did they think that?
8. What is the source for the story that there are 49 terms for snow?
9. Outline the meanings of *ihuma* and *sila*.

DISCUSSION QUESTIONS

1. Why does the word Eskimo rather than Inuit tend to be used in jokes and inaccurate statements about the number of Inuktitut snow terms?
2. How would you characterize the relationship between language and culture?
3. Explain the differences between using the apples-to-watermelons analogy and apples-to-apples analogy when comparing English with Inuktitut.
4. Explain how the cliché about snow terms participates in a general low outsider evaluation of the Inuktitut language.
5. Why is it difficult to translate the words *ihuma* and *sila* into English?
6. What might an early Inuit explorer have said about English speakers when (s)he learned that equivalents for *ihuma* and *sila* did not exist in English?

KEY TERMS

agglutinative	*ihuma*	infixes
inflection	lexeme	linguistic determinism
linguistic relativism	morphemes	phonemes
polysynthetic	roots	Sapir-Whorf hypothesis
Sila	suffixes	suffixing
syntax	visual bias	

CHAPTER FOUR

The Myth of the Blond Eskimo

LEARNING OBJECTIVES

After reading this chapter, you will be able to

» outline the events of the two Stefansson-inspired expeditions to Wrangel Island.

» explain Jared Diamond's theory about what happened to the Greenland Norse and why.

» discuss the connection between the popularity of the idea of "lost races" and the discovery of the Blond Eskimos.

» identify the Copper Inuit.

[T]he Eskimo, whose life is one long fight against the cold, has the warmest of hearts. Mr. Stefanson [sic] says of his newly discovered "Blonde Eskimo," a people still living in the stone age: "They are the equals of the best of our own race in good breeding, kindness and the substantial virtues."
—Sir Bertram C.A. Windle, "A Rule of Life," *The Catholic World* (1915)

"You ever hear about the blonde Eskimo?" a silver-haired woman who works in the Senior Citizen's Center asks us. I think she's going to tell a dumb-blonde joke, which were all the rage in the lower 48 seven or eight years ago.

"No, I haven't," I say. "It's me. My mother was half Danish and half Eskimo, my father was half Norwegian and half Eskimo. They're from the same village. That's how come I'm blonde. I'm the blonde Eskimo."
—Bruce Jackson, "In the Arctic with Malaurie,"
American Anthropologist (1998)

IN 1989, MORDECAI RICHLER published his Booker Prize-nominated *Solomon Gursky Was Here*, a very tongue-in-cheek Wandering Jew story in which Ephraim Gursky, Solomon's grandfather, is the sole survivor of John Franklin's tragic Arctic expedition of 1845. His prodigious progeny of Inuit Jews wandering south can be identified by the fact that they are wearing Jewish prayer shawls. This was not the first time such a far-fetched story has appeared. Except that previously, the author was serious.

Early in the twentieth century, an intriguing tale was being told. Almost instantly, it became the hot "discovery" of the popular press. The story was spun like this: A "race" of blond-haired, blue-eyed Eskimos lived in the central Arctic of Canada. They were the descendants of Vikings from Greenland.

The Blond Eskimo: A Popular Figure

While Vilhjalmur Stefansson came to popularize this story with great flare— he used it to establish his fame and secure funding for his work—the story of the Blond Eskimo did not begin with him.

Christian "Charlie" Klengenberg (also spelled Klinkenberg), captain of the ship *Olga*, was the first person to report on the group who would later become mythologized as the blue-eyed, blond-haired Inuit. It's unclear from the literature whose experience it really was, but he was the first to bring it to notice. Like Stefansson, he was one of the most colourful Arctic characters in his day. In the winter of 1905–06, his ship got stuck in the ice in Prince Albert Sound, a bay that takes a curving chunk out of Victoria Island, like the bite of a large predator. In early 1906, he took a dogsled to Minto Inlet. There he encountered an Inuit group who, so the story goes, had never seen a White man before. These people would become known as the Copper Inuit.

Where is Victoria Island? This is an important aspect of judging the validity of the Blond Eskimo story. The key point is that it is in the middle of the Canadian Arctic, far from Greenland.

North of the mainland of Canada, there is a series of large islands. The largest and farthest east is Baffin Island, which runs from the northeast shores of Labrador across the Hudson Strait from northern Quebec, and much more distantly, across northern Ontario. It stretches almost as far west as does Hudson Bay.

The mnemonic I use for placing the other great Canadian Arctic islands is an alphabetic one that works almost completely. As you move away from Baffin Island in any direction, the initial of each subsequent island's name moves farther along the alphabet. North of Baffin Island is Devon Island, smaller than the other great islands and separated from its southern neighbour by a narrow strait through which John Franklin and his crew travelled to their death in the 1840s while trying to find the elusive Northwest Passage. North of Devon is Ellesmere Island. It is long and big, and its northern tip almost joins up with Greenland's.

Moving west, we have Prince of Wales Island and Somerset Island. They are north of the mainland of Manitoba. Farther west is Victoria Island, a large and somewhat fat island (must be the whale blubber) that runs about the same longitude as northern Saskatchewan and Alberta. The next island to the west is Banks Island (for my system, it should have been called West Island). Then, there are no more islands to speak of until you go past British Columbia, Alaska, the Bering Strait, and parts of Siberia. Then you come to Wrangel Island, the scene of Stefansson's two expedition tragedies.

The Copper Inuit

Copper Inuit is the outsider-imposed name for 14 to 19 communities that formed a pre-contact population of an estimated 800 to 1000 (Condon 1995: xvi). They share a common Inuktitut dialect and a common practice of making snow knives, ice picks, spears, arrow points, and other implements from the copper found abundantly in the area. They had no common name, traditionally. Calling them the Copper Inuit, which began in 1884, is rather like calling the people in the various communities of Caledon (northwest of Toronto, where I live) as Grow-Op People because of all the marijuana busts experienced there recently. The Copper Inuit traditionally referred to themselves by their location names plus -miut: "people of." The northernmost group who live in the community now called Holman (after John R. Holman, an assistant surgeon on two Arctic voyages) call themselves *Ulukhaktokmiut*: "the place where *ulu* parts are formed." The name refers to the large bluff or cliff looming over the community. That bluff is composed of slate, which was traditionally used in the construction of the half moon-shaped and very sharp women's knives or *ulus*.

The name Copper Inuit is linked with the work of Diamond Jenness, who made them the subjects of his most extensive studies. His 1922 report entitled *The Life of the Copper Eskimos* and his more popular 1928 narrative *The People of the Twilight* are still considered classics in the literature.

First Contact

Vilhjalmur Stefansson well knew that the people who came to be known as the Copper Inuit had been in contact with White men previously. Two British expeditions had made contact in the early 1850s. One was under Captain Robert McClure, who reached Banks Island on August 7, 1850. His ship, the *Investigator*, was locked in the ice for the winter of 1850–51. Numerous walking expeditions set out to map the area. One of those expeditions, led by William Haswell, encountered a group of 18 Copper Inuit, probably the *Kangiryuarmiut* of Prince Albert Sound. A friendly meeting ensued, with an exchange of gifts. Haswell noted the copper tools of the people. After returning with an interpreter, a missionary to the Labrador Inuit, he learned that this had been their first encounter with White men. They drew for him an impressive map of the surrounding territory.

McClure and his crew spent two more winters obstructed by ice before they abandoned their sailing ship and were rescued by another exploration vessel. They left behind a treasure trove of supplies and equipment. According to Arctic anthropologist Richard Condon, this comprised 3,720 pounds of salt pork, 12,828 pounds of flour, 6,388 pounds of canned meat, 1,234 pounds of tobacco, 52 gallons of rum, 7 fully equipped whaleboats, 100 empty casks, woodworking tools, sails, clothing, and various textiles (1995: 29). The Copper Inuit were supplied with useful goods for decades to follow. Archaeological sites all over the area reveal remnants of McClure's expedition. Condon interviewed people in the latter half of the twentieth century who remembered hearing wondrous stories about the cache.

The second expedition to the area was under the command of Richard Collinson, whose *Enterprise* arrived in the summer of 1851. They stayed the winter, sent out expeditions, made fleeting contact with the Copper Inuit, and left for Alaska. An eight-year-old Inuk named Pammiungittok visited the *Enterprise* and was interviewed by Stefansson 60 years later. Pammiungittok reported that Collinson and his crew "were excellent people who paid well for water boots," and that they "threw away much valuable stuff which the people picked up" (Stefansson 1913: 287). Stefansson could hardly plead ignorance of early White contact with the Copper Inuit.

Lost Races

The West has an enduring fascination with "lost races." The mythical Amazons and Atlanteans are early and enduring examples. A more recent one is the current intense anthropological interest in *Homo floresiensis*, the recently discovered fossil remains of the 1 metre tall woman who lived 18,000 years ago on the out-of-the-way Indonesian island of Flores. The idea of a "lost race" that had never seen a White man before was exciting stuff in the days of Stefansson's explorations. These "lost races" appeared regularly in the popular literature throughout the late nineteenth and early twentieth centuries. They often become a kind of anthropological urban legend that "should-know-better" scholars and "they-say" reporters fall for. The classic case in the 1970s was the invented peace-loving Tasaday of the Philippines. The person who "discovered" them claimed that they been in complete isolation for generations. Like the Blond Eskimo, they found their way into *National Geographic*, as well as *Reader's Digest*, the *Los Angeles Times* and the *New York Times* (see Hemley 2003). I remember an episode of the 1970s sitcom *Welcome Back, Kotter* (the one that can take the blame for introducing John Travolta to the world) in which the Tasaday were mentioned in a debate between the goody-goody students and Kotter's sweathogs over whether or not humans were naturally peaceful. While the existence of this band of between 20 and 30 people continued to be disputed into the 1990s, both sides agreed that the isolation part of the story is purely fictional.

The most intriguing claim, from stories apparently told to Klengenberg, was that another group of these people had red hair and beards. Interestingly, although they would be named hereafter the Blond Eskimos, no one, not even Stefansson, ever claimed they were blond. The term was merely used to emphasize their putative Viking origin. As the story got told and retold, the dramatic potential of the "lost Europeans" far outweighed any other aspect of the story as far as Klengenberg and later Stefansson were concerned.

In "Lost Tribes: Indigenous People and the Social Imaginary," Stuart Kirsch points out that lost tribe stories persisted into the 1980s and beyond, including a number of cases in the always anthropologically rich grounds of Papua New Guinea (1997). He also notes that the lost tribes of Israel formed the Western template or (following Gananath Obeyesekere, 1992) "European myth model" for later stories of lost peoples.

In the eighth century BC, the Assyrians exiled 10 of the 12 tribes of Israel from their homeland. This Old Testament story was used during colonization to make newly discovered peoples in far distant lands fit into the familiar storylines of Judaeo-Christian, European/Middle Eastern literature. The idea began in published form in 1524, in *Itinera Mundi, Sic Dicta Nempe Cosmographia* by Jewish writer Abraham Farissol (1451–1525), a generation after Columbus's first encounter with the New World. Later in the sixteenth century, Spanish monk Bartholeme de Las Casas (1484–1566) fought for the recognition of the souls and rights of Aboriginal people in part because he believed they had ancient Hebrew connections. Portuguese traveller Antoni Montezinus visited what is now Ecuador in 1642 and felt that the people there spoke a form of Hebrew and conducted Jewish rites. This belief influenced Dutch rabbi and scholar Menasseh ben Israel to articulate a similar view in his book *The Hope of Israel*, published midway through the seventeenth century. English missionary Thomas Thorowgood published *Jewes* [sic] *in America or Probability that the Americans are of the Race* in 1650. The idea was picked up by three religious and political individuals who were foundational figures of the American colonies: William Penn (1644–1718), after whom Pennsylvania was named; Cotton Mather (1663–1728), a leading figure in the persecution of witches in Salem; and Roger Williams (1603–1683), British theologian and co-founder of the colony of Rhode Island. James Adair (1709–83), an important early American writer, prominently featured the idea in his *History of the American Indians* (1775). Joseph Smith (1806–44), founder of the Mormon faith, included the idea that Aboriginal people originated from ancient Israel (although not of the 10 lost tribes) in *The Book of Mormon*, which first came out in 1830.

This idea of ancient Hebrew lineage was not confined to the Americas only. In New Zealand, another part of the colonized world, European settlers and early scholars were connecting the indigenous Maori stories of migration from elsewhere to the lost tribes of Israel (Hanson 1989).

Later stories eliminated the "Israel" part of the lost peoples. The lost races, particularly lost (and subsequently found) White races such as the Atlanteans, classical Greeks, Romans, Egyptians, and Phoenicians were a very popular theme in serialized stories and novels written for young males during the latter half of the nineteenth century and early twentieth century. It can be readily compared to the mania for UFO and alien stories in the late twentieth and early twenty-first centuries. Boys ate up this fiction like they dine now on multi-course meals of virtual-thrill video games of vicarious heroism.

One sub-theme of this turn-of-the-century escapist literature was about lost White races, particularly of Norse or Viking origin, discovered by male adventurers, often boys, in a hidden temperate valley in the Arctic. One popular example was John Green's *The Ke Whonkus People* (1890) about a lost White race discovered in such a valley in the polar regions north of Canada. Earlier that year, John DeMorgan had serialized stories about two boys who uncovered an ancient Nordic race in northern Greenland. It would later be published in 1914 as *Lost in the Ice: Where Adventure Leads*. The wonderfully titled *Across the Frozen Sea: or Frank Reade Jr's Electric Snow Cutter*, published in 1894 and authored by "Noname" (probably the prolific Luis P. Senarens), had Nordic survivors living in the extreme North. In 1895, Harry Prentice published *The Boy Explorers: The Adventures of Two Boys in Alaska*. The eponymous boy explorers discovered Vikings living in the interior of Alaska.

Stefansson Discovers the Blond Eskimo and Finds Funding

As a young, literate, and adventure-seeking boy growing up in the 1880s and 1890s, Stefansson would have doubtless been aware of such stories and was probably well versed in the genre before he ever thought about becoming an anthropologist. Such was also true of many of those he sought as audience for his lectures, books, and articles, and for his pleas for funding.

In addition, he and much of his audience had probably heard Ólöf Krarer speak. She was an Icelandic woman who presented herself as a Greenland Inuit from 1884 to 1935 (see chapter one). In her story, reported in Albert S. Post's 1886 *Ólöf Krarer—The Esquimaux Lady: A Story of her Native Home*, she stated that

> [m]any people are disappointed when they see me, because I am not darker colored, with black hair. More of my people have light hair than dark, and we know that we are naturally a fair-skinned people, because when a baby is born in my country it is just as white as any American baby, and it has light hair and blue eyes. But the mother does not wash it with soft water and soap, as they do in this country, but she goes to work and greases it all over, and the child is never washed from the day he is born till he dies, if he remains in that country. (Post 1887: 13)

Gísli Pálsson notes that a university professor from Cornell evoked Krar-er's name in a letter to Stefansson in support of his notion of the Blond Eskimo. He had invited her over for dinner with his family and noted, "She was short, fair-haired, and blue-eyed, like all her people!" (Pálsson 2005: 205)

In August 1907, Klengenberg met with Stefansson and told him his fantastic tale of discovery. It seems a little strange that Stefansson's diary notes for August 11, when he first discusses the people, made no mention of their "blond" European heritage. That would be saved for later, for a venue more public than his diary. He did, however, talk of the copper. He added the somewhat unusual note that, according to Klengenberg and his shipmates, these Inuit were "the cleanest they ever saw." In the spring of 1910, Stefansson was on his second expedition. He would actually see the Copper Inuit for the first time, and he would also begin to spin his story of the Blond Eskimo. His story begins when the Inuit neighbours to the south tell him that the Copper Inuit looked not unlike him, or so Stefansson claims. This tale appears in his best-selling book *My Life with the Eskimo* (1913). The tabloid style dramatic approach is vintage Stefansson:

> These simple, well-bred, and hospitable people were the savages whom we had come so far to see. That evening they saw for the first time the lighting of a sulphur match; the next day I showed them the greater marvels of my rifle; it was a day later still that they first understood that I was one of the white men of whom they had heard from other tribes, under the name *kablunat*.
>
> I asked them: "Couldn't you tell by my blue eyes and the color of my beard?"
>
> "But we didn't know," they answered, "what sort of complexions the *kablunat* have. Besides, our next neighbors north have eyes and beards like yours." (Stefansson 1913: 176)

Then he came to meet the people themselves. His diary entry of May 16, 1910 recounts that event:

> *Personal Appearance*: I now understand why the Stapleton people take me for an Eskimo. There are three men here whose beard is almost the color of mine and who look like typical Scandinavians. As Billy said: Three of them look like fo'c's'le men, and aren't they huge? And one looks like a Portugee.... In the mainland party I had noted that a large number of men have a few brown hairs in their moustaches and (more rarely) in the chin beard, a few there have moustaches to be described as dark brown. This I have never seen on Eskimos to the west. Here, however, are men with abundant (3 inch long or so) chin beards (reaching a trifle beyond the corners of the mouth), a full brown in its outer parts but darker near the middle of the chin. The faces and proportions of the body remind of ... sunburnt but naturally fair Scandinavians.... The one that

looks like a Portugee has hair that curles [sic] a trifle at the tips—about as much as mine. One woman has the delicate features one sees in some Scandinavian girls and that I have seen only in one half-white girl to the westward—and there to a less degree than here.... [N]o one could fail to be struck by the European appearance of these people (cf. Accounts of ... Klengenberg and of Capt. Mogg and his crew, both white and Eskimo, as previously noted in my diary). I am exceedingly glad we fell in with these people: it has enabled me to verify previously received accounts, and to establish, to my own satisfaction at least, a very interesting fact. More will be written of their eyes, etc. after I have had better opportunities of seeing them. (Pálsson 2001: 203)

These references to Scandinavians make it easy to predict the theory he would drum up to explain what he claims to have seen. He had found the long-lost descendants of the Norse colonists of Greenland about whom much had been said and written, but little was known.

The Greenland Norse and Their Fate

The Norse or Vikings started moving west, tentatively at first, in the late eighth century AD. By 870, they had occupied the previously uninhabited Iceland. By the 980s, they had reached Greenland. Remember Eric the Red and Leif the Lucky? These were leaders of a joint community that lived in Greenland for nearly 500 years, well into the 1400s. The community encompassed two groups on the western coast of Greenland, some 300 miles apart. At its peak, 4000 people lived in the southern community known as the Eastern Colony and 1000 in the more northerly community known as the Western Colony. These settlements were set inland along fjords. At some point, the people just disappeared. In Greenlandic Inuit oral tradition, there are stories of the Inuit defeating the Norse after the Norse attempt to dominate their people. This is a commonly occurring theme in Inuit stories: Evil befalls leaders who try to dominate them (see Thisted 2001). But there is no other evidence to support this history.

In his recent best-seller *Collapse: How Societies Choose to Fail or Succeed* (2005: 178–276), Jared Diamond presents five basic reasons why the community "collapsed" and died off: "Norse impact on the environment, climate change, decline in friendly contact with Norway, increase in hostile contact with the Inuit, and the conservative outlook of the Norse" (Diamond 2005: 266). Several Norse practices can be considered to have been destructive to the environment. They all but completely eliminated the small forest cover of dwarf willow and alder by cutting and burning the soil-holding small trees and bushes to clear fields and to make charcoal (which they needed to produce iron products on a small scale and repair precious implements made of iron). Lacking wood to construct houses, they dug up turf. Turf walls were sometimes as thick as 6 feet, providing much needed insulation. Turf disintegrated and would have to be replaced. These practices caused erosion that diminished the already too-limited fields needed for hay for livestock.

Climate change was drastic. The Norse had entered Greenland during what Diamond terms the "Medieval Warm Period" from 800 to 1300. This was followed by the Little Ice Age of the next 500 years. Not only did the weather become colder, it also became more variable, less predictable. Summer ice blocked highly desired contact with Norway, some 1,500 miles away. Much-needed supplies would not appear for years.

The Inuit were not in Greenland when the Norse first arrived. They showed up around 1200, with a superior technology for living in the area. With their light, skin-constructed kayaks and larger *umiaks*, detachable harpoon heads and sealskin floats, they could hunt whales that were inaccessible to the Norse. Armed with superior knowledge, the Inuit were able to hunt the elusive ring seal in winter, when that species was plentiful and available to those in the know. The Norse did make it to L'Anse Aux Meadows by the northern tip of Newfoundland, which was 1000 miles away but could not be sailed in a straight line. However, they only stayed there for about 10 years. They also hit the coast of Labrador and places perhaps farther south to get wood. However, they met with such resistance from the Inuit and other Aboriginals that such trips could prove too costly in manpower to offset any gains in material.

Their only demonstrated relationship with Inuit in the North was an antagonistic one. They could have learned so much that was necessary for survival. The Norse people were unable or unwilling to adopt a more Inuit-style culture. Ironically, this was a criticism that Stefansson repeatedly made of White people in the north generally.

But as Jared Diamond clearly states, the Norse were conservative. They were Christians who did not feel they could learn from heathens. They were a hierarchical society dominated by chiefs who encouraged people to hunt for luxury goods (walrus hides and ivory, narwhal tusks, gyrfalcons, polar bear hides, and live polar bears as a curiosity). This was also for European trade that returned luxury goods such as bells for churches and European-fashioned clothing that benefited most the status of the chiefs. They did not encourage innovation or learning from the neighbours. The Greenland Norse starved and froze to death. In the Western Settlement, the archaeology shows us that their last meals were of their hunting dogs, small barely edible birds and rabbits, and the spring calves and lambs that were the hope of the future.

During Stefansson's time, the fate of the Greenland Norse was still a mystery yet to be solved. The archaeological research that revealed the information presented by Diamond was yet to begin. Stefansson developed the theory that the Copper Inuit were the mixed descendants of the Inuit and members of the Greenland Norse colony. The *Ke Whonkus* people lived! In an account that sounds like an entry in Seinfeld's *J. Peterman* catalogue, Stefansson gives us the following description of the Copper Inuit. But unlike Peterman, Stefansson was not flogging overpriced yuppie clothes. He was marketing an idea that would make him famous, and he was selling the significance of his work to enable him to acquire funding for another year:

> We had been told by our guide that we should find the Victoria Islanders of light complexion, with fair beards, but still we were not prepared for what we saw—we had believed what we had been told, but we had not realized it. Natkusiak kept saying, "These are not Eskimo; they merely dress and talk and act like Eskimo." And so it seemed to me.

> It is hard, looking back over a gap of years, to call to memory even the intense feelings with which we meet a crisis in life. That morning, when the nine men and boys of the village stood before me in line on the ice in front of their huts of snow and skins, I knew I was standing face to face with an important scientific discovery. From childhood I had been familiar with the literature of the North; I knew that here a thousand and there a hundred men of Scandinavia and of England had disappeared into the Northern mists, to be hid by them forever from the eyes of Europe; and when I saw before me these men who looked like Europeans in spite of their garb of furs, I knew that I had come upon either the last chapter and solution of one of the historical tragedies of the past, or else that I had added a new mystery for the future to solve: the mystery of why these men are like Europeans if they are not of European descent. (Stefansson 1913: 193–94)

Stefansson began to write letters to people about his theory. On August 12, 1910 he wrote to Hermon C. Bumpus and Clark Wissler of the American Museum of Natural History, the institute that funded him, saying that he believed the Copper Inuit were descendants of the lost Norse. On December 12, he wrote to his mentor, Professor James Mavor, about his concern that he would be accused of sensationalism. In a return letter sent almost a year later, Mavor wisely told him that he should "avoid sensational conclusions" (Diubaldo 1978: 49). It is important to note that in 1906, a year before his conversation with Klengenberg, Stefansson had dismissed the idea of Norse assimilation with the Inuit in a short article in the *American Anthropologist*:

> Considering the historical and archaeological evidences together, it seems probable that the Icelandic colony in Greenland was destroyed by the Eskimo rather than assimilated with them. Apparently there are few, if any, traces of early Scandinavian influence upon the culture of the natives.... There are Icelandic traditions, probably not well founded, to the effect that the main body of the Eastern Colony moved over to Markland (America); this is especially discredited by the almost certain knowledge we have that the Greenlanders of the time were in possession of no seaworthy ships. (Stefansson 1906: 270)

The idea of the discovery of lost Norse descendants caught fire in the newspapers, much as Stefansson must have hoped it would. The first sensational article appeared in the *New York Times* in the fall of 1911 (Diubaldo 1978: 49). Following this, his funding was renewed. According to biographer Richard Diubaldo, that prospect would have been much less likely prior to the discovery.

1912 was a good year for believing extravagant claims. That was the year that the English lawyer Charles Dawson announced that he had found the supposedly 500,000-year-old missing link between ape and human. This story is known today as the Piltdown Man hoax. The skull Dawson found was only 600 years old. The jaw was from an orangutan. Up until April 15 of that year, people believed the Titanic to be unsinkable.

So by 1912, the public was primed for the excitement of Stefansson's discovery. On August 13, the *London Times* published an article containing excerpts from his 1910 letter to Mavar. More dramatic was an article by J.J. Underwood in the less reputable *Seattle Daily News* on September 9. It caught people's imagination with the headline "American Explorer Discovers Lost Tribe of Whites, Descendants of Leif Erikssen" (Diubaldo 1978: 49). This was only the beginning of what two Icelandic scholars have recently and rightly claimed was a media circus (Pálsson and Helgason 2003: 166).

Stefansson had rivals for his claim to fame. In the *Daily Alaskan* of August 29, 1913, under the headline "Stefannson [sic] Branded as Faker," appeared the following words:

> The noted trapper Deschambeault arrived here this morning from the arctic regions. He claims to be the original discoverer of the blonde Eskimo, and says it was he that sent word to Stefannson [sic] regarding their existence. Deschambeault sent word to Stefansson immediately upon his discovery of the white race, and now claims that the latter claimed the discovery for his own, thus robbing the trapper of the glory connected with his find. He denounces the explorer as a fraud.

The Icelandic-language media in Manitoba reported that Stefansson had "discovered a race of 1000 white men" and that such a discovery was "anthropologically speaking, the equivalent to finding lost generations of Israel" (Pálsson and Helgason 2003: 162–63).

In December of 1912, a sympathetic writer for *National Geographic* quoted Stefansson as saying "The 200 [Eskimo] visited in Prince Albert Sound differed in general features from the Eskimo of Alaska and of the Mackenzie River. Some of the Wollaston Land natives have blue eyes, 50 per cent have light eyebrows and a few have reddish beards. The characteristics of these people seem to suggest a mixture of European and Eskimo blood" (Greeley 1912: 1224).

Later in the article, a letter Stefansson sent from Langton Bay, Northwest Territories is quoted under the heading "Are the Blond Eskimo Descended from the Lost Scandinavian Colony?"

> A point of some interest is our discovery of people in southwestern Victoria Land who are strikingly non-Eskimo in type; in fact look more like north Europeans than Eskimo. Their speech and culture are Eskimo, though I found one or two words that might reasonably be thought to be from Old Norse ... It seems to me that if admixture of white blood is the explanation of the origin of the fair type in western and southwestern Victoria Land, then the only historical event that can explain it is in the disappearance from Greenland of the Scandinavian colony of 3,000. (Greeley 1912: 1237)

I want to quickly dismiss one aspect of his evidence: the linguistic "proof." Compare word lists of any two languages in the world, and you will see a few pairs of words that seem to be cognates, or related terms. These are false cognates, the fool's gold of linguistics. Human mouths produce a limited set of sounds. With the tens of thousands of words that exist in all languages, the law of averages says that some words will sound similar and have meanings that, with a bit of imagination, may be considered the same or alike. Those who believed that Aboriginal peoples descended from the lost tribes of Israel often found false cognates between words in Aboriginal languages and Hebrew. (Mel Brooks was to spoof this in his film *Blazing Saddles* by playing an "Indian" who spoke Yiddish.) We will discuss false cognates in chapter six, concerning a mythical Welsh prince.

Stefansson's bestseller of 1913, *My Life with the Eskimo*, further popularized his fanciful linguistic discovery. However, he expressed a bit of scientific caution as he put forward the evidence for his claim. He began by simply asserting what he had originally written in his notebooks. Then he stated that the journalists who had served his publicity purposes admirably "did not always ... quote me correctly, and ... at times showed marked originality in their treatment of what I said" (1913: 195–96).

He then identified four key features of the Copper Inuit as evidence for his claim that they were descendants of the lost Greenland Norse: 1) blue eyes; 2) brown beards; 3) brown rather than black hair (although not blond); and 4) a high facial index measurement (see below).

Stefansson presented his evidence in the following way. He placed the greatest emphasis on cranial or skull measurements, expressed as a facial index. This was part of a long Western tradition of measuring the skulls of Inuit. According to Canadian physical anthropologist David Hughes, the first "craniometrical description of a [human] skull" was of an Inuk, measured by the Dane J. Winsløw in 1722 (1968: 18–19). To give his argument extra force, Stefansson invoked the name of the most famous American anthropologist of his day, Franz Boas:

It is, however, not only the blondness of the Victoria Islanders that suggests the European, but also the form of their heads, as shown by my measurements of adult males. Typically, we think of the Eskimo as narrow of skull and wide of face; in other words, his face is wider than his head. This fact is scientifically expressed by a "facial index" of over 100; while if the face is narrower than the head, the index will be less than 100. The proportions of the head are considered by most anthropologists an excellent test to determine what race a group of individuals belong to. In a summary published by the American Museum of Natural History, Professor Franz Boas gives the following facial indices for (supposedly) pure-blooded Eskimo: Herschel Island, 101; Greenland, 105; Baffin Bay, 102; Alaska, 104; East Greenland, 102; Smith Sound, 102. In the same paper he gives the following indices for persons of mixed Eskimo and European descent: Labrador, 96; West Greenland, 95. My own measurements of one hundred and four men of Victoria Island give an index of 97, which places the "Blond Eskimo," when judged by head form, exactly where it places them when judged by complexion—in the class with persons who are known to be of mixed Eskimo and white descent. (Stefansson 1913: 196–97)

In chapter two, we noted that Boas was very involved in the study of skull measurements, as were all physical anthropologists of the time. In scientific and in broader moral terms, there is nothing strictly wrong with that. Questions of ethics arise in how data is collected and skulls treated. Stealing skulls from Aboriginal graves involves highly questionable ethics. Standard practice in Canadian archaeology today is much more ethical. Archaeologists must work with Aboriginal descendants or with the nearest local Aboriginal group to study and then rebury the dead respectfully.

Skull measurement is not just a past practice. It is still prastised today, with positive scientific effect. For example, in December 2005, a study of 81 skulls in Brazil that were thousands of years old suggested that the first Aboriginal people who migrated to the Americas may have come from a different place than those who came later. The fact, then, that Stefansson measured skulls and came to anthropological conclusions should not be held against him. It is the nature of the conclusions that were flawed.

The Blond Eskimo Captures the Literary Imagination

The romantic fire of the Norse survivors' story blazed during this time, given ample fuel by Stefansson's writings. The Anglican Church launched a campaign to send missionaries to convert "Stefansson's Blond Eskimos." In 1912, Nova Scotia-born Howard Lois Dodge (first cousin to the brothers who manufactured the car by that name) published *Attraction of the Compass: A Romance of the North*, in which a medieval Norse civilization lived in a volcano-warmed region of the Arctic. In 1916, a new version one chapter longer was published with the tantalizing title *The Blonde Eskimo:*

A Romance of the North Based Upon Facts of a Personal Experience. In 1919–20, Samuel Scoville Jr. serialized *The Boy Scouts of the North: or the Blue Pearl*, in which a group of boys accompanied by a trapper encountered a Blond Eskimo called Saanak:

> Saanak, the second hunter, was different from any of the rest of the tribe. His face, broader than his head, looked like that of an Eskimo; but instead of having the seal-brown eyes and black hair of that people, his eyes were blue and his hair and beard of a golden-red. Moreover, instead of being squat and short, like an Eskimo, he was tall and well built.
>
> Years later, Will found out that Saanak was one of the blond Eskimo from Victoria Island far away in the frozen North. A thousand years ago, Eric the Red sailed from Iceland and discovered Greenland. There he founded a colony that flourished on the southwestern coast of Greenland until the Black Death in the fourteenth century swept the shipping of the world from off the seas and the colony was lost for a hundred years. When it was found again, the people had disappeared, merged in Eskimo tribes which wandered up until they settled on Victoria Island.
>
> Saanak had about him something of the strength and gloom of those Norse Vikings whose blood ran in his veins, and the boys noticed two lines of tattooing running from the corners of his mouth to the lobes of his ears. These marks, Negouac told the boys, showed that he had killed a whale single-handed. (<http://www.merrycoz.org/annex/pearl/pearl.htm>)

In 1927, Paul Hotspur published *Treasure of the North! A Gripping Romance of Peril and Adventure in the Arctic*, a tale of Viking survivals in the North. Two years later, Arthur Stringer published *The Woman Who Couldn't Die*, about a member of a surviving Viking colony who was discovered frozen and thawed out to come to life.

Jenness Takes Up the Challenge

Once Diamond Jenness entered the scene, he challenged Stefansson's assertions in various areas of anthropology. We see this opposition slowly developing in his field notes, which he fought hard to keep as his own. The subject of Inuit child rearing was the first to show itself in these notes. It was a good thing that he did not hand them over to Stefansson, as the latter had originally expected. The younger, more modest, and gentler man from New Zealand increasingly questioned the soundness of the information presented by his more experienced leader. Jenness would mount his greatest challenge to Stefansson by attacking his idea of the Blond Eskimo.

Jenness's scholarly style was like that of Charles Darwin in the meticulous mounting of his oppositional points. It began in written form in his diary entry of June 3, 1915: "I measured the five Kanghir [*juarmiut*] adults. They show no signs of 'blondness' that do not appear in the more southern Eskimos" (Jenness 1991: 341). Not long afterwards, he cited information given him by Higilaq, one of his informants: "Higilaq remarked about the colour of my eyes [blue] differing from theirs. In reply to my question, he said the Kanghirjuarmiut had eyes like them, not like me. 'How could they, being Eskimos?'" (Jenness 1991: 483).

In 1916, Jenness published his opposition for the first time in a research note to his article "The Ethnological Results of the Canadian Arctic Expedition, 1913–16," which appeared in the prestigious *American Anthropologist*: "Nothing was observed which would indicate fusion with any other race, save that in two or three instances the features seem to have a somewhat Indian cast. Light coloration in the eyes and beard which was noticeable in certain individuals seemed entirely due to secondary causes" (Jenness 1916: 613).

He would identify those "secondary causes" and develop his argument against the Blond Eskimos more fully in his next appearance in that same journal, a full-length article published in 1921—the same year as Stefansson's next major work, the ironically named "Friendly Arctic" (Stefansson 1921). Jenness's work was quite determined and methodical, like an Inuk crawling up on a seal. He began by referring to and expanding upon the work of literally a "major" defender of Stefansson's.

In 1912, Major General Adophus W. Greeley of the US Army wrote an article entitled "The Origin of Stefansson's Blond Eskimo" in the December issue of the *National Geographic* (1912: 1224–38). Like Stefansson, Greeley was an Arctic explorer who had men die under his command due in part to his inability as a leader (see Guttridge 2000). As a first lieutenant in 1881, Greeley had led an American scientific expedition to Cape Sapine, farther north on Ellesmere Island than any White explorer had ever travelled. After three years of simmering conflict, slow starvation, and eventual cannibalism, only six of the original 25 members survived. In his article, Greeley mostly cited the Arctic exploration literature for examples of Inuit who looked other than what was considered typical (i.e., dark hair, smooth faced). It was less than a critical reading of the literature.

Jenness published his critique of Greeley in 1921 in "The 'Blond' Eskimos" in the *American Anthropologist*. In it, Jenness added to the list of "atypical" Inuit characteristics and was careful to include examples from Greenland, and from Labrador all the way to Alaska, not just from the Copper Inuit. His point was not to single out one group (i.e., the Copper Inuit) as different from the others.

In summarizing the results, in so far as they bear on the question of the "blondness" of these Eskimos and the possible infusion of European blood, I have not considered it necessary to separate the Victoria Islanders from the natives of the mainland south of them (although it might easily have been done), because all the tribes in this region constantly intermarry, and in any one group representatives may be found of half a dozen different tribes, both from the mainland and from Victoria Island. (Jenness 1921: 259)

He then proceeded to debunk systematically the evidence that Stefansson had put forward. First, there was the matter of the blue eyes. He noted that of the 82 men and 42 women he studied, 14 of the men had a secondary bluish colouring, while only two women did. He then noted that those with such a colouring were "either middle aged or well advanced in years" (1921: 259). Next, he observed an unevenness about the light coloration: One eye often showed the feature more than the other.

With these observations, Jenness tried to establish a connection between the light colour of the eyes and *arcus senilis* (i.e., old-age ring). This is a cloudy opaque arc or ring at the edge of the iris, typically associated with old age. In addition, along with Dr. D.S. Neuman, health officer of the Bureau of Education in northern Alaska, Jenness concluded that repeated attacks of snow blindness occurred more often with men than women, and became more common with age. When the two researchers examined the eyes of a number of Inuit from the King and Diomede Islands and from Cape Prince of Wales, they noted that most had *arcus senilis* and that with the very pronounced examples, "there was the bluish-grey coloration of the eye I had noticed among the Copper Eskimos" (1921: 260).

Arcus senilis has been correlated with both age and maleness; for younger people, it is correlated with a history of cardiovascular disease (Moss, Klein, and Klein 2000). To the best of my knowledge, it has not been connected with snow blindness since Jenness.

While Jenness left open the possibility that there could be another cause for the variation in eye colour, his most salient concluding point was again that "the eyes of the Copper Eskimos differed in no respect from those of the natives of northern Alaska" (Moss, Klein, and Klein 2000).

Concerning the beards of the Copper Inuit, Jenness questioned the fanciful sources that spoke of their European-type length and fullness. This was something that Jenness had never encountered. More to the point, he focused in on the colour:

> In color it is usually a dark brownish-black, but not infrequently it is a rich brown, especially around the lips. Even in such cases, however, the hair on the chin is almost always a brownish-black, except when it is becoming grey with old age. There is some reason, therefore, to suspect that any unusually light color around the lips is due to some bleaching agent, perhaps the hot blood soup that the natives are always drinking; for in no case that we noticed was the hair of the head other than black, or a dark brownish-black. (Jenness 1921: 261)

He saved the harshest professional criticism for the most scientific-sounding form of evidence that Stefansson had mustered: cranial measurements. Jenness had himself spent a great deal of time and effort measuring skulls. He rejected both what he felt was the lack of comparative data in the measurement index Stefansson had chosen and the index itself, stating that the cephalic index, which relates the length of the head to the breadth, was generally recognized at the time to be superior. Comparing his own measurements of Copper Inuit with the work done by Søren Hansen among the Ammassalik of East Greenland, he concluded as follows:

> Mr. Stefansson's own comparison—breadth of face with breadth of head—is inconclusive, firstly because he had insufficient data of a similar nature from other Eskimo sources with which to compare his data from the Copper Eskimos, and secondly, because it is not recognized by the best authorities as a consideration of major importance in determining questions of race. The principal feature that is employed for this purpose, the cephalic index, tends to show that the Copper Eskimos are as pure as the purest known branch of the Eskimo race of whom we have definite and detailed knowledge [the Ammassalik]. Until, therefore, we are presented with more tangible and significant evidence of the theory of Scandinavian or even European infusion among the Copper Eskimos must be regarded as unproved, and indeed groundless. (Jenness 1921: 267)

Jenness also raised the question of whether the Victoria Island people had more interbreeding with Athabaskan speakers to the south of them. They would have been more likely to have experienced this than the people to the east of them, who had no non-Inuit Aboriginal neighbours, especially the people of Baffin Island.

Jenness was not through with Stefansson yet. The next year, he reviewed Stefansson's *The Friendly Arctic* and renewed his criticism. More devastating was Jenness's scientific report *Physical Characteristics of the Copper Eskimos*, published a year later. He repeated his criticisms of the 1921 paper and dismissively concluded his discussion of Stefansson's ideas with "[t]he theory of any European admixture among the Copper Eskimos may be rejected without further consideration" (1923: 46).

In 1922, two back-to-back research notes appeared in the *American Anthropologist* challenging Jenness's criticism of Stefansson. One of these critiques came from Harold Noice: "Further Discussion of the 'Blond' Eskimos"(1922). Noice, a Stefansson wannabe, had been a late joiner and survivor of the Canadian Arctic Expedition and an on-again, off-again ally of Stefansson. Like Stefansson, Noice craved to be the great White explorer of fame and fortune. They were journalistic mercenaries of the same ilk. Before going on a rescue mission to Wrangel Island (see below), Noice signed a newspaper contract that gave him exclusive rights to the stories of those he would attempt to rescue. Had the four young men lived, they would not have been allowed to speak to the papers.

By 1939, Noice's fame would peak at a minor level. That year, he published *Back of Beyond*, a photographic expedition to the upper Amazon, and he also had his own syndicated radio show, "The Black Flame of the Amazon Radio Program." Listeners to this show could purchase a map of South America, and if they bought gas at participating gas stations, would be given stamps of "Unusual Animals, Savages and Also the Scenic Beauty of the Jungles" on a weekly basis.

The year after Noice wrote his critique of Jenness, he and Stefansson had a falling out. Noice participated in a mission to rescue members of Stefansson's second tragic expedition to Wrangel Island. Stefansson insisted that it was a "relief" mission. Noice found Ada Blackjack, the Inuit woman, alive. But he also found the recently deceased corpse of one of the explorers. The story he told of an ill-conceived and tragic expedition was not the one that Stefansson wanted people to hear. Further alienation of the two like-spirits would come in 1924 upon publication of Noice's *With Stefansson in the Arctic*, in which the author cashed in on the cachet of his mentor's name, but also criticized him.

In his *American Anthropologist* piece, Noice's criticism of Jenness's observations of the Copper Inuit and other Inuit groups was mostly of the "my word against his" type. Noice had spent two winters with the Kilinigmiun (his spelling) of southeast Victoria Island. He was not a trained observer and was well prepared by Stefansson as to what he should see, so his visual evidence was not trustworthy. There is a truism in anthropology that there are none so blind as those who think they see simply because they are there ("I *know* Indians because I live in Northern Ontario"). He also claimed that the people themselves remarked on the differences between the Copper Inuit and other Inuit groups. Without reasonably detailed accounts of the conversations that led to this conclusion, these claims cannot be trusted. They could have been (and probably were) similar in nature to a "Johnny said that he likes school" comment in which a well-intentioned but unaware adult had asked Johnny "Do you like school?" and Johnny had nodded his head, in part to avoid further discussion.

Noice did not comment on Jenness's observation that "blue" eyes were more commonly found among men than women because he hadn't attempted any scientific count to back up his anecdotes. Nor did he respond regarding head measurements, other than to make this dubious commentary: "I do not follow Mr. Jenness in his reasoning about the head form of the Copper Eskimos, but if there is anything wrong with his scientific method (and it seems to me there must be) someone else will probably point that out" (Noice 1922: 228).

The second critical note in the *American Anthropologist*, "The 'Blond' Eskimo—A Question of Method" by Louis R. Sullivan (1922), needs to be taken more seriously. Unlike Noice, Sullivan was an anthropologist, and one respected in the field. He had a Ph.D. in anthropology and had published scientific articles on the anthropometry (measurement and statistical analysis of human body parts) of various Polynesian peoples (Hawaiians, Samoans, and Tongans), Filipinos, Andaman Islanders, and the Sioux. He had even written a manual on anthropometry.

However, while Sullivan was critical of the methods Jenness chose, he did not take issue with his ultimate conclusion that the Blond Eskimos did not exist. Although he went to great pains to point out his neutrality in that debate—"I do not wish to be understood as arguing for or against a European origin of 'blondness' in the Eskimo" (1922: 227–28)—he showed a definite inclination toward Jenness's position. He stated that the "first six pages of Mr. Jenness's article are as logical and critical as might be asked for" (1922: 225). These included Jenness's discussion of eye and hair colour.

His criticism of Jenness's methodology was twofold. First, he took Jenness to task for his use of the cephalic index, as he claimed that both the Inuit and Scandinavians were "long-headed" people. Therefore, no change in head length would indicate interbreeding between the two peoples. His main criticism is of Jenness's rejection of the facial index as not "*standard*" (Sullivan's emphasis). Like a modern forensic anthropologist who attributes Aboriginal or East Asian descent to a newly dug-up skull with a wide face, Sullivan rightly notes that an Inuit face is wider on average than that of a Scandinavian person. Thus, Sullivan points to the significance of two measures: "From an *anthropometric* standpoint absolute face width and the transverse cephalo-facial index [what Stefansson was referring to] are most satisfactory" (1922: 227).

Unfortunately, Sullivan does not criticize how Stefansson conducted his cephalo-facial index measures. To arrive at a correct figure, one must measure from specific points of the skull. Stefansson did not specify how he came up with his figures. This leaves them open to question.

At this point, Stefansson approached his conflict with Jenness as an undercover operation. He quietly tried to have Jenness's *Physical Characteristics of the Copper Eskimos* altered, claiming that the scientific reputation of the expedition would be at stake if Jenness did not tone down his attack on his former leader (Diubaldo 1978: 201–03). He stated that if certain passages of the 1923 report were not changed, he would have to charge Jenness with "deliberate misrepresentation" (Diubaldo 1978: 203). Stefansson wanted Jenness to admit that he had less experience with the Copper Inuit than Stefansson did, that he had not seen the Prince Albert Sound Inuit, and that he should not be so absolute in his criticism. Jenness, unhappy that officials of the National Museum of Canada had given Stefansson access to his report prior to its publication, refused to discredit himself by backing down from what he believed to be true. On April 7, 1923, Jenness issued a memo, "Account of Call from Mr. V. Stefansson and Dr. Prince," in which he stated: "Mr. Stefansson spent about six weeks among the Copper Eskimo and met about forty percent of their number. I spent upward of 18 months and saw 70%. To insert the statement asked for by Mr. Stefansson would be a direct untruth" (cited in Diubaldo 1978: 203).

In 1928, Stefansson published a defence of his position in an article in *Harper's Magazine* entitled, unsurprisingly, "The 'Blond' Eskimos." He again told the story of the Greenlanders and repeated the tales various people told of "strange-looking" Inuit. He seemed to be following the "aliens have landed" principle: By repeating a large number of slightly strange stories, he hoped to build up one very strange theory. He then "doth protest too much" about exaggerations in the press, with which he claims he was "annoyed from the first," referring to the journalists as "my unwelcome champions." Tellingly, he was not as particular about the location of the places where he draws his stories from as he was in a later article criticizing Jenness.

In the *Harper's Magazine* piece, he also cleverly refuted Jenness's criticisms by showing how all his major critics, including Roald Amundsen and Knud Rasmussen, disagreed with each other, implying that since his critics disagreed about *how* he was wrong, he must be *right*. This, of course, was not a direct critique of Jenness's ideas, but it helped to discredit them without scientifically challenging them. His actual critique of Jenness is a rather convoluted one:

> The first scientific traveler to visit the "Blond" Eskimos after my second expedition was Diamond Jenness in 1914–16, then anthropologist of my third expedition and now head of anthropological work of the Canadian Government at Ottawa. In some careful and in general excellent studies he made several points: (1) The "blondness" was in his opinion less than stated by previous travelers. (2) Some of it was of what might be called biological origin. (3) The blue, or grey, eyes were probably caused by snow-blindness or by eye disease. (4) He dismissed the possibility that there could have been any blood connection with trappers, traders, whalers, explorers, or other visitors since the time of Columbus; but he opposed equally the likelihood of any connection with the lost European colony of Greenland. Whatever blondness there was had nothing to do with any European blood, in his opinion.

> That Jenness observed less "blondness" than Klinkenberg, Mogg, or myself is partly explained, at least, by the territorial limitations of his studies. We had reported the largest percentage of "blondness" as well as the most pronouncedly "blond" individuals from Prince Albert Sound and Minto Inlet, a district he had been unable to visit. In preferring a biological to a historical explanation of what "blondness" he did observe, Jenness was not proposing a new theory, but was falling in with what might be called my second choice of solutions, the biological one quoted above from p. 202 of *My Life with the Eskimo*. (Stefansson 1928)

Stefansson's weaknesses here are several. Concerning the second point, Jenness did not admit to a biological origin of difference for the Blond Eskimos. He did not even admit to a difference; instead, he tried to establish that what differences there were among individuals could be found broadly across the Arctic.

Interestingly, his argument that Jenness did not get to see the most blond population actually cut himself adrift like an ice floe from the other commentators, whose range of supposed sightings were broader geographically than this. He was being inconsistent. Finally, at no point did he try to refute the eye colour argument or any other scientific argument that Jenness had put forward.

Stefansson lost this fight and would progressively lose his favoured position with the Canadian government. Jenness went on to become the chief anthropologist of what is now the Canadian Museum of Civilization. From that base, he would achieve great things. He studied and wrote ethnographies on a variety of Canadian Aboriginal peoples (e.g., the Salish, Sarcee, Carrier, and Ojibwa); established the existence of and named two Arctic archaeological traditions, Old Bering Sea and Dorset culture; wrote what is arguably the Canadian anthropological bestseller, *Indians of Canada*; and wrote a five-volume magnum opus on Eskimo administration.

The Return of the Blond Eskimo

While the myth of the Blond Eskimo never completely died (see Willis 1971: 130), it seemed to have remained hidden for a while. In 1959, Bruce Chown and Marion Lewis of the University of Manitoba published their study "The Blood Group Genes of the Copper Eskimo" in the *Journal of Physical Anthropology*. They looked at the blood typing of 320 members of a population of approximately 1000 in a variety of ways: the familiar ABO groupings and the Rh factor as well as the lesser known systems: MN, Ss, MNS, P, Lutheran, Lewis, and Kell. They did not mention Stefansson by name, but they did state that "there is surprisingly little evidence for replacement of Eskimo genes by genes of Whites. Such is present certainly, but not in such numbers in the populations we have studied as seriously to disturb the inherent Eskimo gene frequencies" (Chown and Lewis 1959: 17).

Two recent books by the twentieth-century giants of historical narrative in Canada, Farley Mowat and Pierre Berton, have brought Stefansson and the Blond Eskimo back to the public eye. In *Prisoners of the North*, a book published just before his death, Berton titled the chapter on Stefansson "The Blond Eskimo," using the term to refer to the man himself, not, fortunately, to his extravagant claim.

We weren't so fortunate with Mowat. In 1998, he published *The Farfarers: Before the Norse*. Mowat had heard Stefansson speak 50 years before. With their shared bombastic styles and mandatory flaunting of conventional wisdom, there must have begun a one-way intellectual love affair. The dedication, "For Vilhjalmur Stefansson, Thomas Lee, and Thomas Lethbridge, who lighted me on my way," hinted at the direction the book would take. All three men resorted to questionable techniques or analyses, for which they were largely discredited. Lethbridge, who had achieved respectability as a Cambridge archaeologist, lost a great deal of his credibility when he began to resort to dowsing (divining) to discover sites. Thomas Lee, whom Mowat frequently cites, became more or less a pariah in Canadian archaeological circles when he claimed that the Sheguiandah site on Manitoulin Island was at least 30,000 years old. Mowat defended that idea without knowing that subsequent research had discredited the claim (1998: 279). A more accurate read is between 9000 and 9500 years (Storck 2004). Mowat's *The Farfarers* fits comfortably with the work of his heroes.

In *West Viking*, published in 1965, Mowat introduced somewhat extravagant claims that the Norse moved west into Canada. He views *The Farfarers* (I keep wanting to call it the *Far-Fetchers*!) as an updated correction to that work and makes even more extravagant claims about the so-called Albans, a name he gives to a Celtic group he believes blazed the path to the Canadian Arctic ahead of the Norse and about whom he also makes some wild statements.

His position concerning the Greenland settlers is as follows. After talking about the so-called mystery of the disappearance of the Greenland settlers and pooh-poohing any claim that they could have simply died off, Mowat wrote that "[s]cores of books and hundreds of learned papers have been devoted to finding a solution to the mystery, but only a few authors, Fridtjof Nansen and Vilhjalmur Stefansson, seem to have got close to the truth. Which is that the Greenland Norse *never did disappear*—they just changed shape" (Mowat 1998: 423; emphasis in original).

It is important to point out that although the term "changed shape" referred to intermarrying with the local Inuit, Mowat did not position his Blond Eskimos (a term he doesn't use) on far westerly Victoria Island. While exaggerating the Norse impact in the Canadian Arctic, he seems to want to restrict the interbreeding to Greenland in the main. Certainly, at no point in the book does he claim that Victoria Island was the home of a genetically mixed people. The farthest west he was willing to go was Pamiok Island, near the north shore of Quebec. He supports Stefansson's spirit, but not his actual claims.

Mowat's arguments for the western boundary of his mixed race came from two sources: stonework and skulls. Both are flimsy forms of evidence. Like many of the amateur scholars before him who wrote about structures created by Aboriginal peoples and other non-Europeans, Mowat underestimates their abilities to construct out of stone. First, there are the 45 structures Mowat refers to as "longhouses." The name creates a bias and expectations that may be misleading. These "longhouses" are rectangular stone constructions of a metre or slightly higher and contain hearth pits. They vary in length: Large ones are 25 to 42 metres long and around 5 to 7 metres wide. In response to the fact that the structures show no sign of roofing, Mowat suggests that boats were used for roofs, as they were in some places in Europe. Of course, the lack of a roof is only a mystery if you expected the structures to be Norse or Celtic longhouses. If they had been named "enclosures" instead, as a number of archaeologists have suggested, there isn't as much of a problem.

Researchers can be led toward conclusions by the nature of the material they study. People such as Mowat, who are depending largely on European sources for the development of their perspective and who have visited European sites and museums, will have visions of European-style buildings dancing in front of their eyes when they see constructions in the Arctic. Archaeologists working in the Canadian Arctic are more familiar with Aboriginal cultures and have a better-informed sense of what these people can construct. They are also much better situated to perceive a continuation of simpler construction into more complex crafting. Canadian Museum of Civilization archaeologist Robert McGhee speaks of these elements in his 1984 summary of Native-Norse contact. He praises early Aboriginal Arctic stone structures and comments on the smaller versions of the larger constructions:

> Any archaeologist who has excavated Dorset and Thule culture structures must be impressed by the stonework used in their construction. Indeed, the amount of boulder construction undertaken by the Thule Eskimos of Labrador has led Fitzhugh (1976: 141) to refer to Thule occupation of the region as "practically a geological event, surpassed only by the Wisconsin glaciation." (McGhee 1984: 20)

On the other hand, Mowat's claim that there were skulls of European and mixed-European heritage found on Quebec's north shore needs to be taken more seriously. Mowat speaks of a conversation he had in 1957 with William Taylor, who was then archaeologist at the National Museum of Canada: "I reminded him that archaeologist Tom Lee had found human skulls associated with the longhouse structures on Pamiok; one of them, according to physical anthropologist Dr. Carleton S. Coon of Harvard University, 'probably European' and another 'predominantly, if not full European'" (Mowat 1998: 271–72).

Mowat comments on a picture of the two skulls, saying that one is "typically Eskimoan in character; the other ... predominately north European" (1998: 272). Coon himself is slightly suspect in this area, as he was one of the last physical anthropologists to try to divide the human species into clearly separate races. He failed. One might suspect a tendency to exaggerate on his part. It should also be noted that the probabilistic measurements now used by forensic anthropologists to broadly typologize skulls as "Aboriginal/ Asian," "Black" and "European" were decades away from being standardized. And they are sometimes wrong.

Robert McGhee problematizes the putative European nature of these skulls as follows:

This claim is based on five skeletons recovered from tombs of Thule Eskimo type, located at one of the sites which also contained longhouses. Carleton S. Coon is reported to have identified one of these skulls as "Icelandic," and three others as representing a mixed European-Eskimo population (Lee 1981: 32). However, Coon never published this opinion; in a foreword to one of Lee's publications (Lee 1971), apparently written after he had examined the skulls, Coon summarized the evidence supporting claims for a Norse presence in Ungava but made no mention of the skulls. Hartweg (1974: 286), who examined the skulls in the context of Eskimo skeletons recovered from the Eastern Arctic, states that they are typical of the local prehistoric Eskimo population. Until the skeletons receive further study, it is probably wise to accept this published view. (McGhee 1984: 19–20)

Nothing has been published in the last 20 years to effectively counter that position.

In 2003, both Stefansson and the Blond Eskimo re-emerged to face the public eye. The former surfaced in a sympathetic Canadian documentary entitled *Arctic Dreamer: The Lonely Quest of Vilhjalmur Stefansson*, first screened at the Montreal World Film Festival. In the production company's promotional website (<http://www.whitepinepictures.com/articedreamer. htm>; consulted November 17, 2004), the following words were written: "One of the most famous men of the early 20th century, Stefansson is best known for discovering the 'Blond Eskimo' of the central arctic."

At the same time as this documentary was screening, the CBC was giving favourable showing to genetic research on whether or not the Blond Eskimo existed. Gísli Pálsson, an Icelandic anthropologist acting as Stefansson's biographer and sometime apologist, along with the help of his fellow countryman biological anthropologist Agnar Helgason, took DNA samples from the saliva of 350 Cambridge Bay Inuit in order to compare them with DNA patterns found among people in Iceland. This research began with a position that reads as quite sympathetic to Stefansson, mixing his hypothesis uncritically with more solid scientific research:

There is now strong archaeological evidence for Norse settlements in Newfoundland, but knowledge of Norse interactions with Canadian Inuit and other Native American groups is very limited. Based on stories of feuds and battles between Inuit and Norse groups in Greenland, together with stories of exchange of goods, services, and mates, there are reasonable grounds to examine genetic evidence admixture between these two groups. In order to both shed light on Inuit migration history and the extent of interaction between Inuit and Norse groups, we made plans to obtain DNA samples from Greenland and Victoria Island in Canada. Victoria Island was selected both because it is central to an understanding of Inuit range expansions and also because, *according to Vilhjalmur Stefansson's hypothesis, it represents the most western reach of any credible Norse presence in Canada.* (Pálsson and Helgason 2003: 165; emphasis mine)

In the announcement of their research project in *Trends in Biotechnology,* they referred to the Copper Inuit community as one "likely to have traces of Norse heritage."

The news of Pálsson and Helgason's research was publicized in September 2003, with headlines like "DNA Study to Settle Ancient Mystery About Mingling of Inuit, Vikings" and "DNA Test May Solve Mystery of Blonde Inuit," and catchy opening lines like "An Icelandic professor wants to use Nunavut DNA to solve a 550-year-old mystery." These were followed by headlines of "DNA Tests Debunk Blond Inuit Legend" and "Inuit-Norse Links Discounted." The tests proved negative. However, somehow I feel that Stefansson's fanciful notion will never be completely laid to rest. Stefansson's stature as an explorer and public figure is too large. What will the anniversary year of his "discovery" of the Blond Eskimo bring?

Negative Implications of the Blond Eskimo

Other than being inaccurate anthropology, what are the negative implications of the Blond Eskimo for the Inuit people? One such implication is that it downplays the role of oral tradition among the Inuit. Certainly, if the Norse Greenlanders had managed to trek across Baffin Island to the central Canadian Arctic, the Inuit would have told and remembered stories about it. But that seems not to have been considered. Inuit oral history has only recently been given the respect it deserves. Second, there is the racist notion that Europeans and their culture are indomitable, able to survive in all environments. The implication is that the Arctic survival capacity developed through hundreds of years of Inuit cultural innovation could readily be equalled by Westerners within a short time. If the Inuit can do it, certainly the strong, determined Norse can. Third, the myth distinctly implies a cultural inferiority of the Baffin Island Inuit, a sense that they were either unaware of the Norse Greenlanders travelling through their country (a reflection of the old idea that the land was essentially empty before the coming of the Europeans) or were so intimidated by the "superior" technology and martial spirit of the Norse colonists that they just let them pass through.

CONTENT QUESTIONS

1. How was the Blond Eskimo "discovered"?
2. What Inuit group was identified as the Blond Eskimo?
3. What happened to the Greenland Norse according to Jared Diamond?
4. What evidence did Stefansson present for the existence of the Blond Eskimo?

5. How did Jenness challenge that evidence?
6. What evidence did Mowat present to support his idea of the Blond Eskimo?
7. What is questionable about this evidence?
8. What evidence does Mowat give for his belief that the Norse travelled across the Canadian Arctic?

DISCUSSION QUESTIONS

1. To what can we compare the fascination with lost races in Stefansson's time?
2. Why do you think that North Americans and Europeans wanted to believe in the Blond Eskimo and in the survival of the Greenland Norse?
3. Why does the idea keep coming back?

KEY TERMS

anthropometry	*arcus senilis*	cephalic index
Copper Inuit	facial index	false cognates
informant	*kablunat*	lost races
Tasaday		

CHAPTER FIVE

Elders on Ice

LEARNING OBJECTIVES

After reading this chapter, you will be able to
» outline the myth of culturally determined Inuit elder suicide.
» identify the three fundamental interpretive errors that led to the development of the notion of culturally determined Inuit elder suicide.
» connect the social scientific concepts of altruistic suicide and cultural relativism to the popularity of this myth.
» present the evidence for traditional respect for elders in Inuit culture.
» distinguish between short-term and long-term abandonment of elders in traditional Inuit culture.
» critically assess the evidence presented for culturally determined Inuit elder suicide.
» identify and critique the forms of causality used to explain the myth of culturally determined Inuit elder suicide.

Today we are going to teach about cultural relativism. This involves knowing that you cannot understand the ways of a people without knowing their culture, the context for their ideas and practices. And culture can have a strong impact that can make people do things that might seem strange to you at first glance. Sometimes it even means that you should not judge people of another culture based on what they do. Take, for example, the case of people who live in southern Ontario, specifically the Greater Toronto Area. When times get tough for the males of this culture, they kill their families and then themselves. Now you have to understand the context first. Rent is very high there, and debt is easily acquired. What's more, many of them have to drive on the 401, which is a very harsh highway on which to drive. You have to be good at steering and braking to survive. Thoughts of killing come easily. So their culture has developed a solution for stress. Kill the family. That benefits the culture because then many people can feel better than that person who killed, the housing vacancy rate can go up, and there is at least one fewer car on the 401.

This is cultural relativism, as might be taught in an Inuit classroom.

A Popular Story: Going with the Floes

In the October 2000 edition of the *Journal of the American Medical Association*, a medical student published an article in which he spoke of witnessing a 97-year-old Yup'ik Inuit kill himself by "vanishing into the early morning fog." The August 31, 2001 edition of the Nunavut paper *Nunatsiaq News* later reported that the student had made up the story. He wasn't the first to make up a story like this.

In spring 2001, CBC television aired a special edition of *Talking with Americans*, based on Rick Mercer's regular comedy routine on *This Hour Has 22 Minutes*, in which he lampoons Americans for their ignorance of Canada. It includes such features as asking people to send congratulations to the new Canadian Prime Minister "Jean Poutine" and to sign petitions to end the seal hunt in Calgary. In the special edition mentioned above, Rick Mercer asked interviewees to sign a petition to end the Canadian practice of leaving their elders on ice floes. Thus, a typically Canadian (but also American) myth was reproduced: the image of the Inuit abandoning their elders, a form of culturally approved suicide. The notion of Inuit elder suicide is deeply ingrained in our culture and lives on in the popular media.

In *Our Inner Ape*, an otherwise excellent book about how human behaviour reflects that of chimps and bonobos, author and leading primatologist Frans de Waal refers to a shouting match between top peace advocates at a conference he attended. They were arguing about the Inuit. In response to the confrontational behaviour of the peace advocates, de Waal quipped, "Some of us at the meeting surely would have been put out on the ice," a clear reference to the myth about elders on ice floes (de Waal 2005: 20).

In their insightful look at Inuit suicide, Kirmayer, Fletcher, and Boothroyd noted that

> [s]uicide has become one of the emblematic cultural traits of the "Eskimo." Nearly every popular film with Inuit content contains a scene in which a dutiful and wise elder ends his or her own existence for the good of the group, usually with remarkable equanimity. This "altruistic" suicide [see discussion on Durkheim below] is viewed as a distinctively Inuit practice, albeit one that demonstrates the harsh exigencies of life in the Arctic. (Kirmayer, Fletcher, and Boothroyd 1998: 194)

According to anthropologist Charles Hughes, the stereotypical image of the Eskimo typically comprises "a people living (presumably year round) in snow houses ... eating fish, swallowing raw meat, rubbing noses, swapping wives, *leaving old people out on the ice to die*, being childishly delighted with white man's tools, having no 'government' ... always wandering" (Hughes 1965: 12–13; emphasis mine). Introductory sociology and anthropology textbooks have ably assisted the nurturing of this false image. The following quotation, taken from a recent textbook entitled *Sociology: A Down-to-Earth Approach* (Canadian edition) demonstrates this:

> Shantu and Wishta fondly kissed their children and grandchildren farewell. Then sadly, but with resignation at the sacrifice they knew they had to make for their family, they slowly climbed onto the ice floe. The goodbyes were painfully made as the large slab of ice inched into the ocean currents. Shantu and Wishta would now starve. But they were old, and their death was necessary, for it reduced the demand on the small group's scarce food supply.

> As the younger relatives watched Shantu and Wishta recede into the distance, each knew that their turn to make this sacrifice would come. Each hoped that they would face it as courageously.

> To grow old in traditional Inuit society meant a "voluntary" death. Survival in their harsh environment was so precarious that all except very young children had to pull their own weight. The food supply was so limited that nothing was left over to give to anyone who could not participate in the closely integrated tasks required for survival. (Henslin et al. 2001: 216)

The idea here is that traditionally, when times got tough, Inuit elders committed suicide, possibly with the assistance of others, but as a culturally mandated choice. The practice is assumed to be frequent and familiar, an integral part of Inuit culture.

This is a White lie. That does not mean Inuit elders never committed suicide. On relatively rare occasions, perhaps in times of unusually harsh conditions, they did, having decided that without their mouth to feed, the family or community would more likely survive. It also does not mean that Inuit family members never assisted a suffering elder to a peaceful death. As we will see, euthanasia of seriously ailing, suffering Inuit elders did occur. This is neither unique to the Inuit nor unusual cross-culturally. However, elder suicide and abandonment were not culturally mandated practices, part of the cultural instructions that individuals grew up with. Contrary to what many non-Inuit authors say, Inuit elder suicide was not "dictated" (a word that some authors like to apply to cultures other than their own) by their culture or customs. It wasn't even suggested; nor was it statistically significant. Also, the family and community may not have come to a consensus about whether a specific euthanasia should take place. In the literature, outsiders almost always presume the community was in total agreement. Who knows what people think if you do not ask them?

Compare this possibility with views of euthanasia in mainstream North American society. Think of the Terri Schiavo case in Florida early in 2005 when her husband and her parents were in dispute as to whether "the plug should be pulled" on her life support machines so that she could die. Newspapers published editorials and letters to the editor supporting opposing views. Inuit family members may have had the same kinds of disagreements when faced with decisions about euthanasia of an elder. But we don't get to hear them.

Analogies are useful here. Calling Inuit elder suicide a culturally mandated practice is like saying that husbands and fathers in Toronto are culturally mandated to commit family murder-suicide when they feel economic or personal failure. Sure it happens, but it does not reflect cultural custom. It would also be like saying that when French sociologist Emile Durkheim wrote his famous book on suicide based on statistics gathered in France, he was saying that suicide is a distinctly French practice. He wasn't. And it isn't.

Why Shouldn't You Believe the Story of Culturally Determined Inuit Elder Suicide?

There are a number of reasons why the White-told tale of Inuit elder suicide should be challenged. First—the one that set off my orange caution light— was the close and caring attachment to elders in Inuit culture, often reported in the primary sources. This is well recorded, for example, in the literature about the Labrador Inuit. Dr. Samuel K. Hutton's *Among the Eskimos of Labrador: A Record of Five Years' Close Intercourse with the Eskimo Tribes of Labrador* (1912) gives a sympathetic portrayal:

> In my visits to the Eskimo households I could not fail to be struck by the patience and devotion with which the people care for their aged ones. The old man or woman, feeble and past work, is sure of a home with a married son or daughter or other relative, and if the poor old body has no relations, there is enough hospitality in the hearts of the poorest of the people to make them open their homes to the needy. (Hutton 1912: 111)

Hutton's work is readily available in university libraries. However, it is not one of the primary sources cited by the sociological and anthropological writers (see Ruth Cavan, E. Adamson Hoebel, and Edward Weyer below) whose analyses of Inuit suicide were drawn upon and later quoted by textbook writers. Is that because he presents an uncomfortable fact that does not fit neatly into their pat portrayal of the people?

More peculiarly, the primary sources that *are* frequently cited often say the same thing as Hutton, but these passages are not regularly quoted. Ernest Hawkes's *The Labrador Eskimo*, first published in 1916, is an excellent example. After three years working with the Inuit in Alaska, Hawkes spent the summer and fall of 1914 in Labrador. His reference to elder suicide/abandonment appears as a generalized comment, not based on any of the events he discussed. I can't determine whether he relied on his own research or the narrative traditions of his White predecessors to arrive at this conclusion.

However, like his near-contemporary Hutton, he stresses Inuit respect for elders:

> The aged are treated with great respect, and the word of the old men and women is final. The Eskimo say that they have lived a long time and understand things in general better. They also feel that in the aged is embodied the wisdom of their ancestors. This does not prevent them, however, from putting the old folks out of the way, when life has become a burden to them, but the act is usually done in accordance with the wishes of the persons concerned and is thought to be a proof of devotion. (Hawkes 1970: 117)

Again, we find many statements of respect for elders in other Inuit groups. Danish anthropologist Kaj Birket-Smith, well-known for his work with the Caribou Inuit who lived just to the west of Hudson Bay, stresses the importance of the knowledgeable old hunter: "An elderly, skillful hunter with great experience always enjoys great esteem as *primus inter pares* [first among equals]. When a number of families are gathered in camp, there is often an elderly *pater familias* [family father] who is tacitly looked upon as [*ihumataq*], i.e., he who thinks, implying: for the others" (Birket-Smith 1929: 258–59).

Another work frequently cited by writers such as Cavan, Hoebel, and Weyer is that of Riley D. Moore. In 1912, he visited the Yup'ik of St. Lawrence Island, off the coast of Alaska in the Bering Sea. He tells the same story: "The older members of the family, especially fathers and older uncles, are treated with extreme reverence and respect, accorded them because of their age and the wisdom garnered from years of experience" (Moore 1923: 73).

However, to show that I am willing to examine the work of those who produce facts uncomfortable to my own hypothesis, we will look closely at Lucien Turner's work. He was an excellent ornithologist and collector of Aboriginal material culture. However, because he was stuck at the base of Fort Chimo in northern Quebec, he was unable to actually see the Labrador Inuit culture in its full, lived context, so his observations on their social practices are not at the same high level as if he'd lived with them. He had the annoying habit of using statistically based terms such as *often, usual*, or *sometimes* without the benefit of fieldwork to back them up. In the first paragraph of the following quotation about how the Labrador Inuit treat their own elders, Turner appears to be generalizing from one example.

> Aged people who have no relatives on whom they may depend for subsistence are often quietly put to death. When an old woman, for instance, becomes a burden to the community it is *usual* for her to be neglected until so weak from want of food that she will be unable to keep up with the people, who suddenly are seized with a desire to remove to a distant locality. If she regains their camp, well for her; otherwise, she struggles along until exhausted and soon perishes. *Sometimes* three or four of the males retrace their steps to recover a lost whip

or a forgotten ammunition bag. They *rarely* go farther than where they find the helpless person, and if their track be followed it will be found that the corpse has stones piled around it and is bound with thongs.

An old woman at Fort Chimo had but one eye, and this was continually sore and very annoying to the people with whom she lived. They proposed to strangle her to relieve her from her misery. The next morning the eye was much better and the proposed cure was postponed. (Turner 2001: 186; emphasis mine)

The next quotation concerns Inuit treatment of "Indian" elders. In both this and the previous quote, you get a sense that Turner has a low appreciation of the value of elders to Aboriginal peoples (or to any peoples). If I were a psychologist, I would want to read what his grandparents or aging parents would have written about grandchildren or children (or just about him in particular):

[A]ged Indian men and women, who have been left behind by the parties of young people who are in quest of fur-bearing animals during the winter months, are only too glad to have a camp of jolly Eskimo near at hand. With them they can live as parasites until their hosts are exhausted of supplies, or until they move to another locality to relieve themselves of the importunities of their unbidden guests. (Turner 2001: 268)

Turner's perspective on Inuit elder suicide should be questioned in light of how he views the social position of Inuit elders.

Despite Turner's perspective, I've encountered positive portrayals of Inuit respect for elders over and over again. I believe that there is a fundamental contradiction between such well-recorded attachment to elders documented in primary sources and the story of elder abandonment found in sociology and anthropology books that relied on second- and third-hand accounts. With few exceptions, the secondary sources that develop the hypothesis of elder abandonment do not discuss Inuit attachment to and need for their elders.

When Is Abandonment Really Abandonment?

There is a clear difference between the notion of permanently abandoning someone and temporarily leaving that person behind until plans can be made to return. This reality provides the second reason to question reports of Inuit elder suicide in tough times. Good ethnographers have provided sufficient cultural context to create explanations for elder suicide that are far more solid than those built on the shifting sands of conjecture. The primary sources often talk about the temporary and hope-filled atmosphere when elders are left behind. They stress that families wanted food to be found when elders had been left behind so that the elders would not have to die (see Rasmussen 1929: 160). Based on his first-hand research undertaken in Alaska during the early 1950s, anthropologist Robert Spencer wrote:

> If a relative had to be abandoned, it was "very sad," "a hard decision," but the group might be saved at the expense of one life. The most recent case that any-one could recall took place in 1939, when an old shaman and his wife were left inland to starve. The family head, a son of the old man, was obliged to leave his father and stepmother and go on by team to get food. *He was unable to return in time to save his parents.* (Spencer 1959: 92; emphasis mine)

Elders might be left with what was hoped to be sufficient food to last them until the more mobile members of the family returned to rescue them. The following quotation from Diamond Jenness about his work with the Copper Inuit during 1913–16 demonstrates this:

> Under ordinary conditions the aged and infirm are never abandoned.... Haviron, who died in the spring of 1915, received a regular dole of food from all his kins-men throughout the winter, though he was confined to his hut during the whole period and could do nothing to help himself. Whenever the Eskimos migrated to another sealing-ground he was carried on one of the sleds, usually, but not always, his son's. In Victoria Island he once left Tusayok's old wife all alone for several days with her tent and clothing and a stock of drying meat, because she was unable to maintain the constant travelling. She had an ample supply of food, and was perfectly happy and content, for she knew that her husband and son would rejoin her as soon as they were able. (Jenness 1922: 236)

Mythology, like dreams, can tell us much about the fears, intentions, and desires of a people. Knud Rasmussen, an anthropologist of mixed Danish-Inuit heritage, led a scientific enterprise known as the Fifth Thule Expedition across the Inuit Arctic east to west from Greenland to Alaska. From this expedition came the important works of Kaj Birket-Smith, Peter Freuchen, and Therkel Mathiassen, as well as Rasmussen's own volumes. In *Across Arctic America: Intellectual Culture of the Iglulik Eskimos* (1927), Rasmussen spoke of how, in the traditional stories or mythology of the Inuit of Iglu-lik, tales were told of the abandoned experiencing "some miraculous form of rescue ... with a cruel and ignominious death for those who abandoned them" (Rasmussen 1927: 160). This to me points to the people's sense that abandoning was wrong and not an accepted cultural norm. Elders would be left behind with hope still burning like an oil lamp in a dark place.

The Deep Roots of This Myth: Beginnings as Euthanasia

The myth of elder abandonment and suicide is deeply entrenched in White literature about the Inuit. Stories about Inuit euthanasia of the aged date back to eighteenth-century Greenlandic literature. Late nineteenth- and twentieth-century Norwegian scholar and humanitarian Fridtjof Nansen examined some of these writings. For example, in *Eskimo Life* he quotes Lars Dalager, who wrote the following description of an aged woman sealed in an igloo to die in 1752:

> It sometimes happens that a woman of no great importance, when mortal sickness falls upon her, is buried alive. A horrible case of this sort occurred a short time ago at this very place. Several people declared that they had heard the woman, a long time after her burial, calling out from her grave and begging for something to drink. If you remonstrate with them upon such inhuman cruelty, they answer that when the patient cannot recover, it is better that she should be put away in her last resting-place, than the survivors should go through the agony of death in observing her misery. (Nansen 1975: 136–37)

The idea that the woman was "of no great importance" is, no doubt, a bad judgment call from a cultural outsider. Nansen claimed that practices such as that described above were "very exceptional" (Nansen 1975: 137).

Nansen also cites Niels Egede, another eighteenth-century writer and the youngest son of early Norwegian missionary Hans Egede. Niels Egede spoke to a Greenland Inuit girl about the Christian idea of "love thy neighbour" and she replied:

> I have given proof of love for my neighbour. Once an old woman who was ill, but could not die, offered to pay me if I would lead her to the top of the steep cliff from which our people have always thrown themselves when they are tired of living; but I, having ever loved my neighbours, led her thither without payment, and cast her over the cliff. (In Nansen 1975: 170)

According to Nansen, "Egede told her that this was ill done, and that she had killed a fellow-creature. 'She said no; but that she was filled with pity for her, and cried after she had fallen over.'" And then, with a relativism rarely found in early writers other than Boas, Nansen questioned: "Are we to call this a good or an evil deed?" (1975: 170).

Euthanasia had become a well-known image in 1824, by which time Captain William Edward Parry and his second-in-command, George F. Lyon, had published their accounts of experiences with the Inuit in and around Igloolik Island (between western Baffin Island and the Melville Peninsula). Their comments on the practice had a definite impact. According to W.C.E. Rasing (1994: 3), the work of Parry and Lyon was a major reference point for Franz Boas when he wrote *The Central Eskimo* (1964, originally published in 1888).

What did Boas have to say about the practice? Interestingly, despite the number of times his writings have been cited as evidence for it, he only made one short reference to Inuit elder suicide and abandonment. It appears almost as an afterthought, possibly prompted more by his reading of Parry and Lyon than by his own experience with the Inuit. At the end of his section on burial customs and without mentioning anything he had seen or heard among the people (unlike his typical context-loaded field notes), he wrote:

> I may add here that suicide is not of rare occurrence, as according to the religious ideas of the Eskimo the souls who die by violence go to Qudlivan, the happy land. For the same reason it is considered lawful for a man to kill his aged parents. In suicide death is generally brought about by hanging. (Boas 1964: 207)

Remember, too, that the people Boas lived and travelled with during that time were hard hit by disease. This was no pristine Inuit culture.

During the nineteenth and twentieth centuries, most White travellers to the Arctic seemed compelled to remark on the practice of elder suicide and abandonment, even if they had neither witnessed it themselves nor heard of recent examples from reliable informants (see Jenness 1922: 236). Riley Moore notes that elder suicide was not practised when he was there, but calls it "formerly quite common" (Moore 1923: 364). His observation suggests he learned about it from what he had read prior to his trip to Inuit country. Yet Moore is often cited as a primary source documenting the practice. He was more likely a secondary source, referring to but not citing the words of those who had gone on before him. More careful methods would be expected of scholars and students today.

The writings of American explorer Captain Charles Francis Hall were a major source of stories that propagated myths about Inuit elder suicide, which later became a North American fixation. Based on his experiences of the harsh winters of 1861 and 1862, he wrote his popular epic: *Life with the Esquimaux: A Narrative of Arctic Experience in Search of Survivors of Sir John Franklin's Expedition* (1970, originally published in 1864). The book was reprinted twice in the next two years, so it sold well. In his often melodramatic writing, he discusses at length four deathly ill Inuit elders who were "buried alive" in the "living tombs" of igloos (Hall 1970: 161–64 and 444–53). All but completely absent is the Aboriginal voice that might have given an insider's explanation in the context of traditional Inuit culture or the exceptional circumstances the people might have been experiencing. What conclusions might Inuit writers have reached had they gone to London, England during that brutal period and witnessed the conditions that many of the living and dying poor, both old and young, faced in that industrial city.

Certainly, they would have witnessed enough people abandoned to die that they might have concluded that such was an "English cultural tradition."

Hall's image of Inuit elders sealed in igloos was reproduced on the big Hollywood screen in 1932, in the movie revealingly named *Igloo*. Included in the dramatic advertising text were these telling words: "See: The old sealed in tombs of ice and left to die" (Fienup-Riordan 1995: 67). It starred Ray Wise (stage name Ray Mala), a 24-year-old part-Inuk Alaskan actor, as the hero, Chee-ak. Chee-ak defied "tribal law" by rescuing his sick father from being sealed in his igloo. When his father died crossing an icy ridge, Chee-ak had to plead for forgiveness from the gods, who were offended by his daring action. The image rang true to both audiences and critics. Under the headline "'Igloo' True, Powerful Story of Eskimo Tribe," W.E. Oliver of the *Los Angeles Evening Herald and Express* wrote "You see the old abandoned, according to the law of the tooth and fang" (Oliver 1932). Hall's message had survived.

Growing the Myth

While early accounts of euthanasia brought the deaths of Inuit elders into the Western spotlight, that alone did not create the myth. During the development of the social scientific literature in anthropology and sociology textbooks, three fundamental interpretive errors were committed. The first error was in interpreting elder euthanasia in cases of extreme bad health as abandonment for the good of the group over that of the individual. The second error was in perceiving this rare practice as common because stories of it have been repeated so often. (Again, think of the Toronto family murder-suicide analogy.) The third mistake was in construing elder abandonment as permanent and necessarily fatal when the intent was temporary, with hopes of rescue. Even Stefansson saw this last point. In his review of the movie *Igloo*, he cautioned southerners against believing in the practice of abandoning elders to die when it did not really exist: "They would travel far during a day, a weakling would drop behind, everyone would expect and hope that he would come up to camp during the evening or night, but sometimes he never arrived" (As quoted in Fienup-Riordan 1995: 68–69).

The newly ploughed fields of sociology and anthropology provided fertile soil for the growth of this myth. In 1894, S.R. Steinmetz published a paper entitled "Suicide Among Primitive Peoples" in the prominent anthropological journal *American Anthropologist*. He states in the Introduction that "[i]t is the opinion of many sociologists, who perhaps have not given especial thought or study to the subject, that the act of self-destruction is infrequent among savage peoples. The purpose of my inquiry is to determine whether this opinion has the support of well-authenticated facts, and, if so, to what degree" (Steinmetz 1964: 53). He then proceeded to demonstrate that the

Inuit practised elder suicide, based not on his own fieldwork, but on earlier sources, including Hall and Nansen.

Altruistic Suicide, Mores, and Cultural Relativism

During the late nineteenth century and first half of the twentieth century, a battle to explain human behaviour was going on in the academic world. "Nature or nurture" is the alliterative short form for that battle, and it continues today in different guises. The fledgling fields of sociology and anthropology needed to develop, from their core concept of culture, explanatory "weapons" to fight the influence of the equally new field of genetics, which used its sharp-edged sword of biological race to explain why societies were different. The concept of Inuit elder abandonment and suicide served as such a weapon as it encapsulated a number of classic sociological elements: the social causation of suicide, the compelling nature of mores, and the "walk a mile in the other person's shoes" concept of cultural relativism.

Three years after the publication of Steinmetz's work, Emile Durkheim published his groundbreaking *Le Suicide: Étude de Sociologie* (1897). In this book, the foundational French scholar established that social characteristics such as age, class, gender, marital status, and religion made good predictors of rates of suicide. They correlated to how integrated or connected individuals were with society. Too much or too little integration were the presumed causes of suicide. Note how the first sentence of the following quote from Durkheim mirrors Steinmetz's words:

> It has sometimes been said that suicide was unknown among lower societies. Thus expressed, the assertion is inexact. To be sure, egoistic suicide [i.e., that which comes from too little integration], constituted as has just been shown, seems not to be frequent there. But another form exists among them in an endemic state. (Durkheim 1966: 217)

This other form of suicide he termed "altruistic suicide," which occurs when "social integration is too strong." The individual makes the ultimate sacrifice "imposed by society for social ends" (Durkheim 1966: 220). Moreover, "lower societies are the theatre par excellence of altruistic suicide" (Durkheim 1966: 227). His examples do not include the Inuit, but come from ancient Europe (e.g., the Vikings, Goths, Visigoths, and Spanish Celts), the high-caste Hindus (who practised sati, in which a wife immolates herself on her husband's funeral pyre; see chapter six), and, not surprisingly, the Japanese ritual suicide of hara-kiri. Nevertheless, he was aware of the alleged Inuit practice. Steinmetz is the first citation in his bibliography for the chapter quoted above.

While Durkheim did not use ecology or conservation of food as an explanation for altruistic suicide, other sociologists who accepted his equation of "folk," "lower," "non-literate," or "primitive" societies with altruistic suicide did. The following quotation from a 1980s textbook on the sociology of deviance illustrates this point:

> Among folk societies, suicides tend to be altruistic in that people take their lives with the idea that by doing so they will benefit others....

> Suicides occur in certain folk societies where limited food supplies make an old or infirm person a burden to the tribe. Among the Eskimos and the Chukchee [a Siberian people with a traditional culture similar to that of the Inuit], for example, old people who could no longer hunt or work killed themselves so that they would not use food needed by other adults in the community who produced it. (Clinard and Meier 1985: 278)

You can see the impact of linking Durkheim's concept of altruistic suicide with Inuit suicide on Alexander Leighton and Charles Hughes in their article, "Notes on Eskimo Patterns of Suicide." Published in 1955, this piece was cited as "the first systematic examination of Inuit Suicide" (Kirmayer et al 1998: 189). It combined two sources of information. One was Leighton's fieldwork in the summer of 1940 with the Yup'ik of St. Lawrence Island, Alaska. The other was a review of the literature, both primary (e.g., Birket-Smith, Boas, Moore, Rasmussen, and Thalbitzer) and secondary. It also included some discussion of the Chukchee. So when textbook writers include both the Chukchee and the Inuit together in a discussion of elder suicide (see Mann 1968b and Clinard and Meyer 1985), they almost certainly have read Leighton and Hughes.

Concerning the Yup'ik of St. Lawrence Island, the last case of elder suicide the authors could document occurred in 1902 (Leighton and Hughes 1955: 330), long before Leighton's fieldwork. Still, they felt confident in declaring that "the killing of aged or infirm parents by dutiful children was evidently a common occurrence" (1955: 329). Dealing with the abandonment of elders, the following statement is disturbing not only because it lacks supporting evidence, but because of the certainty with which it is expressed despite that absence: "No clear-cut information on patterns of abandoning the aged (which, if practiced, might have increased the prevalence of suicides, especially among old women) is available, although the practice probably did exist" (Leighton and Hughes 1955: 334).

The authors point to Durkheim for their theoretical support:

> It may be recalled that Durkheim [1951] examined several different forms of suicide, and one generalization he reached was that the form which he called "altruistic suicide" occurs when social integration is too strong. It would seem that Eskimo suicide can be placed in this general class, although one can leave off, for scientific purposes, the value assumption implied in the phrase, "too strong." (Leighton and Hughes 1955: 336)

Culture or nurture then was used to explain the presumed practice of Inuit elder suicide, and that aspect of culture is given a label—altruistic suicide—specifying the force that society can impose on the individual, particularly in "primitive" societies.

EARLY SOCIOLOGISTS SERVE UP SOME MORES

William Graham Sumner was a Yale professor of politics and social science and an American contemporary of Durkheim. In his highly influential *Folkways: A Study of the Sociological Importance of Usages, Manners, Customs, Mores and Morals* (1934, originally published in 1906), he introduced the term "more" (pronounced like the eel, moray) to the sociological literature to refer to norms that are strongly held in societies. In the following quote from chapter seven, "Abortions, Infanticide, Killing the Old," under the heading "Killing the Old in Ethnography," Sumner relies upon the work of Boas, Nansen, and Turner. (I have identified in the text the sources upon which he draws.) Notice how he misinterprets Turner by adding murderous intent to the Inuit moving camp:

> The Hudson's Bay Eskimo strangle the old who are dependent on others for their food, or leave them to perish when the camp is moved. They move in order to get rid of burdensome old people without executing them [Turner 1894]. The central Eskimo kill the old because all who die by violence go to the happy land; others have no such a happy future [Boas 1888]. Nansen [1893] says that "when people get so old that they cannot take care of themselves, especially women, they are often treated with little consideration" by the Eskimo. (Sumner 1934: 325)

By conflating what may be isolated instances that likely have several different explanations (e.g., leaving to return with food or euthanizing those who are suffering), Sumner lent artificial support to the ideas that culture dictates through mores, and that no further explanation is necessary.

In *A Handbook of Sociology* (1964, first published in 1947), under the somewhat exaggerated heading "The Mores Can Make Anything Seem Right," William Ogburn and Meyer Nimkoff wrote the following: "The mores made it right for the Eskimos to kill their old people" (Ogburn and Nimkoff 1964: 148).

This tradition of attributing Sumner's concept of mores to the myth of elder suicide and abandonment was early adopted into Canadian sociology (which bloomed later as a discipline than its American counterpart). In the first Canadian textbook dedicated to the subject of deviance, *Deviant Behaviour in Canada*, edited by W.E. Mann (1968), there is a chapter entitled "Suicide in Canada," written by Mann himself. Note that when he is speaking of "strong and unqualified identification with the tribe," he is referring to one of the "textbook" features of altruistic suicide:

> The mores on suicide have ... varied considerably between cultures.... In many primitive or peasant societies it seems that a great number of suicides are a consequence of the individual's strong and unqualified identification with the tribe or group and its welfare. Thus, among Eskimoes, and the Chuckchee Tribe, it is expected that old people, when the supply of food runs very short, will kill themselves. (Mann 1968: 214–15)

It seems Mann had also read Leighton and Hughes.

This tradition is also evident in more recent Canadian sociological writing. In his *Introduction to Sociology: A Canadian Focus*, in a chapter on "deviance," editor of Canadian introductory sociology textbooks James Teevan wrote that the Inuit

> defined infanticide and the killing of old parents as acceptable means to protect a limited food supply. The rest of Canada does not allow such behavior. The different outlooks can be explained partly by the different amounts of resources in the two societies, but explainable or not, they illustrate the relative definition of deviance, that what is deviant is specific to time and place and circumstances. (Teevan 1982b: 63)

The 1995 version of the textbook said virtually the same thing (Teevan 1995: 115–16).

IT'S ALL CULTURALLY RELATIVE: THE DEVELOPMENT OF A TRADITION

Teevan's quote above exemplifies how the White lie of Inuit elder abandonment is used to illustrate the key sociological subject matter of deviance (i.e., being different from the cultural norm). It has become a convenient way to make the important pedagogical point that deviance is relative. Deviance is culturally constructed. The rulebook of "thou-shall-nots" is different in each culture.

Textbook relativity "one liners" comparing Inuit elder abandonment to mainstream North American practices that the author opposes are not uncommon in the discussion of the cultural relativity of deviance. It is a well-established tradition in anthropology and sociology (see Smith and Preston 1977: 25 for an American example). We can see its impact on anthropology textbook writers in the following two examples. The first comes from Gary Ferraro's *Cultural Anthropology: An Applied Perspective* (1995), in his section on cultural relativism. Note how he draws upon another textbook (Friedl and Pfeiffer, 1977) to justify his statement:

> Some Eskimo groups practice a custom that would strike the typical Westerner as inhumane at best. When aging parents become too old to contribute their share of the workload, they are left out in the cold to die. If we view such a practice by the standards of our own Western culture (that is, ethnocentrically),

we would have to conclude that it is cruel and heartless, hardly a way to treat those who brought you into the world. But the cultural relativist would look at this form of homicide within the context of the total culture of which it is a part. Friedl and Pfeiffer (1977: 331) provide a culturally relativistic explanation of this Eskimo custom:

It is important to know ... that this ... [custom is not practised] against the will of the old person. It is also necessary to recognize that this is an accepted practice for which people are adequately prepared throughout their lives, and not some kind of treachery sprung upon an individual as a result of a criminal conspiracy. Finally, it should be considered in light of the ecological situation in which the Eskimos live. Making a living in the Arctic is difficult at best, and the necessity of feeding an extra mouth, especially when there is little hope that the individual will again become productive in the food-procurement process, would mean that the whole group would suffer. It is not a question of Eskimos not liking old people, but rather a question of what is best for the entire group. We would not expect—and indeed we do not find—this practice to exist where there was adequate food to support those who were not able to contribute to the hunting effort. (Friedl and Pfeiffer, cited in Ferraro 1995: 24-25)

The second example comes from a recently published Canadian anthropology textbook edited by Miller, Van Esterik, and Van Esterik. After a discussion of Jane Goodall's observation of chimps who did not help polio-inflicted members of their own troop but left them behind, the authors state: "Humans also sometimes resort to isolation and abandonment, as seen in the traditional Inuit practice of leaving aged and infirm behind in the cold, the stigmatization of HIV/AIDS victims, and the ignoring of the homeless mentally ill in North American cities" (Miller, Van Esterik, and Van Esterik 2001: 62; also 2004: 166 and 2007: 146).

When anthropologists enter the field of gerontology (the study of human aging), they take this concept of cultural relativity with them. The work of Ellen R. Holmes and Lowell D. Holmes, authors of the American gerontology textbook *Other Cultures, Elder Years* (1995), provides an excellent example. Admittedly, most of their discussion about the Inuit is positive and reflects the respect that elders received, yet they still ask the following question, under the heading "Relativistic Perspective":

Who is to say that locking the elderly up in nursing homes is more humane than allowing them to wander off on the ice floe and freeze to death as Eskimo elders are sometimes permitted to do? Cultural behavior that may imply low status for the aged in one society may mean something entirely different in another. (Holmes and Holmes 1995: 10–11)

These examples illustrate that when Inuit elder suicide is used as an example of the link between deviance and cultural relativism, the idea of cultural relativism can misleadingly come to take on the appearance of an explanation.

CROSS-CULTURAL COLLECTORS SPREAD THE WORD: CAVAN AND HOEBEL

Cross-cultural research is an important part of the anthropological tradition. A number of potential problems arise, however, with this kind of work. Are the researchers comparing things that are parallel (i.e., the proverbial apples with apples)? Is unique cultural context properly considered? Cross-cultural research makes it easy for textbook authors to avoid consulting primary research documents. Two early works of cross-cultural research concerning Inuit elder suicide, by Ruth Cavan and E. Adamson Hoebel, compounded this problem because the cross-cultural compilers themselves did not have direct ethnographic experience with the Inuit.

Sociologist and criminologist Ruth Cavan was influential in connecting Inuit elder abandonment and suicide to the cultural relativity of deviance. She wrote two major works that promoted that connection. The first was *Suicide* (1965, originally published in 1928). Forty years later, she published *Delinquency and Crime: Cross Cultural Perspectives* (1968). In the latter work, cited by Teevan in 1982, she perpetuated the idea that deviance is culturally relative with the following statement:

> [An] accepted method of reducing tensions was in the approved killing of members of the community who were not self-supporting as judged by the amount of work they could do. These persons were the very old whose days of usefulness, were over.... The killing of the old had no sacred connotations; it was a practiced expedient, practiced in only some of the Eskimo tribes. Where it was customary, the son who took his parent to a remote place and left him (or her) with a small amount of food, soon to die from the cold, was regarded as having performed a meritorious act. (Cavan 1968: 19)

Cavan listed 20 primary sources for her discussion of the Inuit in this work. Only three talk about Inuit elder suicide. Significantly, in her telling of the White lie of Inuit elder abandonment and suicide, Cavan made no mention of the respect for elders that was clearly documented in two major primary sources (Birket-Smith 1929: 258–59 and Moore 1923: 373, both quoted above).

Prominent American anthropologist E. Adamson Hoebel also popularized the notion of Inuit elder abandonment and suicide in connection with cultural relativism. His book *The Law of Primitive Man, A Study in Comparative Legal Dynamics* (1965) included a chapter dedicated to the Inuit: "The Eskimo: Rudimentary Law in a Primitive Anarchy" (1965: 67–99). His praiseworthy project in this book was to make the important cultural relativist point that all societies have laws—some are written down, while others are not. Hoebel put what he felt were unwritten Inuit laws in a form familiar to mainstream North American readers. He called these laws "underlying postulates of jural significance in Eskimo culture." For example: "Postulate III. Life is hard and the margin of safety small. Corollary I. Unproductive members of society cannot be supported" (Hoebel 1965: 69). He added to this by stating that "Infanticide, invalidicide, senilicide, and suicide are privileged acts: socially approved homicide" (Hoebel 1965: 74).

Anthropologists Introduce Environmental Causality

In addition to cultural relativism, the environment is often used to explain the imagined cultural custom of Inuit elder abandonment and suicide. The practice is cast as the so-called natural result of living in the tough Arctic environment, where periodic absences of resources required to sustain the lives of everyone in an Inuit family or community "naturally occur." This idea is easy to invoke. We can all imagine how tough the winters are in the Arctic. Don't almost all southern Canadians complain about winter weather at some point?

Anthropologist Edward Weyer (1904–98) was a pioneer in introducing this form of environmental causation. In his oft-cited compilation *The Eskimos: Their Environment and Folkways* (originally published in 1932; reprinted in 1962), Weyer summarized most of the important sources that refer to Inuit suicide and then framed the material in terms of an ecological model. If death is the elder's wish, it is because the elder is a team player, not for any personal reasons. Weyer's perspective is outlined in the chapter tellingly entitled "Reaction to Population Problem," under the heading of "Killing the Aged and the Infirm." Since the related terms "productive years" and "unproductive years" stay undefined in Weyer's work, readers are free to impose their own culture's notions concerning the value of elders.

> Infanticide, we have seen, is customary on occasion in all groups of Eskimos [a questionable assertion], with the effect of ameliorating the stress that accompanies scarcity of food. At the further end of the life span is the period of old age, when people have passed their productive years. Therefore, we may rightly expect to observe some similarity between the group attitude toward the aged and toward infants. Like the newborn babe, the person who is infirm, either by reason of years or physical disability, is likely to be eliminated under the stress of poverty.
>
> Recourse to abandoning or killing outright such unproductive members of the group is a response to stringent, inexorable life-conditions. Such action, it should be understood, does not indicate a wholly heartless discrimination against the helpless. Devotion among friends and relatives comes into strong

conflict with the deliberate elimination of members of a group. The disposing of one who is aged and infirm sometimes seems, indeed, to be more the will of the fated one than of those devoted to him who will live on. (Weyer 1962: 137–38)

Anthropologist Lee Guemple developed his own resource-based theory. In his "The Dilemma of the Aging Eskimo," published in Beattie and Crysdale's *Sociology Canada: An Introductory Text* (1974), he links the idea of survival of the fittest—killing the outsider-defined unproductive—to Hawkes's commentary about elders who feel for personal reasons that they are ready to die:

> [W]hen the elderly became a drain on the resources of the community, the practical bent of the Eskimo asserted itself. To alleviate the burden of infirmity, the old people were done away with. As Hawkes (1916: 117) points out, this was done when life had become a burden but the act was usually in accordance with the wishes of the persons concerned and thought to be a proof of the devotion of the children. (Guemple 1974: 211)

Thus, Guemple essentializes the Inuit according to a capitalist model. He sees the people as the ultimate pragmatists. They coldly calculate the worth of each individual in terms of that person's value as a resource to the community. The elders are not being killed. The community is being "downsized": "This essay is concerned with the social position of old people in Eskimo society. More specifically, it views old people as a kind of exploitable resource that has value to those who run Eskimo society, the adults" (Guemple 1974: 203).

Guemple had engaged in fieldwork with the Qiqiktamiut of the Belcher Islands in southeastern Hudson Bay and appears in the quotation below to be making an indirect claim on an insider's view: "it is best to consider them as do the Eskimo themselves." However, this insider's claim is weak, as no Inuit voice appears in the work. The people aren't doing the explaining here. Guemple is. While he mentions that Inuit elders have worth, he damns that worth with faint praise by making it quantifiable using outsider scales. The word "respect" does not appear.

> Eskimo are extremely practical. They highly esteem those who make the greatest contribution to the welfare of family and community. This is true for the old and the young as well as the adults. Sentiment is not absent in Eskimo life. Although they are not demonstrative, Eskimo do feel very strongly about family and relatives, and will go to great lengths to be hospitable even to a stranger. But the margin for sentiment in the Arctic is very narrow; the pragmatic business of making a living takes precedence over sentiment. People, then, are judged in terms of their worth as producers. If we are to evaluate the position of the old in Eskimo society, it is best to consider them as do the Eskimo themselves, namely, as a special kind of resource. Viewed in this light, the old

make two important contributions: (1) a source of extra labour for the camp, and (2) a source of knowledge and wisdom essential for order and continuity in the society. (Guemple 1974: 205)

Environmental causation remains well respected in anthropology textbooks. Serena Nanda, in the fifth edition of her introductory anthropology textbook *Cultural Anthropology*, wrote the following:

Sometimes, methods of increasing a group's survival seem harsh to us, but they are necessary because of extreme food shortages. In particularly hard years when food was scarce, some Inuit groups, for example, would leave old people on the ice to die. Sometimes it was an old person who suggested this course of action. These suicides or "mercy killings" indicate not a lack of concern for human life but rather a commitment to the survival of the group. (Nanda 1994: 160)

Balikci Uses Psychology to Blame the Victim

In "Suicidal Behavior among the Netsilik Eskimos," published in the first Canadian-focused introductory sociology textbook (Blishen et al. 1961: 575–87), Asen Balikci takes the unusual position of rejecting what he refers to as "the well-known ecological factor." He also is unusual in taking the opposite position to that of Durkheim. Rather than saying that Inuit suicide was the product of too much social integration (i.e., altruistic suicide), he attributed the cause of 50 cases of suicide of both young and old over the previous 50 years to "the framework of such a poorly integrated society, further weakened by in-group tensions and various anxieties" (Balikci 1961: 582).

In 1971, American psychologist William Ryan coined the term "blaming the victim." It refers to the misleading practice of assigning individuals more or less complete responsibility for their own negative circumstances that in fact have broader social causes. Working class or Black children fail in school because they come from families and homes that are deemed culturally deprived. The notion that the schools privilege White middle-class culture does not enter into the discussion. People are alcoholics because they have little will power. Therefore, no biological factors of genetic predisposition, sociological factors of racial or ethnic stereotyping (e.g., "the drunk Indian"), or factors pointing to systematic oppression need be seriously considered. People are on welfare because they don't have a strong work ethic, not because they come from a poor family with the odds of success stacked against them. Criminals commit crimes because they have a criminal mind, not because life on "the street" offered the greatest chance they saw for success.

Balikci tended to blame the victim in his psychological approach to Inuit suicide. In a paper entitled "Research on Arvilik-juarmuit Suicide Patterns," read at the department of psychiatry at McGill University in January 1960, Balikci interpreted the high rates of suicide and attempted suicide among the Arvilik-juarmiut (a Netsilik group) as indicating a "collective inability to control aggressions combined with a low level of social integration" (in Boydell, Grindstaff, and Whitehead 1972: 451).

Guemple Uses Anthropology to Blame the Victim

The "blame the victim" approach to Inuit suicide has also been tailored to address the myth of elder suicide and abandonment, specifically in Canadian gerontology textbooks. The two major writers/editors of these textbooks—sociologists Victor Marshall and Mark Novak—repeat this White lie of Inuit elder suicide. In the first edition of Marshall's *Aging in Canada: Social Perspectives* (1980), anthropologist Lee Guemple, quoted above, contributed an essay in which he attempts to reconcile this perceived paradox: How could the Inuit take good care of their elders, while at the same time practising elder abandonment/suicide?

> The treatment the Inuit (Eskimo) traditionally accorded their old people *during the precontact period* has been a source of some consternation to members of the Euro-North American cultural tradition because of a seeming paradox. We know that Inuit lavished care and concern on their old people and invested considerable interest in them. But we also know that they sometimes abandoned them on the trail (Rasmussen, 1908: 127). Our own notion of what people are like makes it difficult for us to see how they could be so affectionate in one context and cold-hearted in another, when the chips are down.
>
> The aim of this essay is to try to resolve the paradox; to show how the attitude of love and affection is not incompatible with the idea of killing one's own parents or helping them to kill themselves. To do so we must make a brief foray into the cognitive universe of the Inuit—into their own notion of how the world (of people and things) works. Only then can we fathom how they manage to mix sentiment with seeming cruelty without a sense of contradiction. (Guemple 1980: 95; emphasis mine)

In addressing his manufactured paradox, Guemple makes some fundamental errors. First, he locates the practice in the pre-contact period. Yet all of his sources and his own fieldwork are decidedly post-contact (i.e., after whalers, traders, and missionaries had strongly influenced the course of Inuit culture). More destructive is the fact that by isolating his commentary to this point in history, he erases the possibility that colonialism may have forced the people into desperate measures in some extreme circumstances. Second, the idea of respect is not conveyed, in the quotation above or more generally in the article. Treatment of the elders is presented as if it were an act of generosity—like the keeping of a pet—that cannot be afforded during difficult times. He does not entertain the notion that the elders played an important role in their culture. Third, he misreads Rasmussen, whom, as we have seen, explained abandonment as a temporary measure that would ideally be rectified eventually. Fourth, the "brief foray into the cognitive universe of the Inuit" that he alludes to in the above quote emerges later as the assertion "old people do not, in Inuit cosmology, really die" (Guemple 1980: 99). Instead the "name substance" (the spirit of the name they bear) lives on in others who receive that name. This seems to be conjecture on his part, without any Inuit voices being included. Consider his statement in light of the following metaphor: Many North American Christians put their elders into institutions where they are sometimes ignored. They do not do this because they are heartless, but because they believe their elders will not die, but will live on in heaven in the next life. Fortunately, the 1987 edition of *Aging in Society* does not contain this article.

More consistent in its replication of the White lie is sociologist Mark Novak's *Aging and Society: A Canadian Perspective* (Novak 1988, 1997, and 2001), an example of Guemple's influence on gerontology textbooks. In this book, Novak talks about the Inuit as part of an error-filled discussion of hunting and gathering societies. He begins with a more respectful presentation of Inuit elders than Guemple's. However, he then introduces a Guemple-influenced utilitarian spin, followed by a clear description in support of the notion of Inuit elder abandonment and suicide:

> In Inuit society ... older people keep their status as long as they do some useful work for the group. Their status drops if illness makes them dependent. People make fun of the frail elders, say nasty things to them, or ignore them. The "overaged" get the worst cuts of meat, have little money, and have to do without trade goods. A stranger may take in an Inuit who outlives his or her spouse, children, and close relatives, but the old person will get no respect and will have to do the worst work (Guemple 1977)....
>
> The Inuit also abandon their aged when the older person becomes a liability to the group. They do this as a last resort, and they encourage the older person to make the decision (Guemple 1980), but sometimes the group will withdraw its support rapidly, thus hastening death (Glascock and Feinman, 1981, 27). (Novak 1988: 29–30, 31)

Colonial Contact: A Neglected Causality

Colonial contact must be considered one of the major causes—if not *the* cause—of elder abandonment and suicide in at least a few of the instances when it took place. The negative effect of colonial contact on the Inuit is addressed in sociological literature (see Brody 1991: 35), including textbooks (see, for example, Crysdale and Beattie 1973: 34; and Ferguson in Mann 1970: 30). Yet, it is not once connected with the notion of elder abandonment and suicide.

Even in the early years of European exploration, Inuit cultures were not pristine. Later writers often fail to note that these early primary sources were visiting Inuit who had already experienced intense and often lethal contact with Europeans. For four centuries, European and North American whalers have made their mark on the people. During much of the twentieth century, the Hudson's Bay Company (HBC) created an Inuit dependency on Arctic fox trapping that was literally deadly. It led to debt, created a reliance on inferior foods and clothing, and subjected the people to fluctuating prices, to mention just a few of the factors that threatened Inuit society. During the 1920s and 1930s, several people in the field commented how deadly this threat was. Visiting medical specialist Canadian Frederick G. Banting, who would later become famous for his work on the development of insulin for diabetics, had this to say:

> The gravest danger which faces the Eskimo is his transfer from a race-long hunter to a dependent trapper. When the Eskimo becomes a trapper, he becomes, to a large extent, dependent on the white man for food and clothing. Instead of wearing warm, light clothing which time has taught him is most suitable for the climate, he is given cheap woollen and cotton, which the white man would not wear himself under the same conditions. His native food is seal, walrus, whale, fish, clams, bear, caribou, rabbit, eggs, duck, geese and ptarmigan. His only vegetable is the occasional sea weed. In exchange for his furs he is given white flour or sea biscuits, tea and tobacco, which do not provide sufficient fuel to keep his body warm and nourished. (Banting, cited in Tester and Kulchyski 1994: 108)

Diamond Jenness also noted that trapping for trade was immensely damaging to Inuit culture:

> Very few Eskimo now hunt intensively during the winter months; instead they trap foxes, which are useless to them for either food or clothing. In order to maintain their families during that season they buy European food from the fur-traders, largely flour, sugar, and tea. Now a diet of straight seal-meat will keep a hunter or a trapper in good health, but a diet that consists mainly of bannock and tea is practically starvation, so, over large parts of the Arctic and sub-Arctic the Eskimo are now worse clad, and more ill-nourished than in the days of their isolation. (Jenness 1932: 421–22)

When non-Inuit came North to build the DEW (Distant Early Warning) line radar stations, caribou were killed off in record numbers. During that time, government relocation schemes, guided by non-Inuit anthropologists and following the scientifically unsound notion that all Arctic environments are alike, moved Inuit into locations where they were unaccustomed to making a living. Tester and Kulchyski (1994) document and describe these schemes for the time period from the late 1930s to the early 1960s, when the notion of elder abandonment was being developed and replicated.

The idea of Inuit elder abandonment implied that the Inuit were a people to be saved. This notion accommodated the various imperialist policies of governments and the HBC. The following quotation from an influential work by the sociologist Ruth Cavan illustrates how the two go hand in hand:

> Missionaries redefined some of the Eskimo's ways of reducing life tensions as sinful, and police and other government officials defined the same acts as illegal or criminal. These acts, functioned in the Eskimo way of life, but strongly disapproved in the white culture, included the various forms of killing: infanticide, killing of the helpless old…. As various forms of cash relief were developed in the United States and Canada and extended to the Eskimos, some of the old ways of eliminating problems did become useless. In fact, when old people and children began to receive financial aid, their status was reversed. From a burden in the past they now became an important source of income. (Cavan 1968: 33)

How well did the government perform to "save" the Inuit elders? The Canadian Old Age Pension Act was passed in 1927. Yet despite the fact that a 1939 Supreme Court decision made the federal government officially responsible for the Inuit in the Canadian Arctic, it was not until April 1, 1949 that an Inuk first received a pension cheque (Tester and Kulchyski 1994: 94). The Canadian government had abandoned the Inuit elders for more than 20 years.

Farley Mowat Popularizes Inuit Elder Abandonment and Suicide

It is possible to denounce the destructive actions (moving whole communities) and inactions (failure to pay pensions) of the federal governments of the twentieth century and still put forward a myth that shifts the blame away from politicians and bureaucrats. Take Farley Mowat for example. His popular books *People of the Deer* (1968, originally published in 1951) and *The Desperate People* (1975, originally published in 1959) drew international attention to the threat the Ahiarmiut (a group of Caribou Inuit) faced from ill-conceived government practices (see Tester and Kulchyski 1994: 56–57) and from White sojourners to the North who shot and killed many caribou.

However, like other White "travellers" to the Arctic, Mowat overgeneralized from his highly specific and atypical experiences in terms of Inuit culture. He popularized the White myth of Inuit elder suicide in emotional, evocative statements such as the following:

The old people stand at the lowest point of the scale. The men whose arms are no longer strong and the women whose wombs are no longer fecund—these live on the thin edge of time, with death always before them. When the choice of living and dying comes upon a camp of the People; when starvation announces the coming of death, then the aged ones must be prepared to go first, to seek death voluntarily so that the rest of the family may cling a little longer to life. The old ones seldom die a natural death and often they die by their own hands. Suicide is not lawful in our eyes but as it comes to the People it is a great, and a very heroic, sacrifice—for it is the old who fear death most and who find it hardest to die. (Mowat 1968: 172)

In 1975, Mowat published a book of stories called *The Snow Walker*, whose title story was based on a tale of someone "going to meet the snow walker." Mowat used this expression to describe a culturally mandated act of committing suicide by freezing to death. I used to read that story to my anthropology and sociology students to teach them about cultural relativism. I hope they weren't listening carefully. Another story entitled "The Blood in Their Veins," which adds cannibalism to the snow walker mix, enjoyed some popularity in the Dushkin annual anthropology reader *Annual Editions: Anthropology Collections of Articles* (Angeloni 1990: 72–77 and 1997: 63–68).

Inuit Suicide Today

Frank Tester and Paul McNicoll began their recent study of Inuit suicide with the following succinct statement: "The most intractable problem confronting the government of Nunavut in the Canadian eastern Arctic is a suicide rate that, particularly among young Inuit males, is among the highest in the world" (Tester and McNicoll 2004: 2625).

Consider the following figures. In 1992, the suicide rate for the overall Canadian population was 13 per 100,000 (see Health Canada 1995). A Health Canada study (Isaacs et al. 1998) discovered that the suicide rate for Inuit in the Northwest Territories for the years 1986 to 1996 was 79 per 100,000. This is slightly more than six times the general Canadian figure. The Inuit numbers even compare negatively to other Aboriginal groups. In the study's look at the Dene of the Northwest Territories during the same period, the suicide rate was only 29 per 100,000.

The high Inuit suicide rate is not confined to Nunavut in the Eastern Arctic and the Northwest Territories in the Western Arctic. Similar figures can be found for Inuit in Greenland, Labrador, Quebec, and Alaska (see Tester and McNicoll 2004: 2626).

One very real danger of the White lie of Inuit elder abandonment and suicide is that it contributes to the notion that the current high rate of youth suicide for the Inuit is somehow "culturally determined." By appealing to "cultural reasons" to explain this phenomenon, such compelling factors as historic and contemporary colonialism as well as more general social, political, and economic conditions are unrealistically downplayed. It also bears an undesirable tone of "blaming the victim." Kirmayer, Fletcher, and Boothroyd point out this misplaced cultural blame in their excellent article "Suicide Among the Inuit of Canada" (1998). While they unfortunately seem to accept the White lie about Inuit elders in the past (Kirmayer, Fletcher and Boothroyd 1998: 201), they realize that the "culturalist" argument cannot be used to explain away contemporary youth suicide. They are rightly critical of studies that do. They note two such flawed studies (Minor 1992 and Boyer et al. 1994) that follow this logic:

> Minor (1992: 83) states: "In the case of the young Inuit, it may be that the victims were making an effort to return to a traditionally accepted and respected death. Or the burden of life may have been so great and the confusion of cultural transition so frustrating that they acted irrationally. One could argue either that suicide expresses traditional attitudes or is a result of their collapse. I am firmly convinced that there is a traditional component in most of the suicides among the youth." (Kirmayer, Fletcher, and Boothroyd 1998: 200)

In a recent epidemiological survey of the Nunavik Inuit of Quebec, Boyer et al. rely on the short entry on suicide in Boas's work of 1888 as justification for writing the following:

> Suicide could be considered a culturally adapted behaviour because it is associated with an ancient ritual which was performed by the elderly, resourceless people who relieved the community of the burden created by their dependence. Is it not true that current suicides by young people bespeak of Inuit identity and a sense of community belonging? In that sense, could suicide among young Inuit be perceived as the statement of a double paradox, namely the merging with Inuit culture and identity, and the necessity of severing the merging process? In the Inuit cosmogony, violent death enables the soul to reach a better world. (Boyer et al. 1994: 140, as cited in Kirmayer, Fletcher and Boothroyd 1998: 200–01)

Such writers might be expressing a grain of truth in the salt shaker of elder abandonment. This is not to say that suicide is in any way an Inuit cultural tradition. Rather, it is possible that Minor's "traditional component" comes not from the Inuit themselves, but from the traditional approach to Inuit elder suicide used by sociologists and anthropologists who have the power to define and influence the nature of a culture not their own? What if the people themselves, after listening to and reading the "experts," somewhat accept the outsider opinion about their own traditional culture? It is like the old joke about the young anthropologist who asks the Aboriginal how they used to make their canoes traditionally. The Aboriginal says, "I will go to the one who knows," and leaves the room. The anthropologist waits with excitement, expecting that his informant is going to fetch a knowledgeable elder. But such was not to be. The Native returns with a book written about the people by an earlier generation of anthropologists. The elder was White.

Michel Foucault talks about various means by which indigenous knowledges are disqualified. In the first volume of *The History of Sexuality* (Foucault 1978), one such means he refers to is the intellectual model of the "sexual confession." According to this model, the subject being studied (and marginalized in knowledge production) provides information that comes from his or her subjective experience. However, this does not become authenticated knowledge until it is interpreted by an "objective" outsider/expert who is in the inherently privileged position of "pronouncing truth" by virtue of being an expert. The subject being studied in this way is not allowed to have a voice that is heard without translation from the outsider/expert.

A number of Aboriginal writers have commented on the negative effects of outsider-pronounced truths that automatically override the insights of Aboriginal insiders. In his scathing but humorous look at anthropologists in *Custer Died for Your Sins: An Indian Manifesto* (first published in 1969), Sioux intellectual Vine Deloria Jr. spoke of how anthropologists usurp authority about knowledge of Aboriginal ways:

> Over the years anthropologists have succeeded in burying Indian communities so completely beneath the mass of irrelevant information that the total impact of the scholarly community on Indian people has become one of simple authority. Many Indians have come to parrot the ideas of anthropologists because it appears that the anthropologists know everything about Indian communities. Thus many ideas that pass for Indian thinking are in reality theories originally advanced by anthropologists and echoed by Indian people in an attempt to communicate the real situation. (Deloria 1969: 82)

There is good evidence to believe that at least some educated Inuit have listened to the pronouncements of "White elders" concerning their treatment of their own elders. In her powerful and revealing article called "Suicide Is Price Inuit Paid for Tradition of Competency" (2001), Igloolik Inuit writer Rachel Attituq Qitsualik makes an impassioned plea to her people not to follow the traditional path in committing suicide, something she, herself, once considered. Here, she appears to have accepted as authoritative the writings of outsiders:

> Early explorers and anthropologists were shocked at the high suicide rates among various Inuit groups. *It seemed standard* for the old and infirm, believing themselves to be a burden upon their families, to do away with themselves, sometimes going so far as to recruit their own friends or family members in assisting with the suicide. (Qitsualik 2001; emphasis mine)

In Tester and McNicoll's article, they cite personal communication in 2002 with Inuk Peter Irniq, the Commissioner of Nunavut Territory, for the following:

> Only the elders used to do away with themselves. When they felt they were no longer able, then they would do away with themselves, they did this by walking on the land. They felt children and youth should have more food. (Tester and McNicoll 2004: 2627)

This would appear to be one reason why, in an otherwise excellent article that successfully challenges, among other theories, Balikci's "blame the victim" explanation for Inuit suicide and the anthropological construction of environmental causation, the writers fall back upon Durkheim's altruistic suicide:

> The dramatic images of elderly Inuit turning themselves out into the snow to die so as not to be a burden on others has likely coloured *Qallunaat* [White] understanding, not only of elder suicide, but of Inuit suicide in general. As a social construction it may reflect the extent to which the harshness of the Arctic environment impressed itself upon *Qallunaat* observers. Rather than ending their lives because it was too demanding to live as a "burden," the motive was more likely genuinely altruistic. (Tester and McNicoll 2004: 2627)

Part of the path towards understanding the truth of Inuit suicide today is to uncover the White lies of the past.

CONTENT QUESTIONS

1. What is the myth of culturally determined Inuit elder suicide?
2. What evidence goes against this myth?
3. How does the myth differ from elder euthanasia?
4. What three fundamental interpretive errors led to the development of the notion of culturally determined Inuit elder suicide?
5. How did the myth of culturally determined Inuit elder suicide connect with the early sociological ideas of altruistic suicide and cultural relativism?
6. What explanations have been given for this myth?
7. How has this myth been connected with contemporary Inuit youth suicide?

DISCUSSION QUESTIONS

1. Identify and critique the primary sources that popularized the image of Inuit suicide.

2. What role did the idea of social Darwinism (human survival of the fittest) play in popularizing the notion of culturally determined Inuit elder suicide?
3. What is the danger in gathering material for a textbook based on secondary sources?
4. Why might contemporary researchers connect the present high rate of Inuit suicide among youth with culturally determined Inuit elder suicide?

KEY TERMS

altruistic suicide	blame the victim	colonial contact
culturally determined	culturalist	cultural relativism
deviance	environmental causation	euthanasia
mores	Netsilik	

CHAPTER SIX

The Lies Do Not Stand Alone

LEARNING OBJECTIVES

After reading this chapter, you will be able to

» compare and contrast the treatment of Inuit snow terms with those of Hanunoo terms for rice and Nuer terms for the colour combinations of cattle.

» compare and contrast the story of the Blond Eskimo with those of Prince Madoc and the Welsh Indians, and of St. Brendan and his Irish colleagues.

» compare and contrast the story of sati with that of culturally determined Inuit elder suicide.

> This image of the Arctic as a world apart, where the laws of science and society may be in abeyance, is informed not only by what we hear from present-day observers or see when we visit the area ourselves. It is also moulded by a view of the Arctic that comes down to us from the distant past, when the region was as alien and as impossible for most people to reach as another planet.
> —Robert McGhee, *The Last Imaginary Place*, 2004

It is important to recognize that the myths dealt with in the last three chapters do not stand alone as isolated features about how scholars study and present the Inuit. They resemble to a greater or lesser extent comparable myths about peoples who have been historically positioned as "Other" when looked at through the tinted lens of Western scholarship. On the other hand, the unique features of the myths about the Inuit can be illuminated through a look at similar, but also different, myths about other peoples. Finally, by examining how Canada speaks of the Inuit tells us something about non-Inuit Canadians and how they imagine their own identity.

Inuit Snow Terms, Hanunoo Rice Terms, and Nuer Cow Colour Combinations

The "number of terms for" game is not just played with Inuit terms. Two other languages are also at least occasionally cited in anthropological works for their specialized vocabularies: Hanunoo (an Austronesian language spoken in the Philippines) terms for rice and Nuer (and related Nilotic-speaking peoples) terms to describe the colour patterns on cows. The Inuit suffer by comparison. In 1954, Harold Conklin completed his doctoral dissertation "The Relation of Hanunoo Culture to the Plant World" at Yale University. The same year, he published an often-referenced short article entitled "An Ethnoecological Approach to Shifting Agriculture." In this article, we learn that the Hanunoo of the island of Mindoro in the Philippines cultivate 92 named varieties of rice. This is a seminal paper in the development of ethnoscience or ethnobotany; that is, the study of the knowledge that peoples have of the plant life surrounding them. The number leads to important insights about the sophistication of Hanunoo cultivation, as well as the complexity of their botanical knowledge. And, as far as I have seen, no one reporting on Conklin's work mixes up the 92 with 82, 72, or any other number ending in two.

The Nilotic-speaking peoples of Africa have a very close and intricate connection with cattle in their traditional culture. In the words of E. Evans-Pritchard in his classic study of the Nuer:

> Their skins are used for beds, trays, for carrying fuel, cord for tethering and other purposes ... and for the tympana of drums. They are employed in the manufacture of ropes, spears, shields, snuff containers, etc.... Tail hairs are made into tassels used as dance ornaments.... Their bones are used for the manufacture of armlets, and as beaters, pounders, and scrapers. Their horns are cut into spoons and are used in the construction of harpoons. Their dung is used for fuel and for plastering walls, floors ... and to protect wounds. The ashes of burnt dung are rubbed over men's bodies, and are used to dye and straighten the hair, as a mouth wash and tooth powder, in the preparation of sleeping-skins and leather bags, and for various ritual purposes. Their urine is used in churning and cheese-making, in the preparation of gourd-utensils, for tanning leather, and for bathing face and hands. (Evans-Pritchard 1968, 28–29)

Evans-Pritchard noted that there were "several hundred" ways to label cattle colour patterns. These terms were produced with 10 colour terms that could be modified by 27 combination terms. A simple illustrative example is the distinction between *majok* and *marial* among the Western Dinka. The former is a black cow with a white chest. The latter also has a black background, but this time it is the flank of the cow that has the patch of white (Coote 1994). Patterns featuring distinctions among red, black, and white seem to have been especially well received and appreciated by the Nuer and their Nilotic-speaking cousins, the Dinka and Mandari—the cause for celebration by the owner of the cow. In two publications, Evans-Pritchard promised he would provide a complete list of the Nuer terms, but never delivered.

These examples differ in two essential ways from the Eskimo snow terms literature. With the Inuit example, no attempt is made to fit the snow terms into a cultural context. The number is merely repeated and loosely attached to the "commonsense" notion that they live where there is a lot of snow. This makes the idea easier to reproduce. No detailed explanation seems necessary. Compare that with the other studies. First, strings of context are interwoven into the stories of the two linguistic features of Hanunoo and the Nuer. Conklin and others have connected the number 92 to the Hanunoo's extensive diversity of cultigens. With the Nuer and other Nilotic speakers, the cattle terms were interwoven into the pastoralism of the people. Recently, the connection has been made between the number of terms and the general aesthetics of the people (Coote 1994). The way that the people see distinctiveness and beauty in the world is described using the terminology and patterns used for cows. If it looks good on a cow, it looks good generally. However, with the reporting on the Inuit, the snow terms were not connected with anything other than the fact that the Inuit live where there is a lot of snow. The seeming obviousness of the case made it an "apt" example, one that needed little explanation. Also, the myth of the snow terms is easily reproduced—a short word-bite of information. But without the explanation, the possibility for distortion—in practice a reality—was high. The Hanunoo and the Nuer do not have the immediate familiarity of the Inuit for North Americans and Europeans. Their stories require cultural explanations, while people talking about Inuit snow terms have a basic understanding of the environment to depend on. To return to the more technical academic language of the first chapter, Inuit snow terms more readily become simulacra: cultural images, often in the form of stereotypes, that are readily produced and reproduced like material goods or commodities by the media, including scholars and especially those who write textbooks.

The Blond Eskimo: Atlanteans, Welsh Princes, and the Irish

The story of the Blonde Eskimo recounted in chapter four is at first glance merely an ill-founded tale about pre-Columbian Norse or Viking settlers in the Arctic. But it is more than that. It is one of many attempts by people of European heritage to lay claim to very early settlement in the New World. These pre-Columbian stories have been around with varying popularity since the eighteenth century, and they are still going strong today. They include stories of the mighty Atlanteans of Plato's creation. These are reported frequently on the Internet as the archetypal European super race creating or influencing everything of significance in anyone's ancient world. Aboriginal groups that independently invented the flat-topped, stepped pyramids of Central and South America have been denied credit for their ingenuity. On the Internet, credit has been given to the Atlanteans who taught the Egyptians to construct their pointed-top, smooth-sided pyramids. The Atlanteans then migrated across the ocean that bears their name and shared their brilliance with the plagiarizing Aboriginal people, who selfishly neglected to reference their mentors.

We read similar stories in scientific and popular writing in response to recent research such as the discovery of the controversial Kennewick Man. He was discovered along the Washington Pacific Coast in 1996. The controversy centred on the fact that he was found to have a skull that is more long and narrow than the "typical" broader cranium of Aboriginal people of today and of the recent past. He shared that trait with most other ancient Aboriginal skulls dating back 8000 years or more. Rumours began soon afterwards that he was an ancient European who had come to the Americas prior to the Aboriginal people themselves. A stereotypically Californian New Age, Norwegian-American group called the Asatru Folk Assembly even claimed him as one of their own.

JUMPING TO GENETIC CONCLUSIONS

Recent genetic research has led to premature and misleading conclusions about early Europeans. Mitochondrial DNA (mtDNA for short) research traces the DNA of those who share mutations along a female line. MtDNA, which exists outside the nucleus of the cell and does not code for construction of parts of the body, is passed down on the female side. It goes from mother to daughter and so on for thousands of generations. It is passed down this way because each human egg cell contains a lot of mtDNA. Mutations that occur in one generation are passed down to the next. Haplogroups (that is, groups that share mutations) can be tracked to follow the long, winding trail of the female lineage. Why does this tracking only apply to females? The mtDNA in sperm is cast off when the successful sperm cell jettisons its tail, seeming to celebrate for "getting lucky."

Geneticists are currently keeping themselves very busy tracking the mtDNA lineages or haplogroups of different human populations around the world. They have discovered that there are four major female lineages for Aboriginal groups (termed, appropriately, haplogroups A, B, C, and D). But a minor lineage mysteriously called haplogroup X has also been uncovered. Among those recorded as belonging to haplogroup X are the Ojibwa or Anishnabe, most of whom live in Canada (e.g., Quebec, Ontario, Manitoba, Saskatchewan, and British Columbia). This haplogroup is also one of the seven European lineages, albeit a fairly minor one that is predominantly found in Eastern Europe. The ink was barely dry on this interesting finding when people began leaping to hasty conclusions and drawing maps of migration (see, for example, <http://www.mitomap.org/WorldMigrations.pdf>).

On Sunday, June 25, 2005, the Discovery Network aired a show that used the Ojibwa data and little else to suggest that early Europeans found their way to Canada 17,000 years ago. It's an old story, but not in the way that the producers of the show think.

After that hasty conclusion was reached, haplogroup X was discovered in Asia as well, as many physical anthropologists likely would have expected. The location was the Southern Altai region in southwestern Siberia. Unsurprisingly, the people of that region also possess the four major Aboriginal mtDNA haplogroups. Migration in both directions to Eastern Europe (possibly with Genghis Khan and the other Mongols) and much, much earlier to the Americas is significantly more believable than the idea of early Atlantic-crossing Europeans. Corroborating evidence is coming to light by the tracking of y-chromosome DNA passed down from father to son. Two significant Aboriginal y-chromosome haplogroups (Q and C) have also been discovered among the Turkic-speaking Southern Altaians.

THE PRINCE ON THE PRAIRIES: PRINCE MADOC AND THE WELSH INDIANS

More on the lunatic fringe of stories of early European migrations are those of the "Welsh Indians." If you search the Internet for "Prince Madoc," you will find a host of such stories, often with paragraphs headed by telltale non-scientific statements such as "It is said ..." and "Many believe ..." These stories tell of how a Welsh prince, fleeing from a leadership battle in Wales in 1170, sailed across the Atlantic, along with a good number of his followers, and landed in Mobile Bay, Alabama. There is even a plaque situated near the proposed landing site, erected by the conservative women's group, the Daughters of the American Revolution. It reads: "In Memory of Prince Madoc, a Welsh explorer who landed on the shores of Mobile Bay in 1170, and left behind, with the Indians, the Welsh language."

From there, according to most believers, Prince Madoc and the other Welsh travellers headed across Kentucky and Tennessee. They arrived in the upper Missouri River territory of the Mandan, a Siouan-speaking Plains people. The claim is that they interbred with the Mandan. The evidence they present is easily taken apart; for example, the often-cited ridge-top stone forts date from hundreds of years earlier than the life of Prince Madoc and do not contain a single European artifact. Also, a small sample of carefully selected Mandan words appear to be similar to words in Welsh, but a similar comparison could made between any two languages in the world, given the limited range of sounds humans can make and the ease with which meanings could be considered similar. Using this method, you could readily demonstrate that the Aztecs were related to the Aborigines, Incas to Indonesians.

When did this story begin? It first appeared in print in 1583. This fanciful story was repeated so often over the next 300 years and had reached such prominence that it began to appear in American textbooks. Eminent American historian Samuel E. Morison (1887–1976)—a leading debunker of the myth—remembered the story of Prince Madoc in the first history textbook he ever read. He recalled his teacher saying with a smile, "'Oh Yes! The Mandan Indians still speak a kind of Welsh!'" (Morison 1971: 85).

Why would such a story be created? It was required to fulfill legitimacy needs, to overcome uncertainty about royal position and lineage. Beginning in the late fifteenth century, the English monarchy descended from a Welsh line, the Tudors. This line began with Henry VII, then continued with his son Henry VIII, followed by his own short-lived son (Edward VI, 1537–53), then Henry's religiously rigid daughter popularly known as Bloody Mary, and ended with Elizabeth I, the "Virgin Queen." This line had a number of problems proving the legitimacy of their offspring and of their positions. Spectacular achievements of Welsh royalty would help overcome those problems.

The Prince Madoc story was also used to secure a second kind of legitimacy. In the late sixteenth century, the English were working to stake their claim to the Americas, in opposition to the Spanish. Richard Hakluyt's *Principal Navigations, Voyages, Traffiques and Discoveries of the English Nation* (1589) co-opted the mythic royal Welshman for such a purpose, which is rather like Jamaican-born athletes being called Canadian, as long as they pass the drug test.

Welsh nationalism was also a factor propagating the myth. Above all else, Prince Madoc is a creature of Welsh nationalism. The first history of Wales was published in 1584, and Madoc was featured in this work.

Distinguished Welsh historian Gwyn A. Williams, whose many books include *Madoc: The Making of a Myth* (1980), wrote that in the eighteenth century, the "new Welsh nation was manufactured in London" in Welsh literary societies (Williams 1980: 164). In the air of liberation during the 1790s, brought on by the American and French revolutions, a Welsh political club was formed in London. Its anthem was a hymn to Prince Madoc. Also, a French trader came across the Mandan people and pronounced them "white like Europeans." Earlier, other Native nations fictitious and real were identified as speaking or understanding Welsh. The Tuscarora, who speak an Iroquoian language, and the Shawnee, who speak an Algonquian language, are but two of these. But the Mandan, who speak a Siouan language, quickly rose as the main contenders. In Williams's words "a minor outbreak of Madoc fever seized the USA" (Williams 1985: 171). The disease spread to Wales and to the educated Welsh engaged in literary and political societies in London. English political authorities supported the claim because they once again briefly needed a Welsh-British stake in North America. A crisis had arisen with ships being seized around Nootka Sound and displays of parliamentary pugnacity over competing Spanish and British claims to the Pacific coast.

In 1792, John Evans, a young Welsh Methodist minister, "threw up career and family" to join a society that had caught the fever. He intended to meet and reconvert the Welsh-Mandan descendants at all costs. To further this end, he even worked to advance Spanish claims to the Americas. In Williams's breathless summation of Evans's great but futile adventure, we read that:

> He set off alone up an unknown Missouri with $1.75 in his pocket, was driven back, and enrolled as second-in-command to the Scottish explorer James McKay in the greatest expedition Spain ever sent up the river. Evans did indeed reach the Mandans; he lived through one of the worst winters on earth; he held those Mandans for Spain against the Canadians, helping indirectly to fix the future US-Canadian frontier; he drew excellent maps which Lewis and Clark used on their major expedition only nine years later. He died of drink and disillusion in New Orleans at the age of twenty-nine. (Williams 1980: 171)

After spending some time with the Mandan, Evans asserted that Welsh-speaking Aboriginals "have no existence." This, however, did not kill the story. Nor did the negative report that came back from the explorers Lewis and Clark in their early nineteenth-century journey across America.

The painter-explorer George Catlin picked up the story as he went to visit the Mandan in 1832. Like others of that century, he could not believe that the burial mounds and fortifications being discovered by travellers and settlers moving west could have been constructed by "primitive" peoples. The local "savages" must have learned their technology from Europe, specifically from Wales. Catlin wrote:

> Built on the banks of the river, with walls in some places twenty or thirty feet in height, and covered ways to the water, they evince a knowledge of the science of fortifications not a century behind that of the present day. I submit they were never built by a nation of Indians in America, and present to us incontestable proof of the former existence of a people far advanced in the arts of civilization. (Catlin 1975: 225)

Catlin also assigned European origins to the pottery, beads, and canoes of the Mandan people. None of these were of a construction or design unusual to cultures of the area. Then, he published a comparative list of 12 words that to his mind showed a Welsh influence on the Mandan. Some of the word pairs, such as *ne* and *chwi* for the word *you* in Mandan and Welsh respectively, are poor choices to illustrate any connection. An anonymous Welsh speaker and obvious student of linguistics has posted a piece on Christopher Harvey's website The Language Geek with the heading "Mandan Is not Welsh" (<http://www.languagegeek.com/siouan/mandan_is_not_welsh. html>). The writer compiles a list of Welsh and Mandan words that shows the distinctiveness of the two languages. Most notable in the collection are numbers, which are especially good for showing historical relationships as they are very slow to change. He concludes with the following:

Of all these examples, the two languages share only one word in common, "house." Statistically, there is bound to be at least one or two common words between languages, this does not imply they are related. That the word for "many" in Korean is [mani], and "two" is [tu(l)] does not imply a Korean colonisation of England in the distant past. Nor does the fact that the Mohawk pronominal affixes for 1st and 2nd person—/k/ and /s/—match the Hungarian affixes make it reasonable that the early Iroquois settled Hungary. These sorts of similarities are bound to happen. Historically, Mandan "ti" would be related to /tʰipi/in Dakota, while Welsh "tŷ" is derived from Indo-European *tegos meaning cover/roof (English *thatch*). So these two words, although superficially the same, stem from different sources.

The writer ends by articulating his or her frustration that the belief will not go away. Romantically wishful Welsh and their Midwestern and Alabaman intellectual peers do not want the idea to die. Language geek, I share your pain.

LET US NOT FORGET THE IRISH

Another such story similar to the Welsh Prince has an Irish monk in his seventies, St. Brendan (489–577), travelling with 17 other monks in a boat sewn together with oxhides, crossing the Atlantic. Allegedly, they eventually made their way to West Virginia. There they were claimed to have carved Ogham writing (an early Medieval alphabet), telling of their coming. Ogham, which is currently much fancied by the neo-Pagan movement in Britain, consists of 15 consonants formed by straight lines above, below, or through a horizon line, 5 vowels formed by slanted lines through a horizon line, and (usually) 5 somewhat more complicated characters representing diphthongs (e.g., ea, oi, ui, io, ae). Ogham writing, codified by Benedictine monks who came to Ireland midway through the seventh century AD, was used traditionally on grave markers. Strangely, it reads from bottom to top. To my knowledge, it is the only writing system that does so. I have long said that this was just to confuse the English. Of course, the simple nature of these line letters means that any carved or sometimes naturally occurring lines can be interpreted as Ogham if you believe strongly enough. The fact that your readership is not likely to be knowledgeable about Irish Gaelic helps make your case, too.

Barry Fell, a Harvard marine biologist who upon his retirement marketed himself as "American's leading ancient language expert," purported to interpret or "translate" the stone writing (1983) in West Virginia and elsewhere. His interpretation was easily discredited a few years later (Oppenheimer and Wirtz 1989), but that did not seem to diminish his support much.

In his useful book *Frauds, Myths and Mysteries: Science and Pseudoscience in Archaeology*, Kenneth Feder (1990) outlines and carefully debunks a whole host of similar notions of early White explorers in his chapters "After the Indians, Before Columbus?" and "The Myth of the Moundbuilders." He rightfully sees an element of racism when items of material culture, such as mounds and forts, are seen as too sophisticated or "civilized" to have been developed by Aboriginal people.

I think, however, there is more to it than that. One further reason that Aboriginal people aren't credited with their own technologies comes from the fact that over 95 per cent of the history of the Americas is Aboriginal history alone. I believe that this presents a challenge or threat to some non-Aboriginal Canadians and Americans who wish to preserve their own sense of entitlement to be "native" to that same land. It is a case not just of misinformation; it is also a need to maintain that misinformation.

In addition, I feel that the "bias of the book" comes into play here. The bias of the book is a historical prejudice stemming from the fact that some peoples were literate. These people could tell the story in a way that lasted through the ages and earned the respect of the scholars and teachers of the colonial ages. We don't know what the Druids, who can be considered like the Brahmin or priest caste of the early Celtic peoples, thought of Julius Caesar. However, we do know what he thought of them because he wrote it down, and that has been passed along. And the Caesar-influenced picture that springs to the minds of many Europeans when they hear or read the word *Druid* (e.g., a picture of human sacrifices and people burning in huge wicker figures) reflects the dark shades painted by Julius Caesar's writing.

Similarly, for centuries White travellers who viewed the ruins of the Great Zimbabwe in the southern part of Africa were convinced that they could discover its makers in their book, the Bible. It took archaeologists a long time to establish that the Shona, a local Bantu-speaking people, constructed it.

This kind of thinking flows as well from a kind of manifest destiny. We "Europeans" conquered the Americas easily. Therefore, anyone who is European has it in his or her heritage to be able to make the trip across the Atlantic and have an immediate and readily detectable impact upon arrival. It is all in our culture or our genes.

Sati

A good parallel example to the myth of Inuit elder suicide is the Western construction and reproduction of the high-caste or Brahmanic Hindu practice of sati (often spelled as suttee), in which a widow is burned alive in the funeral pyre of her husband. Like Inuit elder suicide, the story of this practice is often reproduced in introductory anthropology (Holmes 1965: 349 and Williams 1990: 84) and sociology (Rose 1979: 130) textbooks. Its roots are equally deep in the sociological tradition. Durkheim discussed it at length in his chapter on altruistic suicide (Durkheim 1951: 219, 223). Books dealing with Durkheim's work (La Capra 1972: 172 and Nisbet 1974: 234) or with the sociological study of suicide generally (Fedden 1972: 19) made distinct mention of it.

I owe much to the highly detailed and enlightening research of Lata Mani (1998) in recognizing the parallels between sati and Inuit elder suicide. Textbook presentations of this practice should be examined on five main points. First, the practice of sati was fundamentally restricted to upper caste women, not Hindu women generally, as is sometimes stated (see Rose 1979: 130). Second, British colonialists recorded it largely during a specific time period (the late 1700s to 1829, when it was declared illegal) and in a particular place (in the area of Calcutta). How long it was practised before and after that time is questionable, as is the question of whether and where it extended to other regions of the subcontinent of India. Third, as with Inuit elder suicide, claims to the frequency with which it occurred need to be challenged. It was often written about in the early nineteenth-century British and Indian press, which did much to over-report the phenomenon. Fourth, there is the question of its religious roots. When the British multinational powerhouse East India Company was inquiring about the practice, they asked the pundits or religious experts of the people to give a legal opinion on how it related to Hindu scripture. In this way, they, like the missionaries that came to accompany them, were imposing a Protestant tradition of scriptural authority for law not directly applicable to the religious texts of Hinduism that were spread across centuries and contexts. The question led to a debate among the people concerning what was a colonial-inspired discourse, not a traditional line of questioning. Just as the Christian West projects some of its "Holy War" intentions on Islam, so British nineteenth-century evangelical Protestants projected their Biblical literalism on the Hindus. Mani shows as well that the driving forces behind sati were primarily economic. Concerns, especially from the widow's in-laws, about inheritance and financial support led some relatives to push for her suicide. When a woman "chose" sati, it best reflected her assessment that her future in terms of family support was weak. But, like with Inuit elder suicide, it has been convenient to say that the culture (in this case, religion) dictated the action. The "Other" is supposed to obey culture mindlessly, while "We" the Western observers challenge our culture rationally.

Finally, and perhaps most significantly, the voluntary nature of the practice, so often reproduced, must be questioned. In *Suicide: A Social and Historical Study* (1972, originally published 1938), Fedden, who assumes that the will of the women and the cultural will were one, writes that "[t]he voluntary nature of these suicides is attested by the difficulty which the British have found in putting a stop to the custom since it was declared illegal in 1829" (1972: 19; see also Rose 1979: 130).

In Mani's postmodern words, "[t]he technology of widow immolation was geared to ensure incineration, not escape" (Mani 1998: 171). The women were often drugged, more often tied down, or almost literally caged in.

The Inuit as a Canadian Construct

There is more to the White lies I've described here than just another example of the misconstruction and misrepresentation of the non-White "Other." In a way, the White lies are a very Canadian production and reproduction. As a group, Canadians will construct the Inuit differently than would the Americans, the Danes (with Greenland), the Russians, and other Europeans because the Inuit are part of how we imagine ourselves. Although most Canadians live in the south, close to the American border, the North is part of our vision of Canada. When citizens of Toronto, Vancouver, Calgary, Winnipeg, and Montreal say that they are "going North," they speak a common language.

Combating the climate of the North is part of our imagined identity. As I mentioned in the first chapter, my first memories of Canadian poetry come from Robert Service (1874–1958): the poem "The Cremation of Sam McGee" specifically (originally published in 1907 in *The Songs of a Sourdough*). It was dramatically read to me and my classmates in grade five, two years after the poet's death. The opening words are imprinted in my imagination:

There are strange things done in the midnight sun
By the men who moil for gold:
The Arctic trails have their secret tales
That would make your blood run cold ...
(Service 1968)

Service inspired my first visions of the North. I know I am not alone in this. Born in Britain, he came to British Columbia the year he turned 22, and before he was 30, he went North to work in a bank in Whitehorse in 1903. He wrote about the White men of the North, mostly those involved with the Gold Rush of 1898. Although I have read many of his poems, I don't remember one mention of the Inuit. Still, the battle against the noble foe of the harsh Arctic climate stuck with me.

The first Canadian poet that I ever met and admired was Al Purdy (1918–2000), who came to my university, Lakehead in Thunder Bay—the place I then thought of as the North! It is apt that the League of Canadian Poets honoured him with the Voice of the Land Award. Here are the opening lines from "Innuit," in his collection entitled *North of Summer: Poems from Baffin Island*:

Innuit
An old man carving soapstone
at the co-op in Frobisher Bay
and in his faded eyes
it is possible to see them
shadowy figures
past the Dorset and pre-Dorset Cultures

5,000 years ago
if you look closely. (Purdy 1967: 32)

Among my favourite lines are those he writes about an imagined Dorset sculptor, an old, lame hunter carving two swans for his granddaughter. After talking about the making of the carving, he writes:

The carving is laid aside
in beginning darkness
at the end of hunger
after a while wind
blows down the tent and snow
begins to cover him

After 600 years
the ivory thought
is still warm (Purdy 1967: 32)

I can't distance myself from this poem. The imaginings although not the original thoughts or words are mine. The Inuit and their Palaeo-Eskimo and Dorset antecessors are part of how I, and many other Canadians, imagine their country.

Best in the Bush

Canadians have respect for those who are "good in the bush," those who master the North that we so readily envision even if only in the abstract and that we see as wild compared to the domesticity of our national railroad, our Prairie farms, our towns, our big cities, our Newfoundland outports, mines, and logging camps. The Inuit are the best by a long shot. No one yet has done what they have done—clearly mastered the far North in this country. We can imagine them doing anything. And this may be where our acceptance of the lies begins. We can imagine them being so tough that they allow their elders to die. Of course, they know snow so well that they develop an unbelievably wordy vocabulary beyond our means. The myth of the blond Eskimo might be what is called "nativistic envy." We would like to call ourselves the natives of this part of the planet. We would like to think that "people like us" could adapt as well. What better way than to merge with the Inuit genetically, if only in our historical imagining?

In his influential work *Imagined Communities: Reflections on the Origin and Spread of Nationalism* (1983), Benedict Anderson famously said, "In an anthropological spirit ... I propose the following definition of the nation: it is an imagined political community.... Communities are to be distinguished by the style in which they are imagined" (Anderson 1983: 15). The Inuit as their antecessors, then, are part of the Canadian imagining, an image inextricably interwoven into their visions of the Arctic.

The growing popularity of the stone figures commonly known as inukshuk (plural inukshuit) as a Canadian symbol is a recent sign of this imagining. An inukshuk appears on the Nunavut flag. I first noticed the growth in popularity of inukshuit on highway 69, along the east coast of Georgian Bay in northern Ontario. Each year more and more of them appear along the Precambrian shield rock along the highway. In the summer of 2006, my wife, Angie, and I travelled to Gabriola Island, near Nanaimo on Vancouver Island. We stopped at a beach, which bore the bricks from an old brick factory. While my wife took pictures, I constructed a brick inukshuk. We wonder now if we would find a whole beach-load of inukshuit if we went there again.

Traditionally, the Inuit used inukshuit in a variety of ways, including to mark where caribou, fish, or seal might be located. More abstractly, they are symbols to show people that others have been in that location before; there is spirituality, hope, and goodwill in that.

Now we see small metal versions, made in Asian countries, appearing in more and more tourist gift shops across the country. The official logo for the 2010 Winter Olympics in Vancouver is a five-piece multi-coloured inukshuk. In a May 2005 article in *Anishinabek News*, Peter Irniq, a former Nunavut commissioner, is quoted in the following way, lending a cautious Inuk voice concerning generalizing inukshuk:

He says every Inukshuk has a meaning and a reason why it was built in a certain location. He says building the figures should not be taken lightly. "Inuit never build Inukshuk with head, legs and arms. I have seen Inukshuk built more recently—100 years maybe by non-Inuit in Nunavut—with head, legs and arms. These are not called Inukshuk. These are called 'inunguat,' [meaning] imitation of man, imitation of a person," he told CBC.

Irniq says the Olympic committee should have consulted with the elders of Nunavut before they chose the design.

"Inukshuk is like survival. Inukshuk's important significance is survival. What we think about Inukshuk is what we think about the Canadian flag," said Irniq. "It is that important." (*Anishinabek News*, May 2005)

Of course, it is possible that Irniq is speculating as much as he is relying upon the cultural traditions of the people. Some inukshuit are very old. It is also possible that he was being more rigid in his views than his ancestors were, but they didn't have to deal with cultural appropriation. The main point is that in imagining the North and the Inuit in the North, Canadians must listen to Aboriginal voices.

One small sign of how the image can be dangerously appropriated comes from a package of dog biscuits made by Northern Pet Products (a company based just a very little north of Toronto). There are inukshuit all over the package, and the text near the bottom of the bag makes no reference to Inuit:

> The "inukshuk" (i-nook-shuk) is a uniquely Northern Canadian art form. Made of stone, they were used for centuries as navigational markers, symbols of safe passage and indicators of cached food.

Conclusion

What do   ut the Inuit? At a fundamental
level, we   out the Inuit First Nations peoples gene   ed in popular culture. Without
looking a   us "facts" were first constructed,
we have   away if they prove obstacles to
storytelli   cond, we learn that frequently
appearin   roduced not because they have
been che   e they provide powerful means
of illustr   e teachers want to get across to
their students. Beware the good example! Third, we learn that the history of scientific disciplines such as sociology and anthropology was at least partially built around intellectual battles (e.g., nature [biology/race] versus nurture [culture]; cultural relativism versus absolutism) in which exoticizing the Inuit or the "Other" was used as a tool of persuasion. And, sometimes, all seems fair in love and intellectual war.

Finally, Canadians imagining who they are and where their identity lies have a duty to acknowledge the role that the Inuit have played (and are playing) in Canadian history. A series of popular books has been published recently, telling of the contributions of a number of different peoples to world culture: *How the Irish Saved Civilization* (Cahill 1996), and *How the Scots Invented the Modern World* (Herman 2003). Recognizing the role of the Inuit in Canadian culture is no less important.

CONTENT QUESTIONS

1. What forms of evidence are used by those who believe in Prince Madoc and the Welsh Indians?
2. What are the basic weaknesses of this so-called evidence?
3. What needs did it fulfill?
4. How do the academic and popular treatment of Hanunoo rice terms and Nuer terms for colour combinations differ from that of Inuit snow terms?

5. How do the stories of Prince Madoc and St. Brendan relate to the story of the Blond Eskimo?
6. How does the Western production and reproduction of the notion of sati compare with its production and reproduction of the myth of culturally determined Inuit elder suicide?

DISCUSSION QUESTION

1. Why do you think that early European pseudo-scientific theories keep cropping up?

KEY TERMS

bias of the book	cultural appropriation	ethnobotany
ethnoscience	Hanunoo	haplogroup
mtDNA	Nilotic	Ogham
sati	simulacra	Siouan languages

Works Cited

Adovasio, J.M. with Jake Page. 2003. *The First Americans: In Pursuit of Archaeology's Greatest Mystery*. New York: Random House.

Andersen, Benedict. 1983. *Imagined Communities: Reflections on the Origin and Spread of Nationalism*. London and New York: Verso.

Angeloni, Elvio. 1990. *Annual Editions: Anthropology 1990–91*. Guilford, CT: Dushkin.

———. 1997. *Annual Editions: Anthropology 1997–98*. Guilford, CT: Dushkin.

Anishinabek News. May 2005. 17,4: 1, no cited author.

Apple, Michael W., and Linda K. Christian-Smith. 1991. "The Politics of the Textbook," in *The Politics of the Textbook*. New York, NY: Routledge. 1–21.

Balikci, Asen. 1961. "Suicidal Behavior Among the Netsilik Eskimos," in Bernard Blishen, Frank E. Jones, Kaspar Naegele, and John Porter (eds.), *Canadian Society: Sociological Perspectives*. Toronto: Macmillan.

———. 1970. *The Netsilik Eskimo*. New York: The Natural History Press.

Banting, Frederick G. 1927. "Private and Confidential Report to Mr. O.S. Finnie." Dept. of the Interior, Northwest Territories and Yukon Branch, Nov. 8, 1927, National Archives of Canada, RG85, vol. 2081, file 1012-4 pt3A, p2.

Barnhart, Terry A. 2005. *Ephraim George Squier and the Development of American Anthropology*. Lincoln: U of Nebraska P.

Barnouw, Victor. 1987. *An Introduction to Anthropology: Ethnology*. Vol. 2. 5th ed. Chicago: The Dorsey Press.

Baudrillard, Jean. 1983. *Simulations*. Trans. Paul Foss, Paul Patton, and Philip Beitchman. New York: Semiotext[e].

Beach, David. 1994. *The Shona and their Neighbours*. Oxford: Blackwell.

Birket-Smith, Kaj. 1929. "The Caribou Eskimos." *Report of the Fifth Thule Expedition*. Vol. V. Copenhagen: Gyldensalske Boghandel, Nordisk Forlag.

———. 1959. *The Eskimos*. London: Methuen.

Boas, Franz. 1888. *The Central Eskimo*. Sixth Annual Report of the Bureau of American Ethnology. Washington, DC: Smithsonian Institute. 388–669 (reprinted in 1964).

———. 1896. "The Limitations of the Comparative Method." *Science* (new series) 4: 901–08 (reprinted in 1940 in *Race, Language and Culture*. New York: The Free Press. 270–80).

———. 1911. *Handbook of American Indian Languages, Part I*. Washington, DC: Smithsonian Institution, Bureau of American Ethnology, Bulletin 40.

———. 1916. *The Mind of Primitive Man*. New York: Macmillan.

Boyer, R., R. Dufour, M. Préville, and L. Bujold-Brown. 1994. "State of Mental Health." *A Health Profile of the Inuit: Report of the Santé Québec Health Survey among the*

Inuit of Nunavik, 1992. Vol. 2. Montréal: Ministère de la santé et des services sociaux, Gouvernement du Québec. 117–44.

Briggs, Jean. 1970. *Never in Anger.* Cambridge, MA: Harvard UP.

Brill, A.A. 1913. "Piblocto or Hysteria among Peary's Eskimos." *Journal of Nervous and Mental Disease* 40: 514–20.

Brody, Hugh. 1991 (1975). *The People's Land: Eskimos and Whites in the Eastern Arctic.* Middlesex: Penguin.

Brown, Roger. 1958. *Words and Things.* New York: Free Press.

Cahill, Thomas. 1996. *How the Irish Saved Civilization: The Untold Story of Ireland's Heroic Role from the Fall of Rome to the Rise of Medieval Europe.* New York: Doubleday.

Carpenter, Edmund. 1973. *Eskimo Realities.* New York: Holt, Rinehart and Winston.

Catlin, George. 1975 (1841). *Letters and Notes on the North American Indians.* New York: Clarkson N. Potter.

Cavan, Ruth. 1965 (1928). *Suicide.* New York, NY: Russell and Russell.

——. 1968. *Delinquency and Crime: Cross Cultural Perspectives.* Philadelphia: Lippincott.

Chagnon, Napoleon. 1992. *Yanomamo: The Fierce People,* 4th ed. New York: Harcourt Brace Jovanovich.

Chown, Bruce, and Marion Lewis. 1959. "The Blood Group Genes of the Copper Eskimo." *Journal of Physical Anthropology.* March 17. 13–18.

Clinard, Marshall B., and Robert F. Meier. 1985 (1963). *The Sociology of Deviant Behavior,* 6th ed. New York: Holt, Rinehart and Winston.

Collins, Henry B. 1962. "Stefansson as an Anthropologist." *Polar Notes,* 4: 8–13.

Conkin, Harold C. 1954. "An Ethnoecological Approach to Shifting Agriculture." *Transactions of the New York Academy of Sciences* 17: 133–42.

Coote, Jeremy. 1994. "'Marvels of Everyday Vision': The Anthropology of Aesthetics and the Cattle-Keeping Nilotes," in J. Coote and Anthony Shelton (eds.), *Anthropology, Art and Aesthetics.* Oxford: Clarendon Press. 245–73.

Crantz, David. 1820 (1767). *The History of Greenland: Including an Account of the Mission Carried on by the United Brethren in That Country.* 2 vols. London: Longman, Hurst, Rees, Orr, and Bram.

Cree School Board. 1987. *Cree Lexicon: Eastern James Bay Dialects.* Baie-de-la-Poste, Mistassini Lake.

Crysdale, Stewart, and Christopher Beattie. 1973 and 1977. *Sociology Canada: An Introductory Text.* Toronto: Butterworth.

Dahl, Jens. 2000. *Saqqaq: An Inuit Hunting Community in the Modern World.* Toronto: U of Toronto P.

Daily Alaskan. 1913. "Stefannson Branded as Faker." August 29.

De Coccola, Raymond, and Paul King. 1986. *The Incredible Eskimo: Life Among the Barren Land Eskimo.* Surrey: Hancock House.

Deloria, Vine Jr. 1969. *Custer Died for Your Sins: An Indian Manifesto.* New York: Macmillan.

DeMorgan, John. 1914. *Lost in the Ice: Where Adventure Leads.* New York: Street and Smith.

De Waal, Frans. 2005. *Our Inner Ape.* New York: Riverhead Books.

Diamond, Jared. 2005. *Collapse: How Societies Choose to Fail or Succeed.* New York: Penguin.

Dick, Lyle. 1995. "'Pibloktoq' (Arctic Hysteria): A Construction of European-Inuit Relations?" *Arctic Anthropology* 32,2: 1–42.

Dickason, Olive. 1997. *Canada's First Nations: A History of Founding Peoples from Earliest Times*, 2nd ed. Toronto: McClelland and Stewart.

———. 2002. *Canada's First Nations: A History of Founding Peoples from Earliest Times*, 3rd ed. Toronto: McClelland and Stewart.

Diubaldo, Richard J. 1978. *Stefansson and the Canadian Arctic*. Montreal: McGill-Queen's UP.

Dodge, Howard Lois. 1912. *Attraction of the Compass: A Romance of the North*. Long Beach, CA: Press of Dove and Cortney.

———. 1916. *The Attraction of the Compass; or the Blonde Eskimo: A Romance of the North Based Upon Fact of a Personal Experience*. Long Beach, CA: Seaside Printing.

Dorais, Louis-Jacques. 1987. *An Analytical Lexicon of Modern Inuktitut in Quebec-Labrador*. Montreal: Les Presses de l'Université Laval.

———. 1997. *Quaqtaq: Modernity and Identity in an Inuit Community*. Toronto: U of Toronto P.

D'Souza, Patricia. 2004. "Aye, There's the Nose Rub—How Madison Avenue Reinvented the Inuit." *Nunatsiaq News*, Feb. 27. <http://www.nunatsiaq.com/archives/40227/news/features/40227_01.html>.

Durkheim, Émile. 1938 (1895). *Rules of the Sociological Method*. Chicago: U of Chicago P.

———. 1966 (French, 1897; English, 1951). *Suicide: A Study in Sociology*. Trans. John A. Spaulding. Ed. and Intro. George Simpson. New York: Free Press.

Ember, Carol R., and Melvin Ember. 1999. *Cultural Anthropology*, 9th ed. Upper Saddle River, NJ: Prentice-Hall.

Enterline, James Robert. 1972. *Viking America: The Norse Crossings and their Legacy*. Garden City, NY: Doubleday and Company.

Eshleman, J. Ross, and Barbara G. Cashion. 1985. *Sociology: An Introduction*. Boston: Little, Brown.

Evans-Pritchard, E. 1968. *The Nuer*. Oxford: Clarendon Press.

Farb, Peter. 1968. *Man's Rise to Civilization, as Shown by the Indians of North America from Primeval Times to the Coming of the Industrial State*. New York: Dutton.

Fedden, Henry R. 1972 (1938). *Suicide: A Social and Historical Study*. New York: B. Blom.

Feder, Kenneth. 1990. *Frauds, Myths and Mysteries: Science and Pseudoscience in Archaeology*. New York: McGraw-Hill.

Federico, Ronald C., and Janet Schwartz. 1983. *Sociology*. New York: Addison-Wesley.

Fell, Barry. 1983. *Saga America: A Startling New Theory on the Old World Settlement of America Before Columbus*. New York: Times Books.

Ferguson, Jack. 1970. "Social Change in the Western Arctic," in W.E. Mann (ed.), *Social and Cultural Change in Canada*. Vol. 1. Toronto: Copp Clark. 27–50.

Ferraro, Gary. 1995. *Cultural Anthropology: An Applied Perspective*. Minneapolis/St. Paul, MN: West Publishing.

Fienup-Riordan, Ann. 1995. *Freeze Frame: Alaskan Eskimos in the Movies*. Seattle: U of Washington P.

Fitzhugh, W.W. 1976. "Environmental Factors in the Evolution of Dorset Culture: A Marginal Proposal for Hudson Bay," in Moreau S. Maxwell (ed.), *Eastern Arctic Prehistory: Paleoeskimo Problems. Memoirs of the Society for American Archaeology*, 31: 139–49.

Fortescue, Michael D. 1984. *West Greenlandic*. London: Croom Helm.

Foucault, Michel. 1978. *The History of Sexuality*. Vol. 1: *An Introduction*. New York: Pantheon Books.

——. 1980. "Two Lectures," in Colin Gordon (ed.), *Power/Knowledge*. New York: Pantheon Books. 78–108.

——. 1994 (1972). *The Archaeology of Knowledge*. London: Routledge; Trans. from *L'Archéologie du savoir* 1969.

Freeman, Derek. 1999. *The Fateful Hoaxing of Margaret Mead: A Historical Analysis of her Samoan Research*. Boulder, CO: Westview Press.

Freeman, Minnie Aodia. 1978. *Life Among the Qalllunaat*. Edmonton: Hurtig Publishers.

Friedl, John, and John Pfeiffer. 1977. *Anthropology: The Study of People*. New York: Harper and Row.

Gagne, Raymond C. 1968. "Spatial Concepts in the Eskimo Language," in V.F. Valentine and F.G. Vallee (eds.), *Eskimo of the Canadian Arctic*. Toronto: McClelland and Stewart. 30–38.

Gallagher, James E., and Ronald D. Lambert (Eds.). 1971. *Social Process and Institution: The Canadian Case*. Toronto: Holt, Rinehart and Winston.

Glascock, A.P., and S.L. Feinman. 1981. "Social Asset or Social Burden: Treatment of the Aged in Non-Industrial Societies," in C.L. Fry (ed.), *Dimension: Aging, Culture and Health*. New York: Praeger.

Goddard, Ives. 1984. "Synonymy," in David Damas (ed.), *Arctic*. Vol. 5 of *Handbook of North American Indians*, Ed. William C. Sturtevant. Washington, DC: Smithsonian Institution. 5–7.

Goddard, John. 1996. "A Real Whopper (Author Farley Mowat Admits to Elaborating the Facts for Some of His Books)." *Saturday Night* 11,4: 46.

Gomme, Ian McDermid. 1993. *The Shadow Line: Deviance and Crime in Canada*. Toronto: Harcourt Brace Jovanovich.

Greeley, Adolphus. 1912. "The Origin of Stefansson's Blond Eskimo." *National Geographic*. December 12, 24–38.

Greene, John O. 1893. *The Ke Whonkus People*. Indianapolis: Vincent.

Guemple, Lee. 1969. "Human Resources Management: the Dilemma of the Aging Eskimo." *Sociological Symposium* 2 (Spring).

——. 1974. "The Dilemma of the Aging Eskimo," in Christopher Beattie and Stewart Crysdale (eds.), *Sociology Canada: Readings*. Toronto: Butterworth. 203–14. Rev. and Abrgd. from *Sociological Symposium* 2 (Spring 1969): 59–74.

——. 1980. "Growing Old in Inuit Society," in Victor W. Marshall (ed.), *Aging in Canada*. Toronto: Fitzhenry and Whiteside.

Gutteridge, Leonard F. 2000. *Ghosts of Cape Sabine: The Harrowing True Story of the Greely Expedition*. New York: Putnam.

Hakluyt, Richard. 1589. *Principal Navigations, Voyages, Traffiques and Discoveries of the English Nation*.

Hall, Captain Charles Francis. 1970 (1864, 1865). *Life with the Esquimaux: A Narrative of Arctic Experience in Search of Survivors of Sir John Franklin's Expedition*. London: Sampson Low and Son.

Hanbury, David T. 1904. *Sport and Travel in the Northland of Canada*. London.

Hanson, Allan. 1989. "The Making of the Maori: Cultural Invention and Its Logic." *American Anthropologist* 91: 890–902.

Harper, Kenn. 1986. *Give Me My Father's Body: The Life of Minik, The New York Eskimo*. Iqaluit: Blackhead Books.

Harris, Marvin. 1987. *Cultural Anthropology*, 2nd ed. New York: Harper and Row.

Hartnagel, Tim. 1992. "Correlates of Criminal Behaviour," in Rick Lindon (ed.), *Criminology: A Canadian Perspective*, 2nd ed. Toronto: Holt, Rinehart and Winston.

Hawkes, Charles, Marc Keirstead, Reg Hawes, Dick Holland, and Dennis Gerrard. 2001. *Images of Society: Introduction to Anthropology, Psychology, and Sociology*. Whitby: McGraw-Hill Ryerson.

Hawkes, Ernest W. 1970 (1916). *The Labrador Eskimo*. Geological Survey of Canada, Memoir 91, Anthropological Series 14. Ottawa: Department of Mines. Repr. 1970, Johnson Reprint Company.

Health Canada. 1995. *Suicide in Canada: Update of the Report of the Task Force on Suicide in Canada*. Ottawa: Mental Health Division, Health Services Directorate, Health Programs and Services Branch.

Hearne, Simon. 1968. *A Journey from Prince of Wales's Fort in Hudson's Bay to the Northern Ocean: 1769, 1770, 1771, 1772*. Toronto: Macmillan.

Hemley, Robin. 2003. *Invented Eden: The Elusive, Disputed History of the Tasaday*. New York: Farrar, Straus and Giroux.

Henslin, James, Dan Glenday, Ann Duffy, and Norene Pupo (Eds.) 2001. *Sociology: Canadian Edition: A Down-to-Earth Approach*, 2nd ed. Toronto: Allyn and Bacon.

Henslin, James, and Adie Nelson. 1996. *Sociology: Canadian Edition: A Down-to-Earth Approach*. Toronto: Allyn and Bacon.

Herman, Arthur. 2003. *How the Scots Invented the Modern World or How Western Europe's Poorest Nation Created Our World and Everything in It*. New York: Crown Publishing.

Hiller, Harry H. 1976. *Canadian Society: A Sociological Analysis*. Scarborough: Prentice-Hall.

Hoebel, E. Adamson. 1941. "Law-ways of Primitive Eskimos." *Journal of Criminal Law and Criminology*, 341: 663–83.

——. 1965 (1954). *The Law of Primitive Man, A Study in Comparative Legal Dynamics*. Cambridge, MA: Harvard UP.

Holm, Gustav F. 1914. "Ethnological Sketch of the Angmagssalik Eskimos." *Meddelelser Om Grønland* 34.

Holmes, Ellen Rhoads, and D. Lowell. 1995. *Other Cultures, Elder Years*, 2nd ed. Thousand Oaks, CA: Sage Publications.

Holmes, Lowell. 1965. *Anthropology: An Introduction*. New York: Ronald Press Company.

Holmes, Richard (Ed.). 1988. *Fundamentals of Sociology*. Toronto: Holt, Rinehart and Winston.

Hotspur, Paul. 1927. *Treasure of the North! A Gripping Romance of Peril and Adventure in the Arctic*. Amalgamated/Boys' Friend Library, New Series No. 90.

Howard, Michael. 1986. *Contemporary Cultural Anthropology*. Boston and Toronto: Little, Brown and Company.

Hughes, Charles. 1965. "Under Four Flags: Recent Culture Change among the Eskimos." *Current Anthropology* 6,1: 3–69.

Hughes, David R. 1968. "An Eclectic Review of the Physical Anthropology of the Eskimo," in V. Valentine and F.G. Vallee, *Eskimo of the Canadian Arctic*. Toronto: McClelland and Stewart.

Hutton, Dr. Samuel King. 1912. *Among the Eskimos of Labrador: A Record of Five Years' Close Intercourse with the Eskimo Tribes of Labrador*. London: Seeley, Service and Co.

Isaacs, Sandy, Susan Keogh, Cathy Menard, and Jamie Hockin. 1998. "Suicide in the Northwest Territories: A Descriptive Review." *Chronic Diseases in Canada* 19,4. Health Canada. <http://www.hc-sc.gc.ca/hpb/ldc/publicat/cdic194/cd194c_e.html>.

Jackson, Bruce. 1998. "In the Arctic with Malaurie." *American Anthropologist* 100,2: 275–82.

Jacobson, Steven. 1984. *Yup'ik Eskimo Dictionary*. Fairbanks: U of Alaska P.

Jenkins, McKay. 2005. *Bloody Falls of the Coppermine: Madness, Murder and the Collision of Cultures in the Arctic, 1913*. New York: Random House.

Jenness, Diamond. 1920. "Papuan Cat's Cradles." *Journal of the Royal Anthropological Institute* 50: 299–326.

——. 1921. "The 'Blond' Eskimos." *American Anthropologist* 23,3: 257–67.

——. 1922. *The Life of the Copper Eskimo: Report of the Canadian Arctic Expedition, 1913–1918*. Vol. 12, Pt. A. Ottawa: Department of Naval Service, King's Printer.

——. 1923. *Physical Characteristics of the Copper Eskimo*. Ottawa: National Museum.

——. 1924. *Eskimo String Figures*. Volume 13: Eskimo Folk-Lore, Part B.

——. 1925. "A New Eskimo Culture in Hudson Bay." *Geographic Review* 15: 428–37.

——. 1928. *The People of the Twilight*. New York: Macmillan.

——. 1928a. "Eskimo Language and Technology, Part A: Comparative Vocabulary of the Western Eskimo Dialects." *Report of the Canadian Arctic Expedition, 1913–1918*. Vol. 15: Southern Party, 1913–1916. 134.

——. 1932. *Indians of Canada*. Ottawa: Dept. of Mines, National Museum of Canada. Bulletin 65. Ottawa: Acland.

——. 1935. *The Ojibwa of Parry Island, Their Social and Religious Life*. Ottawa: Dept. of Mines, National Museum of Canada. Bulletin 78. Anthropological Series, No. 17.

——. 1937. *The Sekani Indians of British Columbia*. Ottawa: Dept. of Mines, National Museum of Canada, Bulletin 84, Anthropological Series, No. 20.

——. 1938. *The Sarcee Indians of Alberta*. Ottawa: Dept. of Mines, National Museum of Canada. Bulletin 90, Anthropological Series, No. 23.

——. 1943. *The Carrier Indians of the Bulkley River: Their Social and Religious Life*. Washington, DC: Smithsonian Institution, Bureau of American Ethnology, Anthropological Papers, No. 25.

——. 1944. "Eskimo Language, Part B: Grammatical Notes on Some Western Eskimo Dialects." *Report of the Canadian Arctic Expedition, 1913–1918*. Vol. 15: 34.

——. 1955. *The Faith of a Coast Salish Indian* (ed. by Wilson Duff). Victoria: BC Provincial Museum. Anthropology in British Columbia, Memoir 2.

——. 1957. *Dawn in Arctic Alaska*. Minneapolis: U of Minnesota P.

——. 1962. *Eskimo Administration, I: Alaska*. Arctic Institute of North America, Technical Paper No. 14.

——. 1964. *Eskimo Administration, II: Canada*. Arctic Institute of North America, Technical Paper No. 15.

——. 1965. *Eskimo Administration, III: Labrador*. Arctic Institute of North America, Technical Paper No. 16.

——. 1967. *Eskimo Administration, IV: Greenland*. Arctic Institute of North America, Technical Paper No. 19.

——. 1968. *Eskimo Administration, V: Analysis and Reflections*. Arctic Institute of North America, Technical Paper No. 21.

Jenness, Diamond (with Rev. A. Ballantyne). 1920. *The Northern D'Entrecasteaux*. Oxford: Clarendon.

Jenness, D., and A. Ballantyne. 1928. "Memoir Series: Language, Mythology, and Songs of Bwaidoga, Goodenough Island, S.E. Papua pt 3, A-1E." *Journal of the Polynesian Society* 37,146: 139–64.

Jenness, Stuart. 1991. *Arctic Odyssey: The Diary of Diamond Jenness, 1913–1916*. Ottawa: Canadian Museum of Civilization.

Jones, Judy, and William Wilson. 1987. *An Incomplete Education: 3,684 Things You Should Have Learned but Probably Didn't*. New York: Ballantine Books.

Keenleyside, Anne, Margaret Bertulli, and Henry C. Frike. 1997. "Franklin Expedition: New Skeletal Evidence." *Arctic* 50,1: 36–46.

Kendall, Diana, Rick Linden, and Jane Lothian Murray. 1998 and 2000. *Sociology in Our Times: The Essentials*. Canadian edition. Scarborough: Nelson.

King, James. 2002. *Farley: The Life of Farley Mowat*. Toronto: HarperCollins.

King, Thomas. 1990. *All My Relations: An Anthology of Contemporary Canadian Native Prose*. Toronto: McClelland and Stewart.

Kirmayer, Lawrence, Christopher Fletcher, and Lucy Boothroyd. 1998. "Suicide Among the Inuit of Canada," in Antoon Leenaars, Susanne Wenckstern, Isaac Sakinofsky, Ronald Dyck, Michael Kral, and Roger Bland (eds.), *Suicide in Canada*. Toronto: U of Toronto P. 189–211.

Kirsch, Stuart. 1997. "Lost Tribes: Indigenous People and the Social Imaginary." *Anthropological Quarterly* 70,2: 58–67.

Kottak, Conrad Phillip. 1999. *Mirror for Humanity: A Concise Introduction to Cultural Anthropology*, 2nd ed. New York: McGraw-Hill College.

Kublu, Alexina, and Mick Mallon. 1999. "Our Language, Ourselves," in *Nunavut '99: Changing the Map of Canada*. Co-published by Nortext Multimedia Incorporated and Nunavut Tunngavik Incorporated [Online].

Kulchyski, Peter. 1993. "Anthropology in the Service of the State: Diamond Jenness and Canadian Indian Policy." *Journal of Canadian Studies* 28,2.

Kulchyski, Peter, Don McCaskill, and David Newhouse (Eds.). 1999. *In the Words of Elders: Aboriginal Cultures in Transition*. Toronto: U of Toronto P.

LaCapra, Dominick. 1972. *Durkheim*. Ithaca, NY: Cornell UP.

Laskin, Richard. 1964. *Social Problems: A Canadian Profile*. Toronto: McGraw-Hill Ryerson.

Leighton, Alexander H., and Charles C. Hughes. 1955. "Notes on Eskimo Patterns of Suicide." *Southwestern Journal of Anthropology* 11,4: 327–38.

Levin, Jack, and William C. Levin. 1988. *The Human Puzzle: An Introduction to Social Psychology*. Belmont, CA: Wadsworth.

Lorimer, Rowland, and Jean McNulty. 1991. *Mass Communication in Canada*, 2nd ed. Toronto: McClelland and Stewart.

Lowe, Ronald. 1983. *Kangiryuarmiut Uqauhingita Numiktittitdjutingit / Basic Kangiryuarmiut Eskimo Dictionary*. Ottawa: Committee for Original Peoples Entitlement, 241.

———. 1984. *Siglit Inuviaaluit Uqausiita Kipuktirutait / Basic Siglit Inuviaaluit Eskimo Dictionary*. Ottawa: Committee for Original Peoples Entitlement, 305.

Lyon, George. 1824. *The Private Journal of Captain G.F. Lyon of H.M.S. Hecla, During the Recent Voyage of Discovery under Captain Parry*. London.

Macionis, John, Juanne Nancarrow Clarke, and Linda Gerber. 1994. *Sociology: Canadian Edition*. Scarborough: Prentice-Hall.

Macionis, John, and Linda Gerber. 1999 and 2002. *Sociology: Canadian Edition*. Scarborough: Prentice-Hall.

Macionis, John S., Mikael Jansson, and Celia M. Benoit. 2002. *Sociology: The Basics*. Scarborough: Prentice-Hall.

Mailhot, Jose. 1978. "L'étymologie de «Esquimau» revue et corrigée." *Etudes Inuit/Inuit Studies* 2,2: 59–70.

Mani, Lata. 1998. *Contentious Traditions: The Debate on Sati in Colonial India*. Berkeley: U of California P.

Mann, W.E. (Ed.). 1968a. *Canada: A Sociological Profile*. Toronto: Copp Clark.

———. 1968b. "Suicide." *Deviant Behaviour in Canada*. Toronto: Social Science Publishers.

Mann, W.E., and Les Wheatcroft (Eds.). 1976. *Canada: A Sociological Profile*, 3rd ed. Toronto: Copp Clark.

Marshall, Victor W. (Ed.). 1980 and 1987. *Aging in Canada: Social Perspectives*. Markham: Fitzhenry and Whiteside.

Martin, Laura. 1986. "'Eskimo Words for Snow': A Case Study in the Genesis and Decay of an Anthropological Example." *American Anthropologist* 89,2.

Mathiassen, Therkel. 1928. "Material Culture of the Iglulik Eskimos." *Report of the Fifth Thule Expedition* 6,1 (1921–24). Copenhagen: Gyldensalske Boghandel, Nordisk Forlag.

Maud, Ralph. 2000. *Transmission Difficulties: Franz Boas and Tsimshian Mythology*. Vancouver: Talonbooks.

McGhee, Robert. 1984. "Contact between Native North Americans and the Medieval Norse: A Review of the Evidence." *American Antiquity* 49,1: 4–26.

———. 2004. *The Last Imaginary Place: A Human History of the Arctic World*. Toronto: Key Porter Books.

McGoogan, Ken. 2001. *Fatal Passage: The Untold Story of John Rae, the Arctic Adventurer Who Discovered the Fate of Franklin*. Toronto: HarperCollins.

McKinlay, William Laird. 1999. *The Last Voyage of the Karluk: A Survivor's Memoir of Arctic Disaster*. New York: St. Martin's.

Mead, Margaret. 1967 (1928). *Coming of Age in Samoa: A Psychological Study of Primitive Youth for Western Civilization*. New York: Laurel.

Medicine, Beatrice. 1987. "My Elders Tell Me," in J. Barman, Y. Hébert, and D. McCaskill (eds.), *Indian Education in Canada*. Vol. 2: *The Challenge*. Vancouver: U of British Columbia P. 142–52.

Memmi, Albert. 1991 (1957; and in trans. 1965). *The Colonizer and the Colonized*. Boston: Beacon Press.

Mercer, Blaine E. 1958. *An Introduction to the Study of Society*. New York: Harcourt, Brace and Company.

Merton, Robert K. 1968 (1949). *Social Theory and Social Structure*. New York: The Free Press.

Miller, Barbara D., Penny Van Esterik, and John Van Esterik. 2001. *Cultural Anthropology: Canadian Edition*. Toronto: Allyn and Bacon.

———. 2004. *Cultural Anthropology: Second Canadian Edition*. Toronto: Allyn and Bacon.

———. 2007. *Cultural Anthropology: Third Canadian Edition*. Toronto: Allyn and Bacon.

Miller, Elmer S., and Charles A. Weitz. 1979. *Introduction to Anthropology*. Englewood Cliffs, NJ: Prentice-Hall.

Minor, K. 1992. *Issumatuq: Learning from the Traditional Healing Wisdom of the Canadian Inuit*. Halifax: Fernwood.

Moghaddam, Fathali M. 1998. *Social Psychology: Exploring Universals Across Cultures*. New York: W.H. Freeman and Company.

Moore, Riley D. 1923. "Social Life of the Eskimo of St. Lawrence Island." *American Anthropologist* 25: 339–75.

Morison, Samuel Eliot. 1971. *The European Discovery of America: The Northern Voyages A.D. 500–1600*. New York: Oxford UP.

Morrison, David A. 1991. *The Diamond Jenness Collections from Bering Strait*. Hull: Canadian Museum of Civilization.

Moss, S.E., R. Klein, and B.E. Klein. 2000. "Arcus Senilis and Mortality in a Population with Diabetes." *American Journal of Ophthalmology* 129,5: 676–77.

Mowat, Farley. 1968 (1951). *People of the Deer*. Toronto: McClelland and Stewart.

———. 1975. "The Snow Walker," in *The Snow Walker*. Toronto: McClelland and Stewart. 131–42.

———. 1975 (1959). *The Desperate People*. Toronto: McClelland and Stewart.

———. 2002. *The Farfarers*. Toronto: Anchor Books Canada.

Müller-White, L. 1998. *Franz Boas Among the Inuit of Baffin Island, 1883–1888: Letters and Journals*. Toronto: U of Toronto P.

Murdoch, John. 1887. "On Some Popular Errors in Regard to the Eskimos." *American Naturalist* 21: 9–16

Nanda, Serena. 1994. *Cultural Anthropology*, 5th ed. Belmont, CA: Wadsworth.

Nansen, Fridtjof. 1975 (1893). *Eskimo Life*. New York: AMS.

Nett, Emily M. 1993. *Canadian Families: Past and Present*, 2nd ed. Toronto: Butterworth.

Nickerson, Sheila. 2002. *Midnight to the North: The Untold Story of the Inuit Woman Who Saved the POLARIS Expedition*. New York: Jeremy P. Tarcher/Putnam.

Nisbet, Robert. 1974. *The Sociology of Emile Durkheim*. New York: Oxford UP.

Niven, Jennifer. 2000. *The Icemaster: The Doomed 1913 Voyage of the Karluk*. New York: Hyperion.

———. 2003. *Ada Blackjack: A True Story of Survival in the Arctic*. New York: Hyperion.

Noice, Harold. 1922. "Further Discussion of the 'Blond' Eskimos." *American Anthropologist* 24,2: 228–32.

———. 1924. *With Stefansson in the Arctic*. New York: Dodd, Mead.

———. 1939. *Back of Beyond*. New York: Putnam.

Novak, Mark. 1988, 1997, and 2001. *Aging and Society: A Canadian Perspective*. Toronto: Nelson.

Obeyesekere, Gananath. 1992. *The Apotheosis of Captain Cook: European Mythmaking in the Pacific*. Princeton, NJ: Princeton UP.

Ogburn, William, and Meyer Nimkoff. 1964 (1947). *A Handbook of Sociology*. London: Routledge and Kegan Paul.

Okpik, Abraham. 1964. "What Does It Mean to Be an Eskimo?" in R. Laskin (ed.), *Social Problems: A Canadian Profile*. Toronto: McGraw-Hill. 129–31.

Oliver, W.E. 1932. "'Igloo' True, Powerful Story of Eskimo Tribe." *Los Angeles Evening Herald and Express*, June 1 (quoted in Fienup-Riordan 1995: 69).

Oppenheimer, Monroe, and Willard Wirtz. 1989. "A Linguistic Analysis of Some West Virginia Petroglyphs." *West Virginia Archaeologist* 41,1: 1–6.

Pálsson, Gísli. 2001. *Writing on Ice: The Ethnographic Notebooks of Vilhjalmur Stefansson*. Hanover, NH: UP of New England.

———. 2005. *Travelling Passions: The Hidden Life of Vilhjalmur Stefansson*. Winnipeg: U of Manitoba P (English edition; originally 2003).

Park, Michael Alan. 2000. *Introducing Anthropology: An Integrated Approach*. Toronto: Mayfield.

Parry, W.E. 1824. *Journal of a Second Voyage for the Discovery of a Northwest Passage from the Atlantic to the Pacific; Performed in the Years 1821–22–23 in His Majesty's Ships Fury and Hecla*. London: John Murray.

Peacock, F.W. 1972. *English-Eskimo Dictionary*. St. John's: Memorial University of Newfoundland.

Peck, Edmund J. 1925. *Eskimo-English Dictionary Compiled from Erdman's Eskimo-German Edition*, 1864. General Synod of the Church of England in Canada.

Pei, Mario, 1965. *The Story of Language*. Philadelphia: Lippincott.

Perron, Paul U. 1996. *Towards a Semiotics of the Modern Quebec Novel: "Agaguk," by Yves Thériault*. Toronto: U of Toronto P.

Post, Albert S. 1887. *Ólöf Krarer—The Esquimaux Lady: A Story of Her Native Home*. Ottawa.

Potier, Pierre. 1920. *Fifteenth Report of the Bureau of Archives for the Province of Ontario*. Toronto: C.W. James.

Prentice, Harry. 1895. *The Boy Explorers: The Adventures of Two Boys in Alaska*. New York: Burt.

Pullum, Geoffrey K. 1989. "The Great Eskimo Vocabulary Hoax." *Natural Language and Linguistic Theory* 7,2: 275–81.

Purdy, Alfred. 1967. *North of Summer: Poems from Baffin Island*. Toronto: McClelland and Stewart.

Qitsualik, Rachel Attituq. 2001. "Suicide Is Price Inuit Paid for Tradition of Competency." <http://www.indiancountry.com> (January 22).

———. 2002. "Word and Will—Part Two: Words and the Substance of Life." *Nunatsiaq News*, November 12, 1998.

Rasing, W.C.E. 1994. *Too Many People: Order and Non-Conformity in Igluliugmuit Social Process*. Nijmegen: Katholieke Universiteti Faculteit der Rechts geleendheid.

Rasmussen, Knud. 1927. *Across Arctic America: Intellectual Culture of the Iglulik Eskimos*. New York: G.P. Putnam's Sons.

———. 1929. "Intellectual Culture of the Iglulik Eskimos." *Report of the Fifth Thule Expedition, 1921–24*. Vol. VII, 1. Copenhagen: Gyldensalske Boghandel, Nordisk Forlag.

———. 1931. "The Netsilik Eskimos." *Report of the Fifth Thule Expedition, 1921–24*. Vol. VIII. Copenhagen: Gyldensalske Boghandel, Nordisk Forlag. 1–542.

Ratajczak, Richard. 1998. *Annotated String Figure Bibliography*. <http://www.isfa.org/rataj.htm>.

Ray, P.H. 1885. *Report of the International Polar Expedition to Point Barrow, Alaska*. Washington, DC: Government Printing Office.

Reid, Anna. 2003. *The Shaman's Coat: A Native History of Siberia*. London: Orion Books.

Robertson, Ian. 1989. *Sociology: A Brief Introduction*. New York: Worth Publishers.

Rohner, Ronald P. 1966. "Franz Boas: Ethnographer on the Northwest Coast," in June Helm (ed.), *Pioneers of American Anthropology: The Uses of Biography*. Seattle: U of Washington P. 149–212.

Rojas, Aluki. 2001. *Iglumi Isumatait: A Reinterpretation of the Position of Inuit Women*. manuscript. Trent University, Canadian Studies and Native Studies M.A. Program.

Rose, J.P. 1979. *Introduction to Sociology*. Chicago: Rand-McNally.

Ryan, William. 1976. *Blaming the Victim*. New York: Vintage Books.

Sapir, E. 1929. "The Status of Linguistics as a Science," in E. Sapir (ed. D.G. Mandelbaum), *Culture, Language and Personality*. Berkeley, CA: U of California P.

Schneider, Lucien, and Dermot Collins. 1985. *An Inuktitut-English Dictionary of Northern Quebec, Labrador and Eastern Arctic Dialects*. Montreal: Les Presses de l'Université Laval.

Schultz-Lorentzen, X. 1967. *Dictionary of the West Greenland Eskimo Language.* Copenhagen: Reitzel.

Scoville, Samuel Jr. 1919–20. *The Boy Scouts of the North: or the Blue Pearl.* New York: Century. <http://www.merrycoz.org/annex/pearl/pearl/htm>.

Senaras, Luis P. (?). 1894. *Across the Frozen Sea: or Frank Reade Jr's Electric Snow Cutter.* New York: Frank Reade Library.

Service, Robert. 1968. *Collected Poems of Robert Service.* New York: Dodd, Mead and Co.

Slezkine, Yuri, 1994. *Arctic Mirrors: Russia and the Small Peoples of the North.* Ithaca and London: Cornell UP.

Smith, Dorothy. 1990. *The Conceptual Practices of Power: A Feminist Sociology of Knowledge.* Toronto: U of Toronto P.

Smith, Eric Alden, and S. Abigail Smith. 1994. "Inuit Sex Ratio Variation: Population Control, Ethnographic Error, or Parental Manipulation?" *Current Anthropology* 35,5: 595–624.

Smith, Ronald, and Frederich W. Preston. 1977. *Sociology: An Introduction.* New York: St. Martin's.

Spalding, Alex. 1998. *Inuktitut: A Multi-dialectal Outline Dictionary (with an Aivilingmiutaq base).* Iqaluit: Nunavut Arctic College.

Spencer, Metta. 1981 and 1996. *Foundations of Modern Sociology.* Canadian edition. Scarborough: Prentice-Hall.

Spencer, Robert F. 1959. *The North Alaskan Eskimo: A Study in Ecology and Society.* Washington, DC: Smithsonian Institute, Bureau of American Ethnology, Bulletin 171.

Steckley, John. 2003. *Aboriginal Voices and the Politics of Representation in Canadian Sociology Textbooks.* Toronto: Canadian Scholars' Press.

——. 2004. De *Religione: Telling the Seventeenth Century Jesuit Story in Huron to the Iroquois.* Norman, OK: U of Oklahoma P.

Steckley, John, and Bryan Cummins. 2001. *Full Circle: Canada's First Nations.* Toronto: Prentice-Hall.

——. 2005. "Pegahmagabow of Parry Island: From Jenness Informant to Individual." *The Canadian Journal of Native Studies* 25,1: 35–50.

Stefansson, Vilhjalmur. 1906. "The Icelandic Colony in Greenland." *American Anthropologist* 8,2: 262–70.

——. 1913. *My Life with the Eskimo.* New York: Macmillan.

——. 1921. *The Friendly Arctic.* New York: Macmillan.

——. 1928. "The 'Blond' Eskimos." *Harper's Weekly*, 191–98.

——. 1936. "Adventures in Diet, Part 3." *Harper's Monthly Magazine*, January.

——. 1964. *Discovery: The Autobiography of Vilhjalmur Stefansson.* New York: McGraw-Hill.

Steinmetz, S.R. 1964 (1894). "Suicide Among Primitive Peoples." *American Anthropologist* 7 (January): 53–60. New York: Klaus Reprint Company.

Stocking, George W. 1974. *Shaping of American Anthropology, 1883–1911, A Franz Boas Reader.* New York: Basic Books.

Stringer, Arthur. 1929. *The Woman Who Couldn't Die.* Indianapolis: The Bobbs-Merrill Company.

Sullivan, Louis R. 1922. "The Blonde Eskimos—A Question of Method." *American Anthropologist* 24,2: 225–81.

Sumner, William Graham. 1934 (1906). *Folkways: A Study of the Sociological Importance of Usages, Manners, Customs, Mores and Morals.* Boston: Ginn.

Talbot, Father Francis X. 1956. *Saint Among the Hurons: The Life of Jean de Brébeuf*. New York: Harper and Brothers.

Teevan, James. 1982a, 1987, 1989, and 1995. *Basic Sociology: A Canadian Introduction*. Scarborough: Prentice-Hall.

——. 1982b, 1986, 1988, and 1992. *Introduction to Sociology: A Canadian Focus*. Scarborough: Prentice-Hall.

Tester, Frank J., and Peter Kulchyski. 1994. *Tammarniit (Mistakes): Inuit Relocation in the Eastern Arctic 1939–1963*. Vancouver: U of British Columbia P.

Tester, Frank J., and Paul McNicoll. 2004. "Isumagijaksaq: Mindful of the State: Social Constructions of Inuit Suicide." *Social Science & Medicine* 58: 2625–36.

Thalbitzer, William. 1911. "Eskimo," in F. Boas (ed.), *Handbook of American Indian Languages, Part I*. Washington, DC: Smithsonian Institution, Bureau of American Ethnology, Bulletin 40: 967–1069.

——. 1941. *The Amassalik Eskimo, Contributions to the Ethnology of the East Greenland Natives*. 2nd Part. Copenhagen: C.A. Reitzels Forlag.

Thériault, Yves. 1963. *Agaguk* (trans. from 1958 original). Toronto: Ryerson.

Thomas, David Hurst. 2000. *Skull Wars: Kennewick Man, Archaeology, and the Battle for Native American Identity*. Toronto: HarperCollins Canada.

Thwaites, Reuben G. (Jr.). 1959. *The Jesuit Relations and Allied Documents*. New York: Pageant.

Tierney, Patrick. 2000. *Darkness in El Dorado: How Scientists and Journalists Devastated the Amazon*. New York: W.W. Norton.

Turner, Lucien. 1894. *Ethnology of the Ungava District, Hudson Bay Territory*. 11th Annual Report, 1889–90. Washington, DC: Bureau of American Ethnology.

Tyler, Christian. 2004. *Wild West China: The Untold Story of a Frontier Land*. London: John Murray.

Vallee, Frank G. 1962. *Kabloona and Eskimo in the Central Keewatin*. Ottawa: Northern Coordination and Research Centre, Department of Northern Affairs and National Resources.

Weyer, Edward M. 1962 (1932). *The Eskimos: Their Environment and Folkways*. Hamden, CT: Archon Books.

Whorf, Benjamin. 1956. *Language, Thought, and Reality: Selected Writings of Benjamin Lee Whorf*. John B. Carroll (ed.). Cambridge, MA: MIT Press.

Williams, Gwyn. 1980. *Madoc: The Making of a Myth*. London: Eyre Methuen.

Williams, Thomas R. 1990. *Cultural Anthropology*. Englewood Cliffs, NJ: Prentice-Hall.

Willis, Thayer. 1971. *The Frozen World*. London: Aldus Books.

Woodbury, Anthony. 1994. "Counting Eskimo Words for Snow: A Citizen's Guide to Lexemes Referring to Snow in Steven A. Jacobson's (1984) Yup'ik Eskimo Dictionary." <http://www.linguistlist.org>.

Index